**Tim Hanlon with Guardiola,
the manager of FC Barcelona**

British journalist Tim Hanlon is based in Barcelona and covers news and sport around Europe for UK newspapers and magazines.

As well as a keen sports fan, Tim has a broad variety of interests from travelling through to politics and current affairs.

Dedication

I would like to thank my family for their love and support throughout this project, as well as the many people who have assisted me in the writing of the book, in particular, Juan Arias, Paul Goldrick and Richard Allen.

A CATALAN DREAM

Football Artistry and
Political Intrigue

TIM HANLON

peakpublish

Peakpublish
An imprint of Peak Platform
New Bridge
Calver
Hope Valley
Derbyshire S32 3XT
First published by Peakpublish 2011
Second Print October 2011

Printed in India

A CIP catalogue record for this book is available from the
British Library

ISBN: 978-1-907219-15-3
www.peakplatform.com

Contents

Chapter One

A New Beginning

It started with an audacious promise to buy David Beckham from Manchester United. A pledge that was doomed to failure but one which succeeded in giving Joan Laporta the profile he needed in his bid to become FC Barcelona's president and begin the monumental task of rebuilding the great Catalan club, a cultural symbol as well as a brand of worldwide significance.

The date June 15, 2003, was a milestone for Barcelona, yet another key moment in the club's turbulent history. Laporta swept to power with more than 50 per cent of the members' votes. A society noted for its conservatism and reluctance to change, where power was the result of reputation and connections, had voted for a young, dynamic board that promised a new start and the return of swashbuckling football, and most importantly, success.

The unexpected rise of Laporta had its roots in the previous decade under the wavering leadership of Josep Núñez and the collapse of the then most acclaimed Barcelona side of all time, the Dream Team, led by the enigmatic Johan Cruyff.

One of Barça's most prized players not just for his ability but his affinity with Catalans, even naming his son Jordi after the patron saint of Catalonia, had converted into the coach of an all-conquering team which offered a new brand of open and attacking football.

Cruyff was the people's favourite but he had one bitter enemy, the president Núñez. Both had strong personalities and were egocentric, accustomed to getting their own way; while the team succeeded they held an uneasy truce but when this came to an end there were bitter recriminations.

After Núñez ruthlessly fired Cruyff in 1996, an open feud between supporters of the pair split the club in two and it was within this climate of political upheaval that Joan Laporta first appeared.

For many, Núñez's treatment of Cruyff was yet more evidence of a president who had lost his way, who had become obsessed with his own power and was out of touch with modern football.

During almost two decades he had shown the political skills to fight off opponents and won the 1997 elections, but fans were not happy and sought a way to force a change of leadership.

The difference between Barça and many clubs is that the members own it and they elect a president. They can force through a vote of no confidence if they are not happy with the administration.

A group of fans stepped up who were not looking for power but simply to force a more transparent leadership. They were called the Elefant Blau.

Other pressure groups had existed in the past such as the Platforma Barcelonista and Grup d'Opinio but these had looked to back a certain candidate who was standing against the president.

The Elefant Blau chose their name because the elephant is a symbol of strength and blau (blue) short for Blaugrana is the nickname for Barcelona in Catalan. Initially composed of around 50 people with Joan Laporta as spokesman they became a popular front against the president.

The campaign gathered momentum and suddenly Núñez found himself fighting a vote of no confidence, which although he won, spelt the beginning of the end.

Finally, in 2000 with mounting criticism of his leadership and the team failing on the pitch, the embattled Núñez resigned.

"We had been working together since the mid-1990s with Elefant Blau and although we did not directly force Núñez to stand down, he managed to survive the pressure for only two-and-a-half years," said Laporta, "I am not saying that it was just down to our pressure, there were other things more important, but the Elefant Blau was one of these reasons."

The 2000 elections though failed to herald the new dawn anticipated by reformers and in fact the situation deteriorated.

There was a two horse race between Núñez's former-vice president Joan Gaspart and the voice for change, Lluís Bassat, whose group included Laporta and many other members of the Elefant Blau. Also on his ticket was the former-Dream Team player Txiki Begiristain who was to have been sports director, a position he did take later under the Laporta presidency.

It was a resounding defeat for the reformers as the traditionally conservative Catalan voters chose continuity. The reason was that the mood was still not ripe for revolution and it took the Gaspart presidency to come crashing down before finally the middle of the road voters accepted that the situation had got so desperate that only a radical change would suffice.

After the initial disappointment of seeing Gaspart win the 2000 elections, Bassat's team regrouped to examine what went wrong and how they could mount a more successful bid. A debate opened up as to whether Bassat was the right leader, a man who had appeal across the board as opposed to a more radical alternative.

"A new generation needed to take over and we looked for a candidate who would be able to take this to the voters. After Núñez went there were so many issues at the club that I think people were distracted from what really mattered. Gaspart then was elected and he continued the legacy of the previous 20 years as he was from the old order," said Albert Vicens, who was later to become a vice president to Laporta.

There was a growing sense during the Gaspart presidency by a section of those who had been in Bassat's camp that a complete overhaul was necessary and they needed to look elsewhere for a leader. Laporta himself told Bassat that he no longer saw him as the right choice for the leadership but Bassat refused to step aside and continued to make plans to stand again.

Out of the ashes of the old Elefant Blau a small team including Laporta, Toni Rovira, Xavier Cambra, Jaume Ferrer, Jordi Mones and Josep Cubells, started working together with the idea that they would have until the end of Gaspart's term to provide a winning formula, which was to be 2005.

"Lluís Bassat said that he wanted to be the candidate again at the next elections. I took it upon myself to meet up with him and discuss the situation. I thought he should know what everyone was thinking and so I put it to him straight that he was not the best candidate to stand," said Laporta.

"Ideally we would have kept a united opposition and included Bassat on board but this proved to be impossible. I was not thinking of the presidency myself at this stage but it was during 2002 that I felt that perhaps the moment had arrived for our generation to step forward."

Gradually the jigsaw came together and a group was formed, the common thread being youthful, ambitious Catalans with a passion for Barça.

Ferran Soriano and Marc Ingla, two experts in the field of marketing and economics who had worked together for ten years building a consultancy business were brought into the fold.

"At the start we had meetings from time to time in my office during the autumn of 2002 before it became more structured. We had no idea how we were going to present ourselves but we knew we would at the next elections some way or other," said Laporta.

Soriano and Ingla were followed into the team by the marketing guru Sandro Rosell who had experience working in the football world.

"When we had news that other groups were planning their candidature we knew that we had to pick up speed and it was at this stage that I spoke with Sandro Rosell who I knew from playing football together many years earlier," said Laporta.

"Jordi Moix (another future director) suggested I met with Rosell because he was talking to the candidates and we wanted to see whether he would be interested in our project. We had a meeting and after I presented the project he explained that he had similar ideas."

It soon emerged that Laporta would be the natural leader as he possessed the charisma and the public image having fronted the Elefant Blau. Perhaps the warning clouds were on the horizon when a group of competitive businessman came together but the battle of egos had not yet come to the surface as they all fought for the same goal of winning the next elections.

Rosell, more than anyone, posed a threat to Laporta's credentials but at this stage he was happy to take a secondary role. He was different to the majority of the figures in Laporta's camp as he was respected within the Catalan establishment. His father had been a Barça director and was a player in local politics.

Rosell had his first major break when he became involved in the Barcelona 1992 Olympic Games Organisation Committee working in the commercial department. Success there saw him take up a position as manager of ISL Spain who looked after the commercial interests of the IOC in that country.

He was then poached by Nike and again established himself as a top player in his field as he negotiated Nike's sponsorship of the Spanish league match balls and FC Barcelona.

His next step was to take over promoting Nike in Latin America, a job he took up after Adidas-sponsored France beat

Brazil, who had a deal with Nike, in the 1998 World Cup Final.

Moving to Brazil, Rosell spent four years practically living with their national team and establishing links that would become invaluable for his role as a future Barcelona vice-president. During the 2002 World Cup Finals in Japan and South Korea he shared the same hotel as the team, was in the dressing room after the final and held the trophy aloft at the celebratory party afterwards.

In Spain, Rosell also had an enviable list of contacts. He was on good terms with former Real Madrid president Florentino Pérez and first worked with him when Luis Figo signed for Adidas-sponsored Madrid and he had to renegotiate his Nike deal.

Rosell first discussed the possibility of playing an active role within the club in the mid-1990s. He recalls how he travelled to Athens to watch Barcelona face AC Milan in the 1994 Champions League Final with friends, who would later also become directors of the club, and the disappointment he felt when Barça were beaten by Fabio Capello's side.

Rosell rued Johan Cruyff's decision to leave out Michael Laudrup, which Capello admitted gave his side a big advantage. For Rosell the defeat could only be compared with that against Steaua Bucharest in 1986, also in the final of the European Cup, and it made him feel that things should be done differently.

"We debated ways to change the anodyne presence of the club internationally and also why our biggest idols always ended up leaving through the back door. We found out that Cruyff had told (the goalkeeper Andoni) Zubizarreta that he didn't want him anymore on the team coach as it went to the airport. This was just another example of how things should not be done either professionally or out of human decency whether in the sporting world or just socially," he said.

"For a long time we thought, especially Jordi Moix, about serving Barça from the inside, as we did not like what was happening and in particular the sad end of the Dream Team. As

I was with Nike, first in Europe and then in Latin America, I could not participate in debates about this, either from a professional standpoint and then later purely from a question of distance. But it is true that I would have liked to have done."

He remained in touch all the same with what was happening on and off the pitch through friends and the media.

"From the other side of the Atlantic I saw and felt the emotion of Jordi Moix, who with experienced Barcelona people and those from his generation like Joan Laporta, took their first steps towards opposition. First being part of the campaign of Angel Fernández (who stood against Núñez in the 1997 elections), then part of Elefant Blau and after that with Lluís Bassat against Joan Gaspart, without winning on that occasion either," he explained.

Rosell explained that Moix tried to get him on board at the turn of the Millennium saying that such a strong candidate with his international experience, and with a father who was a director and a founder of the Catalan political group Convergencia, would be perfect. Rosell's commitment to Nike, though, prevented this happening.

Rosell supported Bassat in the 2000 elections more than anything because he had friends in the campaign and his father also collaborated in it. He felt that it foundered through a lack of cohesion, demonstrated by the fact that although it was claimed they would bring in Johan Cruyff as sports director even though this had not been arranged.

He was also angry at the way Núñez manipulated the situation behind the scenes: "I believe that Núñez did not behave correctly at this point as during the campaign he gave two long interviews in which he called the Elefant Blau terrorists. He never said vote for Gaspart but he did say that those who vote for the Elefant Blau were wrong and this obviously tipped the balance in favour of the official candidature."

7

Rosell was in Barcelona for the elections and after proposed the signing of players to the new Gaspart board but was frustrated that they did not listen to him.

"I suggested two young Brazilian players with big futures, the striker Adriano, who was then with Flamengo, and Lucio the defender of Internacional. Weeks later Lucio signed for Bayer Leverkusen and Adriano for Inter Milan.

"It annoyed me that Barça allowed them to go because I could see they would turn into great players."

After the 2002 World Cup, Rosell returned to live in Barcelona with his family and was moved as were many fans by the dismal performances of the team especially the 3-0 defeat by Sevilla in December, after which Gaspart chose to stand alone in the directors box as whistles pierced the air around him.

Rosell was thinking about giving his support to one of the campaigns. Bassat's appeared to be the most attractive but he was persuaded out of it because of talk that he was interested only in his own ideas and did not know that much about the running of the club.

Moix suggested Rosell himself should run for the presidency, which he refused, but listened to the idea of supporting Laporta and that is how it all began with a meeting at the Hesperia hotel in February 2003.

As Laporta explained, he had played football with Rosell 20 years earlier for Sant Andreu (a local Catalan club).

"The talk lasted almost five hours but a lot more hours and days were necessary in order to discuss the thousands of points which come to light in these situations. Basically Laporta explained the idea of a project for Barça that was not cut and dried because he was not sure when there were going to be elections. He and Moix initially had the year 2005 in mind but we understood that we had to be prepared for whatever contingency as was the case with other candidates like Bassat," he said.

"I came to that meeting with a lot of hope although I was a bit concerned that I did not know Laporta better. All the information I had on him came from Jordi Moix and I suppose he was in the same situation as regards me. However, certainly as the night progressed and we talked passionately about Barça I had more desire to take part and do something. Slowly but surely we arrived at an agreement where we would work together in the same operation."

Rosell explained that he would not go with Bassat and would give everything to the project; that he would always be honest in his work as long as he was listened to and his advice considered. He began to bring in other influential people, starting with Josep Maria Bartomeu, a successful Catalan businessman he knew from his student days.

The presidential campaign also fitted in perfectly for Ferran Soriano who was looking for a fresh challenge and was attracted to the Laporta campaign.

"I've been a Barcelona fan since I was a kid going with my dad but after that I travelled around the world with my business during my 20s and 30s. I came back to Barcelona in 2003 and given the situation of the club from a sporting and social perspective I was willing to invest my time and put my experience at its service," he said.

"I missed Johan Cruyff's period as a player because I was too young but after that I remember going to the stadium for European matches. We did not have a season ticket but we used to go to the midweek games. My father worked at the market and there were people who had seats and couldn't go on Wednesdays due to work.

"I had nothing to do with Elefant Blau as I had my own company with Marc Ingla and I was living and working in many places, in the USA, in South America and in Europe. But by 2003 we had sold our company and we were back in Barcelona at the time of the elections.

"Marc Ingla and I met the team who were preparing for the elections and this was about half a year beforehand. We shared values and a vision and we started working from there. In my personal case I was playing with the idea of putting the experience that I had into something as passionate as football and FC Barcelona.

"At the beginning there was no project, we just had the idea that we could do things better and people were coming from different angles, from a management perspective, from a social perspective and our friends like those from the Elefant Blau, who had a history of being involved in club elections."

The steady construction of a presidential campaign had to step up a gear when it became clear that Gaspart was not going to survive to see out his term of office. One disaster after another had left his position untenable and he had to step down early in 2003.

Vice-president Enric Reyna took his place in a caretaker capacity until elections could be held in the summer. A further twist in the build-up to the elections saw Reyna dig in his heels and it appeared at one stage that, against club rules, he planned to make his position permanent.

He told the media that he was the man that could lead the club out of its malaise but eventually he was forced to listen to reason and agreed to call elections. His stubbornness had already had a negative effect as elections were unable to be held until mid-June and this gave the winner less time to make signings before the start of the new season.

When the campaigning eventually got under way Lluís Bassat was the strong favourite while Laporta was very much an outsider.

Though it was tough to begin with, the Laporta campaign quickly took up speed.

"We were frustrated because we did not know what was going to happen, when the elections were going to be and there was the fear that Reyna would try and stay in power. We were in a battle against time to get things in place," Soriano said.

"I was given responsibility for the political campaign. I concentrated full-time on this. I got in touch with a Catalan woman I knew who worked as a political advisor in Washington, in the United States, and I asked her to give me an idea of how to organise elections because I did not know and I had to learn. She put us in contact with Xavier Roig, who had led several campaigns with Pasqual Maragall (ex-president of the Catalonia local government) and had a lot of experience. He then took up a role in the running of our campaign.

"Working with their help and some natural instincts over the messages we wanted to put forward we arranged everything. Marc Ingla assembled a team of people with whom he and I had already worked and we put together a project as though it was one we had spent ten years doing with our own company.

"We did not know whether we could win but we thought that if the worst came to the worst the experience we would gain would stand us in good stead for another attempt maybe in four, eight or even twelve years."

It is tradition for well-established members to gather together before the club elections to discuss which way they are going to vote, a practice which has its origins in the adversity the club faced first under the dictator Miguel Primo de Rivero.

The club was closed for six months in 1925 and members worked hard to ensure that there was a future afterwards. They were called into action again under the repressive Franco regime, and it is still this same network of families that retain an important power in the overseeing of club affairs.

Before the 2003 elections they met up again but Laporta was not able to convince them to side with him. Instead they were more inclined to go with Bassat.

"The fight against Bassat appeared to be impossible. Everything was in his favour, he had an impressive image thanks in part to his surname and his publicity agency Bassat Ogilvy. He also had heavy-weight Catalans on his side," said Rosell.

"All the same, and it is easy for me to say now, his candidacy at the time reminded me of the Titanic."

The initial polls announced on April 30 also gave little hope to the Laporta camp. Bassat had 42 per cent of the vote with the next candidate having just six per cent. It is incredible to think that just a month and half later Laporta would go on to win.

Soriano said: "We were the last candidacy to present ourselves publicly which caused concern for many but I was quite relaxed. My heart wanted to attack the situation but my head said be calm.

"Our strategy lay in the concept we offered of change. We were qualified to offer this change for three important reasons: we represented the necessary generational shift; none of us were responsible for the situation that the club found itself in; and finally the effort we were giving which no one could match."

The Laporta camp established their headquarters on Passeig de Gràcia, near to the central Plaça Catalunya, so as to draw in as many people as possible and the team worked tirelessly, comparing notes on the progress at the end of each day.

Soriano explained the strategy: "According to our polls we had drawn level with Bassat within three weeks and most importantly our name was growing while that of Bassat was dropping away. Two weeks before the elections we knew that we were going to win because we had moved a little ahead of Bassat and we were still growing."

Even so on May 30 they had to present their votes before Barça's election commission in order to go into the last round. Bassat was in front with 9,894; Jaume Llauradó claimed 6,057 and Laporta was third with just 5,725.

The Laporta campaign constantly reinforced the need for change and focused clearly on each problem afflicting the club. They argued that Barça was no longer one of the top sides in world football and they promised to return it to one of the top five in the world.

They were against selling off club land and they aimed to concentrate on associating the Barça team more with Catalonia and to do this by putting more emphasis on youth and bringing through more Guardiolas and Iniestas. They would buy only a small number of star names, similar to Cruyff's policy in his day as coach, to complement the rest of the team.

In retrospect the difference between the Laporta election campaign and those of his rivals was astonishing.

Against this well-honed political strategy, the rest appeared amateurs. Youthful and cutting edge, the campaign caught the imagination. The videos of Barcelona's European Cup success in 1992 were shown repeatedly as members walked into the Laporta camp's headquarters and models handed out pamphlets about how a vote for them would make the club great again.

Importantly, Laporta was media friendly, never missing an opportunity to talk about his aims in stark contrast to many of his opponents. Bassat's secretary was like a brick wall claiming the front-runner wanted to keep a low profile.

Even at this stage there were rumours that Laporta was egotistical and craved the limelight but in the build up to the elections he was charm personified. He was easily able to sway the voting with his charisma.

In press conferences he looked at ease in front of the camera as he answered questions from national and international journalists in Catalan, Spanish and English.

But if there was one single element that pushed the Laporta campaign to victory it was the announcement that Barcelona were going to sign the England captain David Beckham.

Until that point Laporta was just a name on a list of candidates, but by making this claim he catapulted himself to the forefront. He became the subject of interest internationally. People began to wonder who he was and whether Beckham, the biggest draw in the game, really would move to the struggling Catalan side.

At the press conference when he made the claim there was a buzz of excitement. Laporta stated he had made a deal with Manchester United and on several television screens they displayed an internet page from the Old Trafford club with the agreement displayed officially.

Laporta spoke about what it would mean to bring Beckham to Barcelona, how it demonstrated the direction the club was going to take and the ambition they had. Encouraging Beckham to choose Barça ahead of other clubs he said he would be the star of the team. Laporta stressed the attraction of the sun, sea and the mountains and Barcelona's hedonistic lifestyle.

It was of course just hype. Beckham had already agreed to join Real Madrid as Laporta's camp well knew. But it fed the imagination of members only too ready to be taken in, because the idea sounded so much better than the reality.

"The real importance of Beckham was his value in terms of merchandising. It is true, though, I knew that Florentino Pérez had the player tied down even though the deal was not officially closed," said Rosell.

"To take him away would be a mission pretty much impossible because it is the player who always decides. At the same time, though Beckham was a good player with a big value especially in the Asiatic market, I always pushed for Ronaldinho as Jan (Joan Laporta) knew from the start," said Rosell.

"Initially the name of Beckham was mentioned by Jordi Cruyff (Johan's son and a former Barcelona player) who had played with him at United. To find out exactly the position I spoke with Peter Kenyon, the Manchester United chief executive, and we arranged that on June 10, five days before the vote, the Manchester United website would post an agreement between them and Barcelona if we won the elections and the player agreed.

"The news had a big impact and gave us a lot of credibility. The deal could not be denied in spite of what had been arranged between Florentino and the player's agents because it was not officially authorised by Fifa.

"I do not agree though that it was the key element to us winning. It gave us credibility but the key was the desire from the members for a change."

Laporta's campaign pledge to make Barça one of the top sides in the world both on the pitch and financially, within three years, showed the dynamism which had been lacking from Barça's politics for a long time.

The decision to use Beckham to attract voters when the board knew they had no chance to get him has been criticised.

"He used the signing of Beckham which was a lie but Laporta had a very good campaign which worked well, creating a new atmosphere. The people believed in Beckham, the press believed in it. I said on the television that it was not true and he was going to Real Madrid but no one wanted to believe me," said Josep Maria Minguella, the former agent who had brought Diego Maradona and Leo Messi, among others, to the club and who was an election candidate himself in 2003.

"I presented myself having retired from being an agent and having been a member of Barcelona for many years. I wanted to offer my views on football to the club and give the direction in which I thought things should go."

He also claimed that Laporta made his first signing as president, the Turkish international goalkeeper Rustu Recber, in order that Manchester United agreed to publicly announce a deal had been made with Barça.

"When we had the elections they did not have any players confirmed other than Rustu and this was because at the time his agent was Pini Zahavi, who has influence at Manchester. The Laporta group used him to have contact with Manchester United so as to get them to negotiate for Beckham," said Minguella.

"As a result they signed Rustu who did not fit into their plans in any way just so that Manchester would put on their website that they are negotiating with Barcelona for Beckham. The reason was to try and make it appear that Barça would sign Beckham but in reality they only had Rustu."

While Laporta was courting the international media, Bassat was far more cautious. Having failed before under the promise of change, his strategy now was to follow a similar line to

Gaspart in the previous elections by attempting to conciliate and unite rather than breakaway.

Bassat though for a second time misread the feelings of the Barça members.

Three years of deterioration since the 2000 elections meant the members now were prepared to look for radical change. Gaspart's attempts to moderate had gone badly wrong and in their desperation the members were ready to choose a board with no experience of running a club.

Two days before the election the Laporta camp made its final push, publishing a list of 116 famous Catalans who were supporting their project.

The results showed the hard work had paid off as Laporta won with more votes than any other presidential candidate in the club's history. The count on June 15, 2003, showed he had attracted 27,138 votes – 53 per cent, the first time a president had won with more than 50 per cent.

"We were an error in a system that had perpetuated the existing power base. It was an invisible line of power involving the same well-established groups. For they to lose control meant that they made grave mistakes and it makes me happy to think that I worked to make the history of Barça richer," said Soriano.

"It also meant that as we broke from the system we would always be in danger as the establishment will look to find an equilibrium again. Having lived a long time away from home before 2003 I can consider myself as someone looking in from the outside and I can say that the existing Catalan order had failed."

The true extent of the shift in power was shown when the new board was introduced to the ex-president of the Catalan local government, Jordi Puyol, a renowned figure in local politics who helped oversee the restoration of democracy in Catalonia after Franco. Due to the close-knit nature of the Catalan establishment it is unusual for new Barça board members to need an introduction but on this occasion the only director he knew was Sandro Rosell.

A dynamic board had been elected to take Barça into a new era. Laporta had promised to bring back a football model in the image of the Dream Team and how better to do that than to have its founder Johan Cruyff working in the background pulling the strings.

However the battle of egos and jealousy that would eventually blow the board apart were also beginning to bubble under the surface.

Chapter Two

More Than A Club

Walking through the centre of Barcelona and especially the real Catalan heartland of the city in the 'barrio' of Gracia, ahead of an important match day, it is difficult to imagine this cosmopolitan melting pot without football.

People of all ages and backgrounds with their only common link, their allegiances to Barça and the region they claim it represents, Catalonia, gather in any bars available with a television to nervously await kick-off. Some fans know more about football than others but the over-riding sensation is that watching Barcelona play is an expression of national pride.

The region of Catalonia, in the north east of Spain, has a tumultuous history of battles for its autonomy but did once boast an empire under the Kings of Aragon that stretched across the Mediterranean Sea and included the southern part of Italy up to Rome.

However, now with Catalonia part of today's Spain, for many Catalans Barça is their best outlet to champion their different identity and culture.

To see how Barça came to represent so much more than just football and to become almost a byword for supporting the downtrodden and fighting repression it is necessary to delve into the club's complex history.

From when it was originally formed as football spread to the Mediterranean with industrialisation, to the blows it received during the catastrophic political instability and dictatorships that Spain suffered for an important part of the 20th century.

The major crisis that affected the club in the summer of 2003 was so severe because of its importance to the people of Catalonia.

Go back over 100 years to the end of the 19th century and this is where Barça had its origins. A port city like Marseille, Nice and Genoa it was a hive of activity with foreign traders arriving from overseas and mixing with local workers; and it was out of this breeding ground for new ideas and innovation that football arrived and quickly took a hold.

British colonial workers at the Rio Tinto mines in Huelva on the south coast of Spain played matches among themselves in their spare time and the appeal of the game was contagious as curious onlookers created Spain's oldest team, Recreativo de Huelva, in 1889.

The game spread quickly but it took another ten years before FC Barcelona was officially formed as a result of a letter to the local newspaper from a Swiss man, Hans Gamper (who later changed his name to the Catalan Joan).

A year later another team called Espanyol was formed in Barcelona. They are now the second biggest club in the city and while Barça are considered by many to be the side of Catalonia, Espanyol are the team of Spain.

The truth is far more complex and many Catalan Espanyol fans are angry at the way that Barça tries to have the Catalan cause all to itself and they rightly point out how their team's colours were styled on the mythical seaman Roger de Llúria who led the Catalan-Aragon fleet of the 14th century.

However, Barça did make efforts to identify themselves with the region and put the flag of Saint Jordi, the patron saint of Catalonia, on their club badge while Espanyol if anything went the other way by making King Alfonso X111 their honorary president and renamed themselves Real (meaning royal in Spanish) Club Espanyol. This was especially unpopular as this came just three years after the 'Setmana Tràgica' in which a Catalan rebellion was repressed brutally by the king and the leader Francesc Ferrer i Guàrdia was executed.

"Barça participated in manifestos and cultural events unlike Espanyol and became rather than a club of foreigners, the team of Catalonia. This was the real start of the rivalry," claims the Catalan writer Salvador Duch, but this is hotly disputed.

Iván Rodriguez, a journalist for Spanish radio station Cope, takes a different view: "I am first of all Catalan and then secondly Spanish, I know there are a lot of Espanyol fans who are from Madrid and Andalusia and the rest of Spain but that is the same for Barcelona."

The arrival of the dictator Miguel Primo de Rivera in 1923 saw a crackdown on the Catalan culture with their language repressed forcibly and the flag and national anthem - the Els Segadors and La Senyera - banned. It also saw Barça's first real political conflict with the state.

The club received stiff reprisals after arranging a testimonial game for the l'Orfeo Català, the Catalan cultural music society, which was abolished by the regime in 1925. A British band onboard a boat stationed at the port was brought in to play the Spanish national anthem but in what has become a legendary moment, having received jeers from the 14,000 crowd and unaware what to do they began to play 'God save the King' which was greeted by applause. The state responded by closing down the stadium for six months.

Even so the club was building steadily with a new 25,000 capacity stadium constructed and they won their first league title in 1929.

The stars on the pitch were Ricardo Zamora and Josep Samitier. Zamora is now considered to be one of the best Spanish keepers ever and the shot-stopper who concedes fewest goals each season in the Primera Division is awarded the Zamora trophy; while Samitier is Barca's second highest goal scorer of all time with 326 during 13 years at the club.

But president Joan Gamper was feeling the strain of political pressure from the regime and this on top of difficulties with his business ventures led him to commit suicide. His contribution is remembered each year with the Joan Gamper Trophy, held as a curtain raiser to the new season against an invited club.

The Primo de Rivera dictatorship came to an end but the 1930s were politically shaky times. The reinstated king was soon overthrown paving the way for the Spain's Second Republic which meant the return of local government for Catalonia.

Unshackled, Barça tried to raise membership but they remained at the forefront of political tension that was considerably more than a battle between Catalonia and Madrid rule. As across Europe there were battles of ideology and this was made worse in Spain by its fragile political system.

In July 1936 a failed army coup led to a full scale civil war which was to last for the next three years with Franco's nationalist Falange party, backed by Hitler and Mussolini, against the Republican forces who had the more covert support of the Soviet Union.

Catalonia's Republican local government led by Lluís Companys gradually saw its power eroded as the region spun out of control. Many socialist and communist groups fought for control with anarchists in street battles during the May Days of 1937.

The man given the responsibility to lead FC Barcelona through these troubled times was a wealthy businessman Josep Sunyol, who was also an elected representative of a left-wing Catalan party.

As a Republican politician Sunyol was required to make the perilous journey to Madrid which ran the risk of bumping into pockets of rebel resistance.

In August 1936 he travelled to Valencia and then on to Madrid but he was never to make it back home and instead became a martyr to the Catalan cause.

His Ford car flying the Catalonia flag was stopped by a Franco unit on a mountainous range called the Sierra de Guaderrama, north of Madrid, and the president along with the other occupants were shot dead and their bodies dumped by the roadside.

The truth slowly filtered back to Catalonia and he quickly became a hero even to left-wing groups despite his capitalist background.

In Madrid, a battalion fighting Franco's forces took the name Sunyol as did a regiment of volunteers, ironically based on land where Real Madrid's Bernabeu Stadium now stands.

FC Barcelona was left without a president but a makeshift board led by Rossend Calvet i Mata took control and refused to let go of the reins after being told to become a workers' syndicate.

The Les Corts stadium was actually used to house religious refugees following a bloodbath that saw an estimated 7,000 people connected to the church murdered in Republican areas.

The player Josep Raich was forced out of FC Barcelona by the authorities as he had previously played for a Catholic club Joventuts Catoliques de Molins de Rei.

Despite the onset of the civil war in July, 1936, the league continued in Spain until October at which point the Spanish federation called a halt.

Amazingly, football matches did not stop on either side of the political divide and while a Fascist league was orchestrated in the north of Spain, plans were also made to set up a Catalan tournament.

Differences of opinion over its format actually led to guns being drawn between representatives of the Catalan FA, Barcelona and Espanyol before an agreement was found.

Barça lost several key players including prolific Argentine striker Enrique Fernández (he did return in 1947 as coach and lead the team to two consecutive league titles). Also absent for the start of the 1936-37 season was coach Patrick O'Connell, a former Celtic and Ireland international, but he was back by Christmas after accepting the danger.

In October 1936, before a match between a Catalan X1 and Valencia X1, both captains went to speak to the president of the local government, Lluís Companys, to ensure the safety of keeper Ricardo Zamora, who was rumoured to have fascist leanings.

He was later given a six-month jail term but was smuggled out wearing a disguise and fled to the Argentine embassy and then on to France.

Moving to Nice, he met up with former team-mate Josep Samitier who had experienced similar problems. Samitier was imprisoned in Madrid before escaping to France with only the suit he was wearing. He later did become a friend of Franco.

The fierce rivalry between Barcelona and Real Madrid was to come to the fore in unusual circumstances when due to the instability in the capital, Real asked to play matches in the Catalan mini-league without competing for the title but Barça alone vetoed the idea.

Espanyol went on to win the competition but lost their final game against Barça in a match marred by the Barcelona fans running onto the pitch and attacking the Espanyol players, calling them fascists.

The Mediterranean league was then set up with teams from Barcelona and Valencia. Those from Madrid and the Basque Country, although invited, considered it too dangerous to travel as these areas were under siege from Franco's forces.

A shortage of petrol meant teams that did take part had to travel by train and at night without lights for security reasons.

Barcelona went on to win the league in 1937 and in recent years there has been plenty of debate over whether they should be able to claim it as a national league title. It was never recognised by the Franco regime but president Joan Laporta sought to get this decision overturned claiming that Sevilla's cup win in 1939, which is officially accepted, was from a tournament which only comprised teams in territory under Franco's control.

After their league success, Barça went on a money making tour of Mexico and the United States where they made $15,000 just from the initial stage

Unsurprisingly perhaps with the conditions worsening in Barcelona, only nine of the 20-man squad returned. Star winger Marti Ventrola stayed behind in Mexico and went on to marry the niece of the Mexican president. His son José played for his adopted country in the 1970 World Cup.

The trip saved the club from going bankrupt but had political consequences as 15 months later the Franco authorities imposed a two-year suspension from football on all those involved.

Franco's nationalist forces were gradually moving closer to Barcelona progressing from Madrid to Valencia and then on to the heart of Catalonia with the capitulation at Lleida in the spring of 1938. Among those fighting at the front were the Barcelona players Josep Valle, Juli Gonzalvo, and Antoni Gracia.

The fascists' ability to call on aviation support from Italy was tipping the balance. Mussolini's planes bombarded the city indiscriminately causing heavy loss of life and the club offices were among the buildings hit.

With war looming in the rest of Europe, Republicans fought to hold out as long as possible in the hope they could later receive the support of the Allies but it was not to be and they caved in after losing the battle of the River L'Ebre during the second half of 1938. Catalan industry relied on the river and damage to the supply line led to many years of restricted electricity after the war. Among the dead from the battle was Ángel Arocha, a league winner for Barça in 1929.

The Franco forces made their way into Barcelona by January 1939 and one of the first steps taken by the new regime was to abolish the autonomy for Catalonia conceded by the Second Republic.

Franco then put a stranglehold on the region using a severe economic policy. He decided the only solution for the "Catalan problem" was to ban anything representative of Catalonia, bar their traditional dances and foods. The Catalan language was suppressed and more than 100,000 Catalans passed through concentration camps in 1939.

The president of the Catalan local government under the Second Republic, Lluís Companys, was caught in France by the Gestapo and returned to Spain where he was shot in 1940. His only crime was being a leader under the previous regime.

With a crackdown on all things Catalan, FC Barcelona moved into the most difficult period of its history and a question mark hung over whether it would continue as a sporting entity.

Even referees could not be relied on for their impartiality. Pedro Escartín, a high-ranking official was among those who discovered the body of Josep Sunyol and he publicly ridiculed the former-Barca president for being in the wrong place at the wrong time.

To spread the Franco message through sport the Marca newspaper was set-up in San Sebastian in 1938. The first edition exhorted its readers to 'Raise your arm for the sportsmen of Spain'. It has become the biggest selling sports paper in the country making the transition seamlessly into democracy but it maintains to this day a Madrid bias.

"The intention is that the capital of Catalonia once again functions with Español (the Spanish spelling of the team Espanyol, the club restored it's Catalan name in the mid-90s), Europa, Badalona and Sabadell," it reported in an early edition.

"Of Barcelona no one knows although it would not be strange if they changed the colours of their shirts and their name as well. The intention is to make Spain the protagonist instead of Barcelona."

Then in a further issue it claimed: "Español was a team formed by good and sane Spanish; Barcelona is Catalan to the centre and guilty of making intolerable propaganda."

There was no united Catalan force under the flag of FC Barcelona as has so often been said and Franco was a dictator, if he had wanted to get rid of the football team then he would have done so. It is argued that he retained the club to channel the nationalism of the Catalans into football and away from other more directly political avenues.

Barça were only allowed to reopen after the civil war with a pro-Franco board that denounced Catalanism and pledged itself to a united Spain. It had to acknowledge that its earlier attempts at political separatism were wrong. In order to align itself more closely with Spain it had to change its name from Futbol Club Barcelona to Club de Futbol Barcelona in order to appear more Spanish.

If this was not bad enough, the Francoist president appointed in 1940, Enrique Piñeyro, knew nothing about football and in his first season they only stayed in the top-flight thanks to a final game win over Murcia.

Fortunately the club was financially secure as a result of their trip to the American continent and Piñeyro learnt to respect the traditions of the club. He was, in fact, fined for being too lenient and later it was rumoured that he was not allowed to publish his memoirs.

On the pitch, too, the picture was improving with the team winning the 1942 Generalisimo Cup (the name of the King's Cup under Franco's regime).

Barcelona were entering into one of their most successful periods and they received significant support from the regime financially. For obvious reasons it is glossed over by the club but while Real Madrid were seen as the flagship side for Franco, he was also an honorary Barcelona member.

In those early days the Barcelona stands were not a hotbed for Catalan resistance. Nobody dared say anything in case they were denounced and they certainly would not express their inner feelings to people they met casually at the stadium. In fact many of those who went to the matches were immigrants to Barcelona from other parts of Spain who chose to support the club as a way of being accepted into the closed Catalan society.

Historically, whether in times of dictatorship or otherwise FC Barcelona had never had a fervently outspoken Catalan leadership and that was what made the circumstances of 2003 all the more remarkable when a radical board was finally voted in.

"Until Laporta's group took charge the club had never been in the hands of the hardline, the idea that it was staunchly Catalan is a myth. People came to Barcelona from all over Spain and by supporting the club they could integrate for example in bars with Catalans," said Dr Lee Watson, who has researched the evolution of Catalan culture.

"The idea that you can become a Catalan overnight is false, but supporting Barça gives you an entrance. Really the reason why Laporta and his more radical group were able to take control was because of the extreme problems at the time."

A taboo topic that has largely been suppressed since the end of Franco is the large number of Catalans who supported Franco and whose businesses thrived under the 'Generalissimo'.

Whether for political reasons or purely out of a sense of survival they worked with the state and many of these were involved in the running of the football team.

Joan Laporta's own father-in-law, Juan Echevarría, was an example of a Catalan who became a powerful figure in the dictator's regime and later his son Alejandro helped establish the Franco Foundation in his memory. Laporta made Alejandro a club director and it caused the president major embarrassment when his political activities were revealed.

The matches between Real Madrid and Barcelona were always going to have political overtones and were swamped in controversy. None more so than the two-legged cup tie in 1943 when Barça won 3-0 at home and the Madrid media claimed that Real had received a hostile reception from Catalan fans.

Barcelona travelled to Madrid with tensions already running high. Before the game it is alleged the match referee went into the Barça changing room accompanied by police and said that he would lay down the law severely. By half time the players were losing heavily and felt they were being discriminated against but then the head of state security is supposed to have told them they had better play the second half if they wanted to leave the stadium alive.

Barça lost 11-1 with the team simply going through the motions and afterwards the Barça board offered its resignation.

Even then, however, when Franco was at his most repressive both teams were fined and the following year Barça beat Real Madrid to lift the Concordia Cup that was set up to ease tensions between the sides.

Barça also won the league in 1945, but they were convinced that politics cost them the title the following year. Sevilla fielded an illegal player that would normally lead to a two-point reduction but instead they were just fined and the two points saw them win the title.

By the end of the Second World War, the defeat of fascism in Europe compromised Franco's hardline approach and he steered his dictatorship towards national catholicism which gave Catalonia some, if only limited, hope for the future. Gradually there was a move towards democracy in the running of football and Barça were able to elect their own president in 1946 with Agustí Montal i Galobart taking over.

The legendary Hungarian midfielder Ladislao Kubala inspired the team to their famous five cups in the 1951-52 season when they won the league, the King's Cup, the Martins Trophy, the Duward Cup and a forerunner of the European Cup: the Latina Cup.

Success brought increased support and the need to move from their Les Corts stadium to the Nou Camp, in 1957, which saw another example of direct help they received from the state. They had financial aid and permission to build on public land.

Again, bitter Espanyol supporters feel aggrieved.

"The difference between the clubs is that Barcelona are the team of the workers and Espanyol that of the middle-class and wealthy. Under Franco we did not do that well and in fact we have done better since him. Barça try and fool people into believing that they are the team of Catalonia," said journalist Humbert Cagigal, of the local paper La Vanguardia.

The Francoist organisers even officially opened the Nou Camp on the date of the Catalan festival, the Mercè.

Barcelona's fans point to the transfer of the great Argentine Alfredo Di Stefano to Real Madrid as an example of bias but again there are two sides to the argument.

Barça had the rights to the player from River Plate although he was playing on-loan for Millionários of Bogotá and Real Madrid had a deal with them. Fifa ruled in favour of Barcelona but it was decided in Spain that it should go to arbitration and each team would have the player for two seasons.

Barça's sense of injustice increased in 1955 when the Imperial Order of the Yugo and Flechas was given to the Real Madrid players who had won the Latina Cup despite the fact that nothing had been given to the Barça players when they lifted the trophy several years earlier.

In the final ten years of Franco's life up to his death in 1975 there was major liberalisation and in Catalonia, under Narcís de Carreras and Agustí Montal, the club was gradually reunited with its Catalan heritage. Barça fans, though, still felt that their club was discriminated against.

Former-president of Real, Santiago Bernabéu, was a close friend of the dictator and an opponent of Catalan separatism. After his side lost the 1968 cup final to Barcelona he said: "They are wrong those who say I don't like Catalonia, I like and I admire it, in spite of the Catalans."

In that game Madrid conceded an own goal and from then on Barça defended to the end, as bottles and other objects rained down onto the pitch. Some saw it as Barça playing against the establishment although Real Madrid fans were equally unhappy, protesting at the actions of the referee.

It was at this match that a renowned exchange of words took place in the presidential box. The clearly agitated wife of government minister Camilo Alonso Vega said to the president of Barça, Narcís de Carreras, "Well done, Barcelona is also part of Spain isn't it?" To which the president replied: "Let's not be annoying señora, let's not be annoying." It was a comment that was replayed many times in the Madrid and Catalan press.

Tensions rose as a result of the legendary 'Guruceta scandal' in 1970 when during the second leg of the cup quarter-final against Real Madrid, a penalty was awarded against Barça for a debatable foul that was in any case outside the penalty area.

Having pulled a goal back Barça had been pressing for a second to draw level on aggregate after losing 2-0 at the Bernabéu stadium, when the packed ground was stunned by the calamitous refereeing decision.

The Barça captain was sent off for sarcastically applauding the decision and Real scored from the penalty. Several Barça players then walked off the pitch but were persuaded back by the English coach Vic Buckingham.

In more democratic times the situation could have been simply put down to error, but the crowd was incensed and convinced of conspiracy. They threw objects onto the field and completely lost control when a Barça penalty appeal was turned down, leading to a pitch invasion.

The events have been recorded by Catalans as a manifestation against the state but it could also be considered the actions of an unruly mob similar to what happened more than 30 years later when objects were thrown at the Real Madrid player Luís Figo.

In the days following the Guruceta match it was actually Franco ministers who prevented the football federation's plan to close the Nou Camp. The inexperienced referee Emilio Guruceta was given an official reprimand, but went on to become a respected international referee before dying in a car crash in 1987.

The fact that the president of the referees' association, José Plaza, was a Real Madrid member did little to ease claims of partiality. He was able to dictate who should referee which games and was still in charge into the 1980s.

Local television in Catalonia would highlight the different standards of refereeing between Real Madrid and Barcelona and it was set in the Catalan psyche that they had to overcome the system in order to win.

Catalans remain critical of refereeing decisions. There is always talk that Real Madrid receive preferential treatment but the truth is that both the top sides get the benefit of the doubt more so than other clubs and president Laporta's friendship with the head of the Spanish football league, Ángel Villar, has also helped them.

Although not on the same scale as Italy, Spain has had its own fair share of claims of bias and corruption. The full truth about many of the controversies during the Franco period such as Di Stefano's move to Real Madrid or the friendship Samitier and Zamora had with Franco, for example, will probably never be known.

But what sits uneasily with the idea of a persecuted Barcelona is that between 1940 and 1960 when Franco's government was at its most hardline, Barcelona came out on top with seven league titles, compared to Atletico Madrid's six and Real Madrid's four. There was also help from the Franco government for the transfer of Ladislao Kubala to Barça on top of the other assistance.

By the early 1970s the ageing Franco had already made Juan Carlos, a prince of the Spanish royal family, his successor and major changes were underfoot.

With the opening of borders, Barça were able to look further afield for a talismanic player that would bring by 1973, an end to the 13-year barren spell without a league trophy. Ambitiously, Barça looked for a player who could sow new hope on the pitch and they were ready to break the bank if necessary to bring him in.

They knew it would be difficult but their first choice was the waif like star of Rinus Michel's all-conquering Ajax team.

Johan Cruyff was the biggest name in European football and at the same time it appeared that his spell at Ajax was coming to an end. He had many suitors but his willingness to be associated with the Catalan cause swung the balance and when he did eventually sign after turning down the more successful Real Madrid he was already immensely popular.

Chapter 3

Cruyff

Always prominent in Laporta's presidency was the figure of Johan Cruyff. While on the periphery at first glance and without any real input if you ask any board members, the truth is that his impact was considerable.

For the largely middle-aged businessmen who fought for power in 2003, Cruyff was an idol. They grew up while Cruyff was at the pinnacle of his fame and either saw at first hand or heard about his exploits on the football field.

Cruyff was a godfather figure and what cemented him even closer to this younger generation was a desire to see the end of president Josep Núñez in the 1990s and his influence thereafter.

Many of the members of the famous Elefant Blau group that had sought to discredit Núñez plotted with Cruyff his downfall, while for the 2003 election campaign his backing gave them a powerful ally. He was respected around the world as one of the greatest players of all time but also a football thinker and innovator.

Aged 17 and working part-time in a printers he made his debut for Ajax in 1964. A year later saw the arrival of coach

Rinus Michels and he was to have a dramatic effect on the development of Cruyff and the philosophy of the Dutch game with the onset of 'total football'.

The manner of a 5-1 victory over Liverpool in the 1966 European Cup announced to the world the arrival of a new brand of attacking football, and for the first time put Dutch football at the forefront of the game.

Michels developed his tactics through studying other coaches and by trial and error. He introduced the idea of the team going forward and defending in unison, one in which players could function in several different roles. He even used the concept of confrontation to bring the most out of players, sometimes deliberately winding them up at half time.

Michels had the luxury of a sublimely talented Cruyff, but the slender built forward was able to offer even more than that. Cruyff had a thoughtful approach to the game and he would spend plenty of time with Michels discussing tactics and ideas during and after training sessions.

Michels' system took a set-back when Ajax were roundly beaten in the 1969 European Cup final but he was still building the blocks towards European domination which the team achieved by winning three European Cups in succession.

The approach revolutionised the game and victory in the 1972 European Cup final was perhaps the greatest hour for 'total football' when Inter Milan, and their defensive 'catenaccio' style, were defeated.

By 1973, the mood at Ajax was changing. Michels had already left for Barcelona and Cruyff realised his time was also up. Ajax's success had been based on selflessness and player versatility. Cruyff had been at the centre of this and was given license to roam anywhere on the pitch with others filling in for him.

However, the Ajax dressing room was turning sour through egos and jealousy, particularly of Cruyff's elevated role in the team and the final straw came when Cruyff lost the captaincy.

Barcelona paid a world record one million dollars to bring in Cruyff and with anticipation sky high he helped the team to win the league in his first season.

Playing the attacking football for which the club is now renowned, they went 27 matches unbeaten but the real moment to savour for the Culés (Barcelona fans) was a 5-0 away win at the Bernabeu stadium. Cruyff was amazed at the way fans would actually thank him rather than just sing his praise.

After such a great start though, Cruyff was never able to recapture the same success at European level he had enjoyed at Ajax. The best Barça reached was the semi-final of the European Cup, but Cruyff's football talent alone ensured he would never be forgotten.

In some ways this was in keeping for a player who put style over results. Despite losing the 1974 World Cup final to West Germany he and many other Dutchmen found plenty of solace in the fact they had played the purest football in the competition.

Confidence bordering on arrogance was also part of Cruyff's make-up and it almost led to him quitting Barcelona in 1976 after a bust-up with coach Hennes Weisweiler over being substituted. His stature at the club and fan protests eventually led to the coach leaving instead.

Then in 1978, Cruyff refused to go to the World Cup in Argentina for reasons that were never explained at the time.

Stories banded about of a sponsorship dispute, poor conditions provided by the Dutch FA or that he took a political stance against the Argentine dictatorship.

More recently his former assistant Carles Rexach explained it was his wife's decision and, maybe to defend himself against the claim, Cruyff dramatically announced on Spanish radio that he had been kidnapped and held at gunpoint just months before the competition. This had altered his outlook and instead of going to the World Cup he decided to spend more time with his wife.

Cruyff did leave Barça at the end of his contract in 1978 and after a spell in the United States brought his career to an end in Holland.

It was not the end of the story for Cruyff as he returned ten years later with the club in crisis and his impact was to shake the football world.

During the 1980s Barça had fallen into a slump. Despite money invested in two of the biggest names at the time, Diego Maradona and Bernd Schuster, they did not bring success and instead unsettled the club leaving a trail of disputes and infighting.

Maradona arrived in 1982 from Boca Juniors already a world star having debuted for Argentina aged just 16 but in an eventful two years at the Nou Camp he lived a chaotic lifestyle brought about by illness, injury and excess.

Too few were the chances for him to show his talent.

In his first season he missed three months through hepatitis but on his return he helped the team to win the King's and League Cups, and was applauded at the Bernabeu stadium by the home fans in a similar way to Ronaldinho 24 years later.

The following campaign started badly for Maradona as a brutal tackle from Athletic Bilbao's Andoni Goikoetxea saw him break his leg and tear ligaments. Barça reached their second consecutive King's Cup final but this was to end in defeat and shame for Maradona.

League champions Athletic Bilbao were the opponents and they had a fierce rivalry with Barça led by the coaches César Menotti and his adversary Javier Clemente. In the build-up to the game there were insults thrown back and forth between the tough disciplinarian Clemente and Barça's laid-back trainer.

Emotions were intensified on the pitch with Maradona facing Goikoetxea.

Bilbao won the match 1-0 but after the final whistle frustration got the better of Maradona who launched himself at the Athletic player Miguel Sola and a free-for-all resulted involving both sets of players while the king waited to give out the cup.

The Barça board were already at the end of their tether with Maradona due to the off-the-field problems and this was just another nail in his coffin as they considered off loading him.

Living in a rented house provided by the club in the exclusive area of Pedralbes, he had developed the 'Maradona clan'. About 20 people all moved in, from his wife, father and childhood friend-turned-agent Jorge Cyterszpiller, through to the family of his brother-in-law and other hangers-on.

Many of Maradona's problems resulted from inexperience and poor advice from his incompetent agent Cyterszpiller.

While Maradona was spending vast amounts of money on himself and those around him he was earning less than his contemporaries at the club and was building up debts. Cyterszpiller's response was to set up an image rights company with luxurious offices that acted as an attempted cover-up against judicial demands for unpaid bills. In the end the club was forced to bail Maradona out agreeing to give advance payments and advice over his legal disputes.

Maradona's fate was sealed immediately after the 1984 Cup final.

Club directors spent the night in the lounge of their Madrid hotel waiting for news about a coach crash in which six fans had been killed and at the same time discussing what they should do with Maradona; one suggestion was a swap deal with Atletico Madrid's Hugo Sánchez. Then at dawn, Maradona strolled in with an entourage having been out all night despite the defeat.

His amazing talent was not enough to sway the Barça directors, with only four out of 21 voting to keep him, and he was eventually sold to Napoli after protracted negotiations lasting over two months between vice-president Joan Gaspart and Napoli president Corrado Ferliano.

Barça also parted company with their chain-smoking coach Menotti, a perfect double act for Maradona who enjoyed the nightlife and changed training sessions to the afternoon.

Núñez felt it was time to look for a disciplinarian coach and his search took him to England. Speaking with the then England manager Bobby Robson, he advised him to choose the promising trainer Terry Venables, an unknown quantity in Spain.

Venables was not the exponent of the typical English long ball style of the time that many feared but then neither was he the tough enforcer that Núñez sought. However, he did bring initial success.

Fans had wanted to see the club buy Mexican, Hugo Sánchez, but Venables plumped for the self-confident Scot, Steve Archibald, and the decision paid off when the team won the league in his first season, 14 years since their last championship success.

But the following year defeat in the European Cup final produced a backlash from which Venables was never able to recover.

The match against Steaua Bucharest, in Seville, was pivotal for Venables' Barcelona.

The coach brought back Archibald from injury at the expense of the popular Pichi Alonso, who had scored a hat-trick in the semi-finals and the gamble failed. Barcelona failed to win their first European Cup in the most heartbreaking fashion, losing in a penalty shoot-out.

The season went on to be even more disappointing as Barca also lost the final of the King's Cup to Zaragoza and finished runners-up in the league.

Venables was unable to reinvigorate his team the following season. The gifted but confrontational German, Schuster, who had stormed off at the end of the European Cup final, was separated from the squad and eventually sold as the situation deteriorated.

Venables' biggest mistake was to rely on players he knew from Britain. He staked his name on Mark Hughes and Gary Lineker ahead of Ruud Gullit and Marco van Basten, who went to AC Milan.

Hughes, nicknamed 'the bull', was a major failure. He struggled to adapt to the less physical nature of the Spanish game and fans failed to appreciate his ability.

Defeat in the Uefa Cup to Dundee United marked the end for Venables who was replaced by Luis Aragonés in 1987.

This was not the solution, though, and the mood in the dressing room hit a new low with the 'Hesperia Motion' where players, meeting at the hotel of that name, called on the president to resign in a dispute about who should be paying an extra tax levied on their wages.

Núñez's presidency was on the rack with the team failing and the fans as well as the players rallying against him. But he went on to show the survival qualities for which he became famous during his 22-year reign and out-played his opponents.

His desire for power was greater than any grudge and his trump card was to bring back Cruyff, with whom he had never got on well, but they agreed to work together.

As popular as ever at the Nou Camp, Cruyff had been the choice of Núñez's opponents as the new coach but none thought that he would go for Cruyff himself.

"The pair had not seen eye-to-eye during Cruyff's time as a player but they were clever enough to work together to benefit their own interests," says journalist Miki Santos.

"When Cruyff left the club in 1978 he had not paid up all the money he owed to the Spanish tax authorities and so Núñez also agreed to pay this money after negotiating a deal with Cruyff.

"He paid the money and won the elections, but this situation is not unusual in politics, where people who don't like each other, work together for a common goal, but the problem is that after a while it usually turns sour."

It was the last throw of the dice for Núñez but Barça fans had not forgotten Cruyff the player and how he had always championed the Catalan cause.

Brought in to win votes, few would have anticipated quite the impact that Cruyff was going to have a second time at the club, although he had made a bright start in his first coaching job at Ajax.

His ideas have been credited for changing the approach to European football and his style has since been taken on at Barcelona by future trainers Frank Rijkaard and Pep Guardiola.

The Ajax system introduced by Michels, where football for the first time was considered an art form, was the cornerstone of Cruyff's own coaching.

"I prefer to win playing well and if we lose I prefer to do it playing well," he was famously quoted as saying.

Using the idea of player versatility, Cruyff turned the Ajax team into one of the most attractive to watch in Europe.

He brought through young players like Marco van Basten, Rijkaard and Dennis Bergkamp and helped them to make the most of their skills.

With hindsight it is easy to see what Cruyff had achieved at Ajax, but after two disappointing years into his job at Barça the jury was still firmly out on his tactics and he had plenty of critics. His popularity from his playing days only went so far, and he struggled against the weight of opinion that claimed he was egocentric and that his unorthodox new system had not actually brought any league titles to Ajax.

At this time in Spain there was little tactical analysis - it was the result that came first and foremost. Few people stopped to consider the new approach Cruyff was introducing and it was typically treated with contempt.

While football in England has been derided for being 'long ball' with no build-up through midfield, in Spain it has been traditionally defensive along the lines of the Italian model.

It was to take another decade for new, younger coaches, influenced by Cruyff's Barça and Arrigo Sacchi's all-conquering AC Milan side, to lift the game to a new level and for the media to begin to look at football in a different light by taking an interest in analysis.

"Before Cruyff arrived there had been many problems and so when things also went wrong for him there was a real crisis.

A new debate started up with everyone in the firing line; we had 30 players in the squad and more-or-less 20 ended up leaving," said Carles Rexach, who became Cruyff's assistant in 1988.

One of Cruyff's first steps after the 1988 elections was to ensure the future of captain Jose Alexanco at the club. He saw the benefits of having a strong figure in the dressing room despite the fact Alexanco had been a leader in the Hesperia Motion and was considered an unruly element.

A particular skill of Cruyff's was to bring through young players and mould them into what he was looking for, but Barça were demanding immediate results. As Cruyff approached the end of his second season his time appeared to be running out. His only trophy had been a Cup Winners' Cup a year before and the upcoming King's Cup final against an all-conquering Real Madrid team was expected to be his death knell. To have lasted so long was surprising as Venables had been sacked despite winning the league and reaching the European Cup final.

The thunder and lightening that night in Valencia mirrored the stormy atmosphere at the club, as Barça looked to upset the form books and beat Real Madrid in the final.

Before the match there was little hope among Barça fans and Cruyff himself feared the worst. Coming to the end of his contract, the club was looking to replace him, with César Menotti about to be offered the chance to return.

On the touchline Cruyff confided to a colleague as he looked up to the press box: "they look like vultures circling their prey."

The opponents Real were enjoying a purple patch in their history led by the 'Quinta del Buitre', five stars of the team led by the most charismatic, Emilio Butragueño. In 1990 they won their fifth league on the trot and were expecting to brush aside Barcelona in the cup before the majority of the team headed off to the World Cup in Italy.

When Barça set out to play a three-four-three formation against such a formidable opposition, one board member in the stands thought to himself this would be the final 'Cruyffism'. Another director admitted later: "it was really difficult to keep backing him because his decisions seemed like madness."

But Cruyff, reverting back to the Dutch 'total football' of his playing days, knew exactly what he was doing. Barça came out 2-0 winners with goals from Guillermo Amor and Julio Salinas. It saved his job and possibly that of the president Josep Núñez.

Chapter Four

The Dream Team

The Masia is a traditional farmhouse in the shadow of the Nou Camp that was renovated to house the Barça youth players. Leaving their families behind they were able to concentrate on honing their football talent and with the stadium standing large in front of them, wonder whether one day they would have the chance to play for the first team.

One 13-year-old who moved to the Masia and progressed through the youth ranks before becoming an integral part of Johan Cruyff's team was called Pep Guardiola.

The Masia, a listed building that was constructed in the early days of the 18th century, was used as a club office before president Josep Núñez cleverly decided to convert it into accommodation for youth players.

Cruyff was always a firm believer in bringing through local players from the youth academy and it was a popular move as Barcelona's homegrown talent has always been treated with special affection by the fans who consider them as their own. Similarly, expensive foreign imports are viewed with suspicion and have to prove themselves before being accepted.

A perfect example was Cruyff's assistant, Carles Rexach, born in Pedralbes, a stones throw away from the Nou Camp.

Known as 'Noi de Pedralbes', our own from Pedralbes, he was a talented winger who played alongside Cruyff in the 1970s and having stayed closely bonded to the club he is now considered one of its elderly statesman.

Rexach had a gift for nurturing young players, working as a youth coach, before becoming Cruyff's assistant and he complemented the Dutchman's philosophy.

By 1990, after two years their dedication to the formation of players was beginning to pay dividends and the success in the King's Cup Final against Real gave Cruyff a lifeline allowing him to continue his project.

"When we got the job in 1988 we needed some time to settle in. We had to work on the team spirit and get the players working together more." he said, "The first year we won the Cup Winners' Cup, then we went backwards just winning the King's Cup but after that it really took off."

The introduction of youth players had a big part to play in this turnaround. Guillermo Amor was the first to make the breakthrough from the academy under Cruyff and for youngsters at the Masia it was their goal to follow in his footsteps.

Amor was brought to the club at 12, two years before the permitted age, but the rules were waived to one side once the coaches saw his potential.

Equally famous for his homesickness at the Masia having had to leave his family behind in Benidorm, he made exemplary progress through the youth ranks and went on to become the engine in the midfield in the first team with an enviable work-rate.

Guardiola first came to the attention of Rexach when he was a youth coach but he still had a long way to go. Growing up in the Masia, five years younger than Amor, Guardiola was one of the kids hoping that one day they would be able to emulate him.

Guardiola endured the many doubts and frustrations of a prospective footballer before moving to the Barça B side and from there he quickly made his debut in 1990.

The figure of Jan Molby in the career of Guardiola is a curious anecdote but Cruyff's decision to stand-by the emerging star instead of signing the Dane from Liverpool had a major impact on both Guardiola and the subsequent fortunes of the club.

Real Madrid's capture of Luis Milla opened up a space in midfield and with the club planning to bring in Molby, Rexach spoke to Cruyff saying that at least first he should take a look at the emerging waif-like Guardiola.

As luck would have it, Guardiola was left on the bench for the next Barcelona B game and Cruyff was left asking how he could put his trust in a player even if he wasn't a regular in the reserves.

He did, though, accept Rexach's judgment and with also Ronald Koeman injured and Amor suspended, Guardiola made his debut.

"Molby played a massive part in the success of Barcelona as the club was about to sign him when Cruyff persuaded he didn't need him and promoted Guardiola to the first team. I doubt very much that if Molby had come, Guardiola would have had the success he went on to have, while Molby is a name which has now been lost in history," said Jordi Basté, a journalist for the radio station RAC 1, and a close friend of Guardiola.

"Pep went on to make his debut against Cadiz. I knew beforehand but he didn't and during an interview in which he denied he would play, I bet him a meal that he would. After the game we arranged to have a meal together and we have been good friends since."

And so, aged 19, Guardiola took his first steps down a road that was to bring plenty of reward but also many difficult moments.

Barça looked for even balance of youth and experience.

"Along with the members of the youth team like Amor and Guardiola that we brought in, we signed other players such as José Mari Bakero and Hristo Stoichkov. Our aim was to have a third of the team Catalan, a third Spanish and a third world-class players," said Rexach.

"Those that we bought had good technique, were able to adapt to the new style of football and also were able to bring with them their own skills and characteristics. When it fell into place we had four or five years of great success and people finally recognised what we had been looking to achieve."

At the time a typical Spanish defence would be composed of two centre-halves, a libero (a further free defender), two wing-backs and a covering midfielder. Cruyff would often field just three defenders and he would always play a creative midfielder, first Luis Milla and then Pep Guardiola. He had two wingers who would be encouraged to remain out wide and have little defensive responsibility.

Cruyff would look at the team as a whole and not its individual elements so for example it was the job of the team to close down the opposition as a group starting from the forward line.

Players were signed to fulfill a specific role within his system.

"We used to base our play in the opposition half, with our defence in the centre of the pitch," said Bakero, who was brought in from Real Sociedad, "he would tell us we were specialists in the job that we did in the team."

In 1991, Barça won their first league title under Cruyff with a team assembled meticulously but which from a distance could appear to be a side of misfits.

It was headed by Koeman, a stocky and immobile defender but at the same time one of the finest ball-players that the game has seen. He was able to dictate the game from centre-half.

Technique over athleticism and this meant it did not matter to Cruyff that many players like Albert Ferrer, Sergi Barjuan, Eusebio Sacristán, Amor and Bakero were not physically imposing. Guardiola was also light-weight and with little pace but he more than made up for this by being an intelligent and instinctive passer.

From Juventus came Michael Laudrup who had failed to prosper in the Italian game, which was heavily weighted in favour of defence. At Barça his talent on the wing was fully appreciated and his inability to defend excused. Gary Linekar and Julio Salinas were both converted from strikers to wingers where Cruyff felt they would be of more benefit to the team.

Aggression came in abundance from the temperamental Bulgarian Hristo Stoichkov in attack, who achieved notoriety by stamping on a referee's foot for which he received a lengthy ban.

Under the phlegmatic leadership of Cruyff, Barça went on to win the league again for the next three years and the real crowning moment for his new approach to football was the European Cup victory against Sampdoria at Wembley.

"He will touch it to Stoichkov, Bakero will stop it and Koeman will shoot, goaaaaaal," screamed Joaquim Maria Puyal of Catalunya Radio, on the night of May 20, 1992, after 111 minutes of football. The moment has become etched in Barcelona history.

Finally, after so many years of being in the shadows of Real Madrid, Johan Cruyff had built a team that was the best in Europe.

Barcelona fans travelled in the thousands to London to watch the European Cup final against Sampdoria. The club had of course been at this stage before in 1986 when with Terry Venables in charge they suffered the heartache of defeat. But this time with the team heading for a second consecutive title there was more confidence.

Before the game Cruyff gave his players the legendary simple message, that now they had arrived this far, they should just go out and enjoy themselves.

It turned out to be a dour match that in any other circumstances would be instantly forgettable.

With few chances for either team and no goals after 90 minutes the game was finally decided by a trademark Ronald Koeman free-kick in extra-time.

After the match the players changed from their away strip into their traditional colours to walk up the famous Wembley steps to greet the Uefa president Lennart Johansson, who gave the cup to captain José Alexanco.

Later Barça vice-president Joan Gaspart famously jumped into the Thames amid the celebrations.

It was the pinnacle moment for Cruyff as he had at last brought to the club as a coach what he had achieved as a player at Ajax but never been able to deliver at Barça during an illustrious career.

The team went on to inherit the nickname, the Dream Team, after the all-conquering American basketball side, which won Olympic gold in Barcelona that summer. A star line-up from the NBA including Michael Jordan, Magic Johnston and Larry Bird had swept all before them on the basketball court.

The names of Guardiola, Stoichkov, Laudrup, Koeman et al have become immortalised by the club and the city, in a similar way to England's World Cup winning players in 1966. Although more recently Barça have won further Champions Leagues under Rijkaard and Guardiola, the first will always be held in a special light.

Even when Andres Iniesta scored an injury time goal to knock out Chelsea from the 2009 Champions League, many papers in Spain rushed to compare it with Barça's last minute strike by José Mari Bakero against Kaiserslautern which saw Barça go through to the next round of the 1992 edition.

The victory has also been used for political gain. An aspiring presidential candidate in 2003, Joan Laporta, used the success to sell his own ambitions. When voters walked into his campaign headquarters in the city's Passeig de Gracia they would see videos of the game being beamed at them from all angles.

"I always remember the confidence we had especially the season we won the European Cup, it was the same in the final even though it was the chance to win the competition for the first time," said full-back Albert Ferrer.

"Once we started winning the dressing room became very positive, everyone there knew what Johan wanted and there was no pressure from the outside.

"We felt as though we were innovators. We were doing something different and that is a good feeling. On top of that it was a fantastic group of people and I had the best time of my career.

"Cruyff had a special personality and what he did well was to keep players concentrated and under just enough pressure to ensure they played their best all season. I would say that was his best quality.

"It was very competitive; while there were say three or four who always played, the rest knew that they had to work hard to stay in the team."

The following season, the Brazilian Romario, one of the most gifted strikers of his generation, joined the all-conquering side.

In his first season he won the Fifa World Player of the Year and was top scorer in Spain but he was also a constant handful for Cruyff as he was one of the many Barça players past and present who also enjoyed the city's nightlife.

The Barcelona Dream Team will always be remembered for introducing a new style of attacking football but there was plenty of myth as well as substance in their reputation as they were far from perfect.

Apart from their first league success in 1991, the other three all went down to the wire. In 1992, Real Madrid only had to draw away at Tenerife to win the league but they lost while Barça won their match against Athletic Bilbao.

The most memorable finish, though, was a year later when Barça's title rival Deportivo la Coruña had to beat Valencia in the final match of the season. In the last minute Miroslav Djukic missed a penalty that would have won them the league.

But while many of the successes the team enjoyed were down to good luck, Koeman also feels mental strength had a part to play.

"We won championships in the final minutes because we believed in ourselves and we thought that we were the best," said Koeman, although adding: "the Dream Team had a lot of failings but the thing is that people remember the good things and not the bad."

If an important element to the Dream Team was confidence then it was the 4-0 demolition by AC Milan in the final of the 1994 Champions League final which shattered this. After that Cruyff's team was never to be the same.

Despite winning the league in 1994 it was as though AC Milan had given Barça a lesson in playing football and this was not the Milan side at its pinnacle under Arrigo Sacchi but a poorer version now under the leadership of Fabio Capello.

Afterwards the team lost direction and were never able to correct the slide. Romario and Stoichkov, stars of the 1994 World Cup in the United States, returned to Barcelona as shadows of their former selves.

The Brazilian had a number of run-ins with Cruyff especially as a result of turning up late for training and eventually was to leave through the back door as so many other Barça stars have done. He was transferred to Flamengo in January, 1995, after Cruyff had run out of patience.

The wheels really had come off and the team's only success from the 1994-95 season was the Spanish Super Cup while they didn't even qualify for Europe.

The following campaign was to be the last for Cruyff and his sacking led to a complete and lasting fall-out with president Núñez.

Barça once again were unable to produce and while Cruyff successfully brought through highly-rated youngsters like Iván de la Peña, his signings, with the exception of Luis Figo, failed to pay off.

"When they lost the final in Athens against AC Milan it was the beginning of the end not just because of the defeat but the manner in which they were torn apart and by then people were expecting more," said As journalist Miki Santos.

"There were too many egos in that side and when he realised that he had to freshen up the squad, those he signed were not good enough. That, though, was not all his fault as he was not given the money. He was interested in Zinedine Zidane and Rui Costa, who at that time were still emerging on the world stage.

"Núñez had other plans and thought it was time for Cruyff to leave, so he told him that the cash was not available."

The situation was not made any better for Cruyff when allegations were made by Spanish radio that a public and players' display of support for him with banners and placards during one of the final games of the season, was staged by Cruyff trying to force a face-off with Núñez.

"What happens is that fans, players, coaches and boards take everything for granted and begin to think that winning is easy and that it will continue. But little by little things started to go wrong," said Rexach.

"The problem with Barcelona historically is that, if you compare football to a stock market, they try and get every last bit of money out of the shares. You have to sell beforehand and in football you have to change players.

"There were no attempts to gradually change the team but even if there had been it would still have been difficult to compete in the transfer market with the money we had available.

"It meant that in the end there was major upheaval and a complete overhaul was necessary. When that happens there is always plenty of criticism and unrest from fans, and it takes time and effort to rebuild the team.

"We waited for too long to change things and the result I think is that we gave away the final of the Champions League in 1994 and the Spanish league the following year."

With three weeks to go until the end of the 1995-6 season Cruyff was dismissed and his assistant Rexach took control of the team, which finished in third place.

Unsurprisingly then, the marriage between Núñez and Cruyff, based on convenience, had fallen apart.

"Even during the success there were moments of debate and argument. They remained together basically due to the success of the team and so when the things started to go wrong it meant real trouble," said Josep Maria Minguella, the former agent, who later ran for the 2003 presidential elections.

"Núñez used to have regular meetings each week with Cruyff, Rexach and the vice-president Joan Gaspart. Núñez was a president who liked to discuss football and tactics but on top of all the other problems when Cruyff suddenly decided he did not want to continue doing this, it made the situation worse.

"He said he did not have to discuss these things, which was true enough, but this decision led to a further deterioration in their relationship.

"Football though comes in cycles and it is normal that teams like the great Ajax and AC Milan sides have a period of success then another team takes over."

Chapter Five

The end of Núñez

In the latter years of the 1970s Spain was in a state of flux and the move to democracy saw a rise in Catalan nationalism. They were once again able to openly express themselves in their own language and quickly went about tearing down the vestiges of the Franco era.

It was strange then for Barça to elect a non-Catalan president in 1978.

Josep Lluis Núñez Clemente was born in Barakaldo, in the Basque Country, and his family moved to Barcelona when he was still a young child.

He grew up to become a successful construction magnate but despite being a familiar face in the business world he struggled to be accepted within the close-knit Catalan establishment, something that irked him.

His desire to be accepted and leave a mark led him to run for the elections where he showed he was a natural politician and swayed the popular vote. He went on to run the club for the next 22 years with an iron rod and now the word 'Núñezism' is common parlance for his style of leadership.

An ambitious and enterprising man he survived many moments of crisis along the way but he will always be remembered as the president when the Dream Team made Barcelona an icon for attacking football.

Largely due to the length of time he was in control, he has gone down as Barca's most successful president, winning 30 football trophies along with many others in the different sports in which the club participates.

He also maximised the potential of the club by extending the Nou Camp to hold 106,000 spectators and oversaw the construction of the Mini Estadi, the small stadium to the side of the Nou Camp where the reserve team plays.

Núñez introduced a solid economic policy taking into account the benefits of marketing and publicity. Another of his decisions was to open the FC Barcelona Museum in 1984 - now the most popular museum in Catalonia with more than one million visitors a year.

His strength of personality has left a lasting impression on the club and ten years since he went, his influence still remains strong at the club.

Núñez showed his capacity for survival following the 'Hesperia Muntiny', when he refused to bow to player dissatisfaction over his leadership, and also demonstrated his steel with his handling of Cruyff both as a player and coach.

However, the decision to remove Cruyff in 1996 was to haunt Núñez to the end and it played a major part in his eventual downfall.

"Núñez got rid of Cruyff in the most cruel of ways, three games before the end of the season, and without warning," explained Josep Maria Minguella, the former agent and closely bonded to the club.

"The way he did it could hardly have been worse, with the vice-president (Joan Gaspart) going down to the dressing room a day before a game to explain the situation to Cruyff."

Gaspart told Cruyff that they were in talks with the former England manager Bobby Robson to replace him. He asked if he wanted to stay until a deal was agreed or preferred to walk away now. Cruyff took the second option.

"Núñez held a press conference to say that Cruyff was leaving and accused him of being in football negotiations but when he was asked what they were he refused to say any more," said Minguella.

The fallout from the feud was a fissure through the heart of the club. Assistant coach, Rexach, found himself in the middle but he did agree to take over the coaching of the team in the final games of the season.

There was a storm of protests from players at Cruyff's dismissal but Núñez was unrepentant.

After the last game of the season Rexach had to choose whether to stay with the club and accept the offer of being Bobby Robson's number two or stand down and show loyalty to Cruyff.

The Dutchman felt he should leave out of solidarity but Rexach was angry that Cruyff was happy to see his son Jordi stay at the club. Initially he accepted the deal from the club but then after speaking with Cruyff was persuaded out of it.

Into the melting pot walked Bobby Robson whose whole appointment was a perfect example of Núñez's Machiavellian politics.

Having got rid of Cruyff, who he saw as a threat to his power due to his strong public support, Núñez deviously brought in an unwitting Robson as stopgap figure.

Robson bore the brunt of the fans' anger at the way that Cruyff had been treated, despite bringing plenty of success on the pitch.

The 1996-97 season saw Barça win the Cup Winners Cup, the Spanish Super Cup and the King's Cup but the achievements were lost on the supporters especially as they missed out on the major trophy, which was the Spanish championship.

Ronaldo, who Robson had known from his time at PSV Eindhoven, was the big star and he bagged 47 goals that season including the only goal, a penalty in the Cup Winners' Cup final against Paris Saint Germain.

Perhaps unsurprisingly, Rexach puts this success after Cruyff and he had left down to an increase in investment.

"They chose to start again with Robson buying big players with quality. They signed Ronaldo, who had a spectacular impact at the club, and other big names including Fernando Couto, Gheorghe Popescu and Luis Enrique who helped to make Barça big again," he said.

"It was a year in which Barça won everything it could have done except for the league but there was war between Cruyff and Núñez and the people were against the new coach.

"Robson had an excellent season and he is now very popular here. People recognise that they behaved very badly towards him then. Robson was always a gentleman and I got on well with him, but the majority of the fans acted badly."

Of course it later emerged that Núñez had been playing Robson along and in reality he was looking for someone to fill-in for a season until one of Europe's most highly regarded young coaches, Ajax's Louis van Gaal, became available.

At the end of the season, Robson was due to go on a trip with the club to Brazil and incredibly he wasn't told until shortly before they were to leave about what had happened.

Minguella explained: "Bobby was in effect a bridge for Núñez and when this came out it made a bad atmosphere worse. The club found themselves in a ridiculous position as Robson had been successful and so he was given the strange position of director of international football."

Robson was forced into the meaningless role, which he accepted for a season before cutting ties with the club. The man he brought with him, Jose Mourinho, as an interpreter and then assistant coach, stayed after Van Gaal saw enough in the young Portuguese to make him his assistant.

"I think that Jose Mourinho has the same mentality as me, he was my assistant for three years and from what I have seen since he has the same approach," said Van Gaal, who admits that he never thought Mourinho, who is now rated as one of the top coaches in the world, would go on and do so well.

"You never know what is going to happen but I certainly did not expect it although he was a good trainer. When I came to Barcelona he was very angry about everything. Bobby Robson had won all that he could have won practically, and he was supposed to leave along with Robson but I decided to keep him on and he learned a lot."

Mourinho himself speaking to El Mundo Deportivo in 1996 admitted that it would be difficult to get to the top but he showed he had the desire.

"There is a long way to go before I could become the first team coach of Barça. I would describe myself as ambitious, organised, spontaneous and the worst loser in the world. In a game I would not think twice about giving my father a kick," he said.

Van Gaal had been part of Núñez's long term plan, he wanted to bring in a coach that would take over all the functions of running the club, following the British model again.

"The president wanted a complete break from the past. When I arrived with Cruyff I knew how the club was organised with different roles from the youth team coaches upwards, as it had always been the same but Núñez wanted someone who would take over everything," said Rexach.

"Van Gaal had complete control, more, probably, than anyone else in the club's history before or since but it all went wrong and the reason was that he fell out with too many people. There were too many wars."

Van Gaal had enjoyed a modest career as a player but moved quickly into coaching, eventually taking over his hometown club Ajax, where he led a young and talented team to the league title in 1996. The side that boasted some of the most promising players in Europe including Patrick Kluivert, Clarence Seedorf and Edgar Davids really hit the headlines a year later when they won the league again and became European champions.

Van Gaal's football philosophy, like Cruyff's, was founded on the coaching of Rinus Michels.

"He was almost a godfather for the people in Holland. Michels created a structure for Dutch football and his book called 'Team Building' was a bible for coaches," said Van Gaal.

"More important than all the titles he achieved, was the fact that he was a very sympathetic human being and not many people understood that. I was a supporter of his approach. When I was young, at training sessions I paid a lot of attention to his coaching ideas."

Fresh from success at Ajax, Van Gaal arrived at Barcelona expecting to employ the same methods but this led to immediate clashes.

In Holland he had made his name bringing youth players through the ranks and his previous experience as a teacher complimented this role perfectly.

However, his disciplinarian approach did not go down well with the experienced internationals at Barcelona who resented being treated like children.

The fans, too, did not take to Van Gaal, who they considered to be abrasive and aloof. They did not like his style of football and were unhappy at his unwillingness to embrace the Catalan culture.

While Van Gaal and Cruyff both championed attacking football the main difference was that for Van Gaal everything had to be planned from the players' movements to the length of the grass on the pitch.

Barça fans had been spoilt watching the individual skills of Romario, Laudrup and Stoichkov; now Van Gaal offered what appeared to be a dour alternative with his constant chime that the route to success was through effort and organisation.

The fact he was a self-confessed Real Madrid fan as a child did not ingratiate him to Barcelona from the start but he made his relationship worse by comments such as: "Catalonia is a good place to live but not to work in," a swipe at their laid back lifestyle.

He was frequently mimicked on Spanish television especially on their equivalent of the British show Spitting

Image, where he was portrayed as a talking brick due to his obstinacy.

His most famous phrase was: "you are always negative, never positive," which he repeatedly told journalists at press conferences after matches in his heavily accented Spanish.

His inability to speak Spanish fluently, never mind Catalan, made him an easy target for jokes while encouraging fans to see him as distant and aloof.

Van Gaal's crucial error was to try and run roughshod over the local media. With almost blanket coverage of Barça from newspapers, radio and television, he needed to appease them but instead his belligerent stance meant he was under constant attack.

"At times he was very aggressive with the media, saying that they did not know what they were talking about and that they were being manipulative. Obviously they just had to wait their moment for things to start going wrong on the pitch, it only took a short drop in form, and then everyone came out against him," said Rexach.

"If I look at the situation in the cold light of day, and being a Catalan, I can see that the media is never reasonable here and the team is either amazing or terrible. If you have such an extreme media and then someone like Van Gaal, who doesn't care about what they say, then there are going to be problems."

Van Gaal went about building the team around his ideals of order and discipline. In his first two years he got rid of 16 players, bringing in 13, including a large number of Dutchmen – Ruud Hesp, Winston Bogarde, Phillip Cocu, Michael Reiziger, Boudewijn Zenden, Patrick Kluivert and the De Boer twins Frank and Ronald.

He fell out with the Brazilian, Rivaldo, arguably the most talented player he brought to the club, who had to endure long spells on the bench.

Rivaldo was a difficult player to manage and the fans turned against him at what they saw as his lack of commitment and the way he would invent injuries so as to return to Brazil.

Van Gaal had little time for creative players who lacked discipline and refused to give him an inch.

Many players who worked under Van Gaal were not enamoured with his style of coaching but they did appreciate his direct approach and honesty.

Albert Ferrer, a survivor from the Dream Team immediately found his position marginalised.

"I had played under Cruyff and Robson but the first thing that Van Gaal said to me was that he had signed Michael Reiziger from Holland and he trusted him so he would play ahead of me. He told me if I wanted to find another club then that would be fine," he explained.

"In the first year I didn't leave because I had confidence in myself from what I had achieved previously and I thought I could prove myself. In the second half of the season I did play regularly but at the start of the next season I was a substitute again and so I had no choice when an offer came from Chelsea.

"I just think that Van Gaal never understood he needed a different approach when training adults at one of the world's biggest clubs. He was dictatorial and it wasn't nice for us. However, while he didn't give me the chance to play at least he was upfront about it."

While there was plenty of dissatisfaction with the way the club was being run, it lay dormant with the team winning two consecutive leagues.

Club elections were held in 1997 but there was no heavyweight opposition and Núñez beat Ángel Fernández comfortably.

A new threat, though, was emerging for the ageing Núñez from a group of predominantly younger, radical Catalans who were fighting against his autocratic leadership.

Núñez had become an imperious figure at Barça who ran the club practically on his own and this new group, the Elefant Blau, with Joan Laporta as its spokesman, sought to highlight the lack of democracy.

To the Catalan establishment Laporta was an outsider but he was extremely ambitious and ready to fight the system.

His rebellious streak had seen him expelled from school for stealing an exam paper and then he was forced to leave a military academy after escaping to watch Barcelona play Steaua Bucharest in the 1986 European Cup Final in Sevilla.

Barcelona and Catalan nationalism were always his passions and he joined the Elefant Blau, which at that time was just a platform for opposition rather than offering an alternative.

They engaged in an examination of the board's activities looking to gather evidence that the financial situation was worse then Núñez claimed.

Amongst other successes, the Elefant Blau forced Núñez to back track and accept that he paid close to £20m for striker Sonny Anderson instead of the £13m previously stated.

It was also uncovered that the board considered selling off club land to raise money – an option Núñez had sworn never to pursue. In the grandiose Barça 2000 redevelopment plan for their Nou Camp stadium it was found that Núñez sought to loan out patrimony for a period of 50 years. Another proposal looked into the possibility of floating Barça on the stock exchange.

Close to the Elefant Blau group was Cruyff, who was an iconic figure to many of the members and he too had the aim of ousting Núñez.

The Elefant Blau put forward a 'motion of censure', a vote of no confidence, and although it failed to achieve the two-thirds majority to force Núñez out legally, they did receive the backing of 15,000 votes, which left Núñez hanging on.

Cruyff had the untouchable position of writing a weekly column in a local paper and making comments to other media. With the vast support he still retained he was ready to put the knife in.

"Since he stopped being a coach, he has always offered his opinion and he was against Núñez and never liked Van Gaal," said Rexach.

Time was running out for both Núñez and Van Gaal and Núñez's decision to offer Van Gaal a new contract followed by the Champions League semi-final defeat by Valencia in 2000 were the final straws.

The Nou Camp was filled with whistles and white handkerchiefs after their European exit and Núñez's decision to resign was followed three days later by Van Gaal leaving out of solidarity, even though he still had two years left on his contract.

Van Gaal gave his final press conference with a parting shot at the press: "Friends, well done, I'm going, you'll all be happy now."

Núñez left an error-ridden legacy from his last few years. Time caught up with him as his decisions went more and more awry.

He failed to move for players like Zinedine Zidane, Rui Costa and Predrag Mijatovic, and while he did bring in Ronaldo it was with such a low buy-out clause it created immediate problems. Crucially though Núñez could not afford to treat Cruyff, the people's hero, so badly.

"Núñez thought the trainer was wrong when it was not actually his system but the players. It is the people on the pitch that win games and so you need to have quality in the team. The tactics can be very good or very bad but it is the players' ability that decides matches," said Rexach.

Elections were called again in 2000 and for the first time since 1978 Núñez was not involved.

His spirit though remained very much alive in the elections, which centered on a continuation of Núñezism or change. The dual was between Núñez's former vice-president Joan Gaspart and the successful publicist Lluís Bassat.

Gaspart offered conservatism, while Bassat headed a group looking for a new start. With Bassat were the Elefant Blau, including Joan Laporta and other respected Barcelona figures like Josep Maria Minguella and Ángel Fernández.

Although Gaspart denies he was offered a place in the Bassat camp, they claim they were willing to include him but he wanted to be president.

"We looked for integration with Gaspart but not as leader so he went his own way and won the election," said Minguella.

"Perhaps the members were not yet ready for such a big change; after all they had just seen Núñez remain in the seat for 22 years. Also, Gaspart was the man with experience in signing players, but he had not been the man in charge, that was very much Núñez.

"Crucially, Bassat and Laporta were not brought on board by Gaspart. They remained in opposition, waiting in the wings."

The end of Núñez did not see a conclusion to the internal battle or Cruyff's destabilising influence from the sidelines. Gaspart found himself inheriting the enemies of Núñez and was in for a torrid three years as president.

Chapter Six

Barça in Crisis

No sooner had Joan Gaspart been elected president than he found himself swamped in one of the biggest controversies ever to beset Spanish football.

Coincidentally, Real Madrid had also held club elections in the summer of 2000 but in very different circumstances to Barcelona with the club on a high after winning their eighth European Cup in Paris.

Lorenzo Sanz's five years as president were dogged by accusations of vote rigging, corruption and club debts. Success on the pitch, however, with the club winning two Champions Leagues made him clear favourite to be re-elected.

The construction magnate Florentino Pérez was the outsider. Having failed in a bid for the presidency in 1995 he was desperate not to suffer the same fate a second time but the polls running up to the elections put Sanz ahead with a sizeable majority. Pérez was viewed as a more financially sound choice who highlighted the debt the club was under, but Sanz, the members felt, was the man to bring trophies.

Peréz needed to conjure up something close to a miracle if he was going to rein in Sanz and that is what he did by putting a proposal to fans that they did not believe possible.

Luis Figo was the emblem and most important player at Barcelona. Signed by Cruyff, he was the current European Player of the Year and was playing the best football of his career. As Barça's only real response to Real Madrid's success he was a favourite of the fans and even a 'penya', a supporters group, had been named after him.

Peréz planned to raid Barcelona for their star player, a move considerably more controversial than any previous transfer between the clubs because of what Figo meant to Barcelonismo.

Culés never thought he would go to Real, although with interest from other big spending European clubs like Lazio, who had just spent £31m on Christian Vieri, they realised that because of the club's problems he could well move on.

A deal was struck between Peréz and Figo's agent José Veiga that the player would sign for Real if Peréz won the elections and if either side failed to comply with the agreement they would have to pay £20m.

"If I am president and Figo doesn't come to Madrid then I will pay the season tickets for all the fans," Perez was able to say to incredulous supporters who were at the same time hearing Figo flatly deny any plans to leave Barça.

Both Figo and Rivaldo had been told to await talks on new contracts until after the Barça elections on July 27, but while the Brazilian was prepared to hold on, Figo felt that the club was undervaluing him.

Crucially the Real elections were a week before those of Barça and so a deal was done and dusted with Figo before a new board was elected at the Nou Camp to deliver a counter-offer.

And so Figo's move to Real went into the history books as probably the most controversial transfer of all time. When he retired in the summer of 2009 despite being one of Portugal's finest ever players he was remembered for the way he left Barça.

While the Catalan club did bank £37.5m, the amount in Figo's buy out clause, it was nothing compared to the feeling of humiliation felt by the loss of their standard bearer. It was almost as though the Figo move showed the impotence of Barça, just as the De Stefano transfer had in the 1950s.

The resentment may not be quite as palpable now but discussion of 'caso Figo' still raises strong emotions.

What was particularly vexing for fans was that Figo had spent the summer denying that he was looking to move. In particular he appeared in one interview with the local newspaper Sport wearing a Barça shirt and categorically saying he was going to stay, while in fact he was on the verge of joining Real.

In Veiga's autobiography he blamed the Catalan media for making Figo say he was going to stay.

The newspaper Sport hit back immediately with journalist Toni Frieros claiming that he was called by Figo to make the interview in which he posed in the Barça shirt.

"Luis Figo rang me at 10pm saying that he wanted to meet up and make some comments the next day which was June 7th (2000). What he said caused a commotion and José phoned me up, furious, asking why he had not been consulted because Figo was stupid. I told him to speak to Figo because it was he who wanted the article," he said.

Figo is now more prepared to talk about what happened and he claims to have a clear conscience about what took place but admits that he did make a mistake by doing the interview with Sport.

"I did not lie when I said I wanted to stay at Barcelona my only error was that in one interview I said that I was not going to go," he said. "I behaved correctly, I told the club what I was doing but I was not valued by them and then when I left it caused a lot of pain."

Although Figo admits that he does not travel to Barcelona for safety reasons he does hope to do so in the future: "I met my wife there and I have a Catalan daughter; Barcelona has a lot of emotional importance for me."

Figo has taken the threat to his himself and his family seriously and he paid 250,000 euros a year for around the clock security on his house in Madrid even while he was playing in Italy.

Whatever Culés feel about the behaviour of Figo it is true that the incoming board manipulated the situation to their gain. Gaspart successfully built up the image of the Portuguese as a traitor and covered up the fact that he should have been offered a new improved deal a long time before the elections.

Gaspart's handling of the Figo transfer was to prove indicative of his actions over the next three years as he lacked the temperament and the skills for the job.

"I will not forget this, whoever is responsible will pay for it. We will see how and when. Figo gave me the impression this morning that he wanted to do two things – make more money and stay with Barcelona. He thinks money is the most important thing in life," was Gaspart's emotional response afterwards.

Looking back Gaspart remains adamant that there was little he could have done under the circumstances to retain Figo.

"Peréz is a friend of mine but he was arrogant in thinking that money could buy everything. In this case it could, although the deal was not entirely legal. I was unlucky to take charge of Barcelona after he had taken over at Madrid and of course he was able to use his own money not that of the club," he said.

"After that we were not able to forget the Figo incident and we made some bad signings but it is also true that we were unfortunate that by taking charge at the beginning of August most transfers have already been made."

Gaspart, who was the face of high-profile signings like Maradona and Stoichkov, denies that he wanted to be president and that he was never offered a role in Bassat's presidential campaign.

The fans' impression that a breath of fresh air at the club through a new leader was all that was needed was very wide of the mark. Gaspart proved unable to close the chasm which had emerged between supporters of Núñez and Cruyff while at the same time was catastrophic in the transfer market.

67

Having vowed to get his own-back on Peréz he showed a lack of rational and calmness when handed the 37.5m pound pot of money from the Figo transfer.

Arsenal's then vice-chairman David Dein could scarcely conceal a smile when Gaspart immediately flew out to London not in a bid to tempt away Thierry Henry as feared but to offer £30m for Marc Overmars and Emmanuel Petit.

Remembering former-coach Louis van Gaal's praise of fellow countryman Overmars, Gaspart lined up the Dutchman. The new coach Llorenç Serra Ferrer then proposed Petit.

"It was outrageous, Dein realised he had the chance of a lifetime and he pushed Barça as far as he could, making them pay far more than the players were worth. It was a difficult situation because clubs knew that Barca had a lot of money to spend and so pushed up the price," said Minguella.

"It was all the more strange because Gaspart had so much experience of negotiating for players, but he paid over the odds for an injury-plagued Overmars. Gaspart never really recovered from that disastrous deal."

But it was only the start of Gaspart's fumbling in the transfer market.

In his first season as president he brought in Gerard Lopez, Alfonso Perez and Richard Dutruel, none of whom lived up to expectation. Then the next year, in big money buys, Javier Saviola came for a rumoured £25m, Giovanni for £13m, Philippe Christanval for £11m and Fabio Rochemback for £10m.

Highly rated Argentine, Saviola, was expected to be the cream of the signings. Arriving from River Plate he was fresh from winning the U-20 World Championships and finishing top scorer with eleven goals.

"He is my successor, I could kill him for being from River (Plate) but he is a great player," said Maradona at the time.

"When I see him play he gives me goose pimples. He has the quality of a midfield conductor and finishes like Van Basten. Breaking from deep he can destroy any defence."

It all may sound difficult to believe now after his career stalled at the Nou Camp and since then fell apart. After several failed moves, he became a bench warmer for several seasons at Real Madrid before moving to Benfica.

Gaspart not only paid exorbitant prices, he then paid the players excessive salaries. Still suffering from a Figo complex, he was worried they could leave just as the Portuguese had done.

This led to other players wanting parity and so wages started to spiral out of control with the club already in debt.

"Gaspart was desperate to keep Kluivert and so Barça gave him a two part contract made up of his deal as a player and a supplement he was paid not to leave. This was incredible because Kluivert was good but not like Ronaldo or Messi at their best," said Minguella.

As if Gaspart wasn't exasperated enough with Peréz after the Figo affair the Real supremo started constructing his galacticos side. At the same time as Barça were signing average players at extortionate prices, Real were bringing in the likes of Zidane and Ronaldo and trophies to boot.

The crowning moment came with victory in the 2002 Champions League Final and although the policy of only buying galacticos was ultimately flawed, it was not until after Gaspart's reign had ended that it became evident on the pitch.

In Gaspart's first season the team could only finish fourth in the league. They were knocked out of the Champions League by Leeds United and beaten by Liverpool in the Uefa Cup before Serra Ferrer was fired and Carles Rexach took over.

There were problems in the dressing room with Rivaldo close to abandoning the club after falling out with the media and fans especially over a trip to see a doctor in Brazil due to an alleged injury.

"If they don't want me then I won't earn even one peseta, I will give up all the money I am owed and I will go back to Brazil with my family and those who do love me," said a hurt Rivaldo.

After 17-years at the club, Josep Guardiola decided to move on before the end of the season. It caused major heartache for many Catalans who had lost their flag bearer on the pitch.

"Barça need him and I am very sorry he has left. He is an emblem and a leader for Catalans," said the local government president at the time, Jordi Pujol.

With no upturn in the club's fortunes in sight, Guardiola thought it was time for a new start and the chance to win more titles before he retired.

He bid an emotional farewell in April, 2001, but his contribution to the club was never forgotten and he was to be welcomed home with open arms when he returned later as a coach.

"I am very proud to have grown and matured here but I am now 30 and my career is escaping me. Looking at the situation and balancing up my options: stay here or look at new leagues, cultures, team-mates and rivals; I believe it is right to leave. I don't know where yet as I have not listened to any offers," he told a press conference at the time.

"At a place like Barcelona it is difficult to find the right time to announce this and I do not know whether this is the correct moment but I have to look to my future. I was clear that the first person I wanted to tell after my parents was Joan Gaspart and then make it public as soon as possible afterwards."

It was another example of the exodus of quality players while despite plenty of investment the recruits were not up to the task in hand.

The following season Barça were beaten in the Champions League by Real Madrid and only qualified for the following year's competition thanks to a spectacular hat-trick from Rivaldo in the final game of the season against Valencia.

In two seasons Gaspart dismissed two coaches as Rexach followed Serra Ferrer in being shown the door. Rexach feels they were both scapegoats for deeper underlying problems.

"I have been appointed coach of Barça a number of times but always like a fireman, when there is a fire I am someone they can call on. I went into the blaze and had a very difficult season with injuries to Overmars, Luis Enrique and Rivaldo," he explains.

"We still though got to the semi-final of the Champions League and we played against Real Madrid who went on to win the final against the Germans (Bayer Leverkusen).

"It was very difficult because every day there was news against me, the players or the president. The problem with having several coaches over a short period is that each brings their own players and so you are left with a massive squad with many players not wanted by the coach, and this is what happened at Barcelona."

Rexach left in the summer of 2002 and despite the fact that confidence in Gaspart's presidential capabilities was already low, fans and media alike were not prepared for the news that their nemesis Louis van Gaal was set to return.

With Van Gaal's parting words of "I'm going, you'll all be happy now," still ringing in their ears, they saw the Dutchman's return as clear desperation but the then director Javier Pérez Farguel did not agree with this view.

"We felt that Rexach was not a strong enough man for the job. In truth he had not had that bad a season and was always popular as a local, but we wanted someone with more discipline to control the dressing room and stop players partying etc," he said.

"We made an exhaustive search and had about five or six possibilities which included Sven Goran Eriksson, Fabio Capello and Klaus Toppmoller. Capello wanted too much money and so we ended up turning to Van Gaal who although seen as unfriendly offered a lot of what we were looking for. He knew the club, had enjoyed success and was a disciplinarian; he did have a problem with the press but this was something we hoped we could change.

"It didn't work; he was unable to change the way he was and on top of this his poor relationship with Cruyff increased the number of his enemies."

Gaspart's presidency, which aimed at diplomacy and bringing people together was becoming synonymous with quick fixes and no real long term planning. They clearly failed to comprehend the animosity towards Van Gaal.

Fresh from failure to take Holland to the 2002 World Cup, Van Gaal, the man with the notebook, was to take over in what was soon to descend into a comedy sketch, only the humour was lost on the Culés.

To make matters even more farcical it was actually Van Gaal himself who revealed he would be returning to the club after being taken in by a Joan Gaspart impersonator in a spoof call from a Spanish radio station.

It cannot be very often that a new coach is greeted at the airport with hostile banners before he is even officially offered the position. Due to the bad feeling towards Van Gaal the club had not even announced at what time he would be arriving at the airport.

The repercussions were felt immediately in the dressing room as Rivaldo announced he was leaving. Rivaldo's individualist style was never in line with Van Gaal's footballing model and having failed to see eye to eye with the Dutchman in his first spell at the club he was not going to hang around for his second.

"Van Gaal is my reason for leaving; I do not like him and without doubt he feels the same way about me because of our previous time together," Rivaldo told reporters.

"He thinks he is the only star and does not want to listen to the opinions of the players. A trainer cannot show you how to kick or control a ball and the opinion of the players must be taken into account."

The Barça board's incompetence had led to a number of signings before Van Gaal was even in place and when he saw who had been brought in he was not happy.

After a failed attempt to sign Fernando Morientes from Real Madrid in a down market bid to revenge the Figo transfer, Barça brought in Gaizka Mendieta, Juan Roman Riquelme and the keeper Robert Enke.

Van Gaal tried to mould the players into his style of footballer.

"It was a system which demanded a lot of everyone. For me there was more emphasis on defence so I had to trackback and could not concentrate on attacking," said Mendieta.

Having arrived on a season's loan from Lazio, Mendieta struggled to adapt and lost confidence as did Riquelme.

Accustomed to being adored by the Boca Junior fans, the move to Europe was a big step for the introverted Riquelme and Van Gaal made it clear to him from day one that he did not want him.

Riquelme had to contend with long spells on the bench and when he did play it was in a position further forward than his favoured role in front of the midfield where he could build the attack.

The backbone of the side remained the same as when Van Gaal left the club with the heavy Dutch influence of Frank de Boer, Michael Reiziger, Phillip Cocu, Patrick Kluivert and Marc Overmars.

Hopes were at a low ebb at the start of the 2002-03 season but they were to hit rock bottom when almost immediately they crashed out of the King's Cup against third division Novelda. The discord in the dressing room was clear with Frank de Boer quick to criticise an inept performance from Robert Enke.

The media mocked Van Gaal's meticulous preparation, which had come to nothing against the lower league side but true to form he hit back.

"We won the Copa del Rey when I was coach here before and I don't remember anyone taking much notice at the time but when we lose everyone is talking about it," he said, tearing into reporters at the press conference.

"The result was due to human errors but I can forgive them because of individual circumstances. We all know that the pitch was small and that Novelda set out to defend."

Unfazed, he promised to stick to a 3-4-2-1 system, saying it would bring success in the end.

The post-match reaction from Van Gaal and the recriminations from the press set the mood for his second stint at the helm.

"They are out of the cup but even now Van Gaal wants to justify the defeat. The team does not know how to score, the defence is a shambles and the keeper is not up to the job," was the frank assessment of the Catalan newspaper Sport.

The only man to back Van Gaal was Gaspart because he knew only too well that unless he could turn around the fortunes of the team his own position as president was in danger.

Evidence that Barça had still not got over the departure of Luis Figo was once again shown in November with the visit of Real Madrid, and it was almost as though the frustration with everything that was going wrong at the club was taken out on the Portuguese.

If possible the screams and abuse directed at Figo were worse than the year before but to his credit he remained calm and even continued to take the corners while missiles rained down from the stands.

In a game of little excitement on the pitch, the fans' ire grew when a Barça goal was ruled off-side but it really boiled over when Figo next attempted to take a corner. Objects were thrown at him including a bottle of whisky, a golf ball and a pig's head; leading to the game being suspended for ten minutes.

Following the 0-0 draw, Van Gaal was criticised for using negative tactics amid claims that Barça should have gone out to win the game.

"I always have to justify myself. It is strange, I have to defend myself when Barcelona had 28 shots and Madrid one, I have not been defensive," was his acerbic reply.

"The game has been a big disappointment but we are going to bounce back. We dominated and created chances so what more do you want? I am disappointed by the result but not the play."

Gaspart incredulously blamed Figo for being provocative and dawdling before taking the corners.

"Figo tried to wind up the fans and the problems resulted from that, I do not want people to come to our stadium and cause trouble," was his astonishing response which left even passionate Barca fans perturbed as they were not the comments expected of a president.

Figo responded at Barcelona airport saying: "Gaspart has not served his club well by saying that. It is ridiculous. I took the corners like I would at any ground in Spain and I had no sporting reason to do it differently. This was a game of football and only mad people think differently."

The Spanish minister of the interior Ángel Acebes claimed that only the professionalism of the police prevented a catastrophe and there were widespread calls for a severe punishment to be meted out to Barça.

What was most worrying was that the Barcelona hierarchy had clearly been permissive in their handling of the hooligan element of the fans. Blame was directly attributed to Gaspart, who in a bizarre relationship had a close affinity to Barça's ultra group the Boixos Nois, widely blamed for causing most of the trouble during the match.

The Boixos Nois were some of the most dangerous ultras in Spain, involved in corruption and murder, but Gaspart always stood by them.

He himself became a member of the Boixos Nois in 1996 and a year later, notwithstanding the fact he was vice-president, Gaspart went from the directors' box to join the Boixos Nois behind the North Goal of the stadium to show his sympathy following the death of one of the group's leaders. Sergio Soto was a man with a criminal record and was reputed to be a neo-Nazi but the club still gave him a minute's silence.

When another fans' group, the Sang Cule, did not respect this, the Boixos Nois attacked them.

The Boixos Nois had returned this loyalty in a typically unruly way during the 2000 election campaign. Gaspart held a meeting with them at his campaign headquarters and on the day of the elections his rival candidates suffered disturbances at their camps.

"They are crazy. They are not proper fans of the club. All they want to do is to cause trouble and many are involved in crime," said one passionate fan, Uri, "I will always be loyal to Barça but for them it is different; they use the name of the club for their own interests."

Journalist Miki Santos explains: "When Gaspart became president he was forced to be more covert but he remained the same. In the Nou Camp there was a special room for the Boixos Nois to keep the things that they would use during the match, like banners, flags and fireworks.

"He had always denied that he looked after them but when Laporta became president they found the room with the banners and everything else from the Boixos Nois. The reason Gaspart backed these people was because he realised the club needed extremists.

"Normally the stadium does not have that much atmosphere and they gave more support and colour but at the same time you cannot control them."

Before the Real game fans must have come into the stadium armed with objects to throw which the security staff had turned a blind eye towards.

In the event, Barça were dealt with leniently by the football federation, ending up with just a fine after appealing against a two-match stadium ban. Many claimed it was another example of bias towards the big two as Betis and Villarreal had both seen their stadiums closed for crowd trouble.

The mainstream Barça fans were becoming increasingly restless. A defeat by Sevilla in December marked their fourth match on the trot without victory and afterwards the crowd jeered and waved white handkerchiefs at the directors' box. In what was likened to Napoleon's last stand, Gaspart chose to remain behind alone for several minutes and listen to the whistles before eventually leaving.

Afterwards he said that the supporters had the right to voice their opinion but while many expected it to be his finale, he refused to stand down and denied he had made mistakes.

All he would offer the disgruntled fans was an assembly meeting to discuss the running of the club but did not even set a date.

Gaspart's presidency was crumbling and days later vice-president Gabriel Masfurrol stood down claiming differences over the direction of the club.

By the time Barça played Mallorca in the run up to Christmas, Gaspart had secretly come to accept that Van Gaal was a liability. The team was languishing in eleventh place and just two points above the relegation zone. Scouring the market for a replacement, the board was lining up a move for the successful Argentine coach Carlos Bianchi.

But in typically shambolic style the club made a last minute U-turn. Barça beat Mallorca 4-0 and following a meeting with the players, in which they gave their support to Van Gaal, Gaspart decided to keep him in charge. Bianchi was to have been unveiled the following Monday but in the end was never given the job.

"We couldn't change the coach just after the team won and scored four goals so Bianchi stayed in Argentina. Later when we approached him he decided to remain at Boca Juniors as his grand-daughter had just been born and he wanted to stay there," said former director, Javier Pérez Farguell.

Van Gaal bullishly tried to play down the problems pointing out that the last time the club won the league in 1998 they had suffered a 'black November' when they failed to win a match but the difference was that now there was no sign of them bouncing back.

The fact that Barça had strung together ten wins out of ten in the Champions League, the best run since AC Milan in 1993, was incidental against the storm of opposition based around his personality, the poor standing in the Spanish league and their style of football.

Whereas a player or manager can move to most clubs and have little or no interest in the culture and history of the city this is not the case with Barça.

Van Gaal appeared detached to Barça fans and it grated with their sense that the club was also a Catalan institution. It led to his downfall the first time round and was a large factor on his return.

The fans were not happy also at the way he had brought in so many foreign players, especially Dutch, and the pressure put on them during games was considerable all-be-it from a half empty Nou Camp.

Some players coped well while others struggled. Frank de Boer, at the centre of defence, appeared to almost wallow in the vitriol of the crowd when he made an error.

For Marc Overmars it was more difficult as he had to justify an exorbitant transfer fee and he also had an unfortunate run of injuries that were eventually to end his career. Apart from this, though, his style of play where he would look to beat a full-back for pace was out of synch with Barça fans preference for short, sharp passing.

Full-back Michael Reiziger showed the strain after realising in a press conference that he said the game was on Sunday instead of Saturday.

"I'm going to be taken apart in the papers tomorrow as they'll say he doesn't even know what day the game will be on. Would you want to play out there in that atmosphere? You're welcome to take my place," he ironised.

Another Dutchman Patrick Kluivert had the public on his back but this had a lot to do with the way he enjoyed the Barça nightlife.

On one typical occasion he turned up late for training, explaining how he had not slept well but then photographs emerged of him out drinking and vomiting in the street the night before.

"I am not a difficult person and I had good relationships with all the coaches I had at Barcelona. The problem was that there was a press with so much control who manipulated the situation," he said.

Kluivert had been rescued by Van Gaal and brought to the Nou Camp in 1998 after his dramatic rise in the game at Ajax had stalled following an unsuccessful move to AC Milan.

He had a healthy strike-rate with Barça, 90 in 182 games, but he failed to bring in trophies and was on a big salary.

"Barça is a big club and expectation is very high, I can now speak openly about the time I was there and the atmosphere if you won was amazing but you got a lot of abuse if you lost, so it was not always easy," he said.

"Van Gaal had a very big influence on my career, I was at Milan for a year where I was not doing particularly well and he gave me the chance to come to Barça. I have known him a long time, since I was a youth team player, and so when the offer came it was easy to take because of his style of football.

"He knows what is right for the team. During training he does everything with the ball and that is what it is all about. He is a trainer with his own mind: he has a strong personality and some people don't understand the way he thinks."

Van Gaal's failure to integrate caused irreconcilable differences. The surreal atmosphere at the club was summed up by a press conference when Van Gaal was asked his view on the criticism he had received from the well-respected Catalan singer Joan Manuel Serrat.

Van Gaal confused Serrat with Placido Domingo, a member of the famous three tenors and incidentally a proud Real Madrid fan whose recording of their club anthem is played every time the players come out onto the pitch at the Bernabeu stadium.

It was almost too easy for the Catalan press to attack him.

"Serrat is just one other member of the club along with the other 100,000 and I cannot argue with each and everyone. I am not an expert on music. I can just say what I like and what I do not like. I like the music of Serrat, Pavarroti and Carreras and I have a CD of theirs at home," said Van Gaal.

There is no doubt that Van Gaal was treated harshly and he does have a strong emotional tie with the city. He still has a house in Sitges on the outskirts of Barcelona.

He was close to tears when he was given the chance of returning to the club but instead he was portrayed as a man without feelings who would sit on the bench during matches with his notepad writing down tactics.

Kluivert is also critical of the way that the press claimed Van Gaal overlooked local players.

"Of the five coaches when I was there I think Van Gaal was better than most in introducing youth team members. It is normal for any coach to sign players that he knows but he also brought in Catalans like Xavi Hernandez and Carles Puyol," he said.

"I also believe it was wrong the way they went on about his personality. It is true that he had a more of an authoritative approach than say Frank Rijkaard, who I knew before from Ajax and the national team, but Rijkaard was very laid back in the way he did things."

In mid-January Barcelona lost 4-2 at home and afterwards members of the Boixos Nois smashed windows and doors at the stadium. They then attacked journalists and a van was hit by a firecracker.

Van Gaal was to last only one more game, another loss away in Galicia to Celta Vigo. Sitting in 12th, they were just three points from the relegation zone and suffering their worst ever start to a campaign.

The following Monday rumours began to circulate that Van Gaal was going to leave and it prompted a large media pack to assemble at the club offices hoping to hear some news.

They were in for a long wait.

The hastily convened meetings behind the scenes by the Barça board went on until the early hours of Tuesday morning. Eventually about 2am Van Gaal and Gaspart appeared before the press for the Dutchman to give his parting words to a Catalan audience eager to write his obituary.

"On the flight back (from Vigo) I believed that I was still the person to do the job and that I could solve the club's problems but I have been talked out of that view and now we have reached an agreement. I am the one responsible," he said.

"There is a negative atmosphere at the club caused by supporters of Cruyff and this is influencing fans, directors and the press. I want to ask the people here and those involved, especially the press, that they back the next trainer because if they do not they will have the same problems."

Van Gaal had tears in his eyes as he spoke to a charged pressroom but it did not put off a final assault from the media.

"You failed the first time, you've failed a second, how does that make you feel?" asked one reporter.

"I did not fail the first time. I would not call winning the league twice and the Copa del Rey, a failure," replied a defiant Van Gaal.

Then it was the turn of an embattled Gaspart and he vowed to stay on, saying he had the experience to help the team through its problems.

"I'd make the same appointment if I had my time again. I thought he was the right choice and so I have no regrets," he said. "Unfortunately things did not work out. Personally as director and vice-president I have lived through moments like this and I am remaining here, we are in a sporting crisis."

Van Gaal had stayed loyal to his 4-2-3-1 system until the end and apart from his personality, his approach to football including comments like: "the game must be based on a system of positions, lines and triangles for perfect coverage during different spells of the match" also determined his downfall.

So the hunt was on to find a replacement but the board had still not learnt their lesson and it was conducted in a similarly unprofessional way to when they considered the appointment of Carlos Bianchi.

Rexach and César Menotti, who had managed Barcelona for a year in 1984, were both touted for the job and in fact the latter was about to board a plane for Spain when it was officially announced that Radomir Antic was to be given what had become a poisoned chalice.

Antic had not managed a club for two years since leaving Oviedo but he was experienced and charismatic, and the board above everything else did not want to make another unpopular choice.

The Serbian claimed that the current team could be a lot more successful with Saviola and Riquelme at the centre. He was convinced the team had the capacity to work harder and more effectively and this was enough to persuade an indecisive Gaspart.

In Antic's first game, though, against Athletic Bilbao the team could only manage a draw after going two-goals up.

"I know what Barcelona need and that is what I am giving to them. Football is a collective game and my work is to put the idea across that the players need to sacrifice themselves for the team," he said in upbeat mood.

"For something to function it is necessary for all the pieces to come together. A trainer must know his players to get the best out of them while players must be aware how to improve their weaknesses."

The turbulent times at the club were reflected by an announcement on the day Antic took over that there would be a board meeting to discuss a date for an extraordinary general meeting, after an ex-director Ramon Fusté proposed a motion of no-confidence in the board.

The former-director was looking to break the bond Gaspart had formed with his five vice-presidents and had been preparing his move for some time.

Fusté had to get the backing of 4,505 members for a motion of no-confidence and he achieved this unlike another member Ivan Carrillo who had made a similar bid a month before.

"He is the worst president in the history of the club," said Fusté at the time. "I think Van Gaal was responsible in the area of his command but the debate is whether he had a squad which a club like Barça deserves.

"He was not the only one responsible as the main achievement of Rexach and Serra Ferrer before him was qualifying for the Champions League."

Gaspart originally fought to block the Fusté motion claiming it was the second to be brought in a year but before the legal argument gathered momentum, he decided to resign on February 13, 2003, to be replaced by vice-president Enric Reyna, on an interim basis before elections at the end of the season.

"The problems at Barça are not just sporting and people need to be less selfish and think of the club. I have a great desire to be a director and president but there are times in life when, for good or bad, you have to be responsible." said Gaspart.

"The president has to look seriously at his errors and his responsibility and take a decision. Certain members might think that you should take a decision earlier or later but you are the one that has to decide."

"How will I feel if Barça win after I go? I will feel the same as any member who wanted me out. There are things which are not negotiable in life such as your family but Barça is something about which you can choose to be involved with."

The timing of his decision was possibly due to outside pressure, not so much from fans but from the authorities. The local government described the next home game as high risk because of the animosity fans felt towards the board.

The head of sports in the local government, Josep Maldonado, told Gaspart he would be unable to say that he had not been warned if there was a death or serious injury at the Nou Camp.

Police said that while they could guarantee the safety of the directors travelling to and from their houses to the game there was a fear that fans were planning to get into the directors' box.

On top of this, Fusté was attempting to drum up opposition by providing coaches so people could travel to protest.

And so finally 'Circus Barça' as the press had begun to describe the club, was coming to an end and Gaspart for all his good intentions left a sorry record as president.

His final signing before the appointment of Antic summed up his dealings in the transfer market. Full-back Juan Pablo Sorin, an Argentine signed from Lazio, offered little on the pitch during the six months he was at Barça and his most memorable impact was to cause consternation when spotted dancing in a heavy metal disco while injured.

Gaspart was part of the old order along with Núñez and he failed to keep abreast of the modernisation of football

A team with a massive world wide following was failing badly in bringing in revenue from merchandising and sponsorship while Gaspart allowed some Boixos Nois into the ground free so that they could create more atmosphere.

He spent 180 million euros on players without winning a trophy and he left with the club saddled with a 230 million euros debt.

Ex-directors Xavier Aguilar and Gonçal Lloveras also claimed in January 2003 that the club would have made extra losses of over 21m euros the previous season had it not sold off facilities.

On the other hand, ex-director Javier Pérez-Farguell felt that while mistakes were made, the situation was portrayed as far worse because the board had enemies who were able to influence the media.

Involved in the economic running of the club, Pérez Farguell, worked under Gaspart and then the first year of the new Laporta regime before his non-political position was made obsolete.

"All clubs have economic problems and owners have to be prepared to lose money. Barcelona is in a better position because of its fan base and ability to draw publicity and sponsorship but even so it is difficult to balance the budget," he said.

"The club had a lot of money after Figo was sold but the cash was spent very quickly. It would have been better to sit back and plan ahead but it had all gone in about four weeks. It was not good but the situation financially was still not terrible compared to a lot of clubs.

"I think it was probably good, though, to have elections when they did because the club needed a new start and to begin again calmly. There were six candidates and the election had a big turn-out in."

The date of the elections remained unclear as it became apparent that Reyna was offering himself as an alternative president on a permanent basis even though club rules stated an election had to be called within three months of him taking over. He even considered buying players before he was eventually persuaded to arrange elections for mid-June.

Antic had accepted a six-month contract with his goal to achieve a place in Europe the following season.

"When I arrived, as you would expect, the team was under a lot of pressure. I wasn't interested in what had happened before or giving my opinions on Van Gaal or anyone else, I came into do a job," said Antic.

"I came with the concept of forgetting it was a short term deal but thinking I was going to be there for a 100 years.

"It was a difficult job made more so by the number of injuries like that to Luis Enrique who was a charismatic captain. I do remember, though, that Carles Puyol was also very important to the team as a leader."

Antic initially stated he would make Juan Román Riquelme the centre-piece of his team but he, like Van Gaal, ran out of patience with the Argentine playmaker.

"Barça need champions and Riquelme needed to work harder to improve. He was under a lot of pressure and so always looked for the killer pass. If a player cannot cope with the pressure then they should not be at Barcelona," Antic said bluntly.

Riquelme only scored three goals all season for Barça and ended up being loaned out to Villarreal. He is a complex character, who although appearing shy and retiring is also very proud, which has led him to have run-ins with many coaches.

In the end Antic achieved his aim of European football with an away win on the final day of the season against Celta Vigo but the Uefa Cup was a long way off satisfying the demands of the fans.

Antic could have done little more as under his direction the team picked up 43 points from a possible 54.

Chapter Seven

The Laporta Revolution

Laporta was left saturated in Cava as he danced with election planners and future board members while television cameras and photographers recorded the scene by Barça's second smaller stadium the Mini-stadi, used mainly for reserve games.

There was a real sense of witnessing a historic occasion, a changing of the order, as Laporta's maverick new team was ushered into power with a landslide victory.

Amid the camera flashes and slaps on the back, Laporta attempted to prepare himself as he walked to the main auditorium where the election results would be read out.

On the stage after being officially made president he once again outlined a fresh new plan for the club, which promised success while at the same time providing transparency for the socios, the members.

In the club offices over the coming days the celebrations came to an abrupt halt when the new board realised the size of the task ahead.

They had pledged to bring Barça back to the elite of the game within three years both in terms of footballing success and financial wealth but a quick examination of the club's books made grim reading.

The club was in a far worse state than previously imagined and was leaking money with debts over 200m euros.

Newly installed vice-president Ferran Soriano, who took control of economic direction, claims the books had been cooked to make the financial situation appear better and training facilities had been sold to raise money.

"The accounts were masked with the sale of patrimony," said Soriano, "we were left with the options of planning a steady, long term recovery or the more risk laden path of spending our way out of trouble to achieve a dramatic change in the club's fortunes."

They chose the latter, which meant that they would also be able to comply with their promises to bring in new world-class players. They would look to cut unnecessary outgoings while seeking new ways to increase income, with this money to be spent on the team rather than to be used to pay off the debt.

Their ambitious plan was to generate 200m euros a year and they considered many different avenues from raising seat prices at the Nou Camp to even shirt sponsorship. Barça had always shunned the idea of using the shirt for commercial interests but during the election campaign Laporta admitted that he would consider it as a last resort and fans were prepared to accept this such was the economic crisis at the club.

The directors were given the job of going out and trying to sell the club to clients.

They renegotiated television deals to make them performance related, if the team did well then the club would earn more. Their own television channel was rebranded Barça TV and given a facelift.

Then there were marketing strategies to maximise revenue from the appeal of the club such as by playing lucrative friendly games abroad and producing more Barça merchandise.

"When we arrived we had the feeling that the whole operation was stuck in the past and that working together we could make dramatic improvements," said another vice-president Marc Ingla.

The club debt meant that they didn't even have the money to pay the interest on loans some of which had spiralled to 27 per cent. Led by the expert Xavier Faus they looked to renegotiate loans armed with a firm business plan, which demonstrated clearly that in the first year they were going to make a loss but after that they would start to make money.

"We spoke with national and international firms showing them our financial plan to restructure the debt and they liked what we were offering. The Catalan bank, La Caixa, who have traditionally been close to the club and supportive worked with us on a daily basis," said Soriano.

The board believed that a successful club model required a sizeable amount of money to be spent on transfers.

"If you look at the case of Manchester United and Tottenham; in 1992-93 they both had the same budget of 25m euros. Ten years later United's was two-and-half times that of Tottenham and you can see the difference that made. What clubs spend in the transfer market will have a correlation with how many titles they have, as long as, of course, they make astute purchases," said Soriano.

"At Barcelona we had the same income as Manchester in 1995 but from then on we fell away more and more. It really started with the arrival in 1997 of Louis Van Gaal as coach, as by then the Núñez model was not working well.

"A good way to tell how well a team is doing is to see if they are able to hang on to their top players and the answer with Barça was clearly that they could not. You only have to look at the sales of Ronaldo and Figo to see that. The problem with the system at the time was that they lacked imagination.

"The world of football was changing with more money coming into it through television deals and publicity. The model that the Núñez directors followed meant that they balanced everything and so were not necessarily in debt but were not taking advantage of the new openings. It was like a grocery store that is doing fine but then a supermarket blows them out of the water.

"In order to compete, during Van Gaal's first two years in charge the spending became more than the income and this gap then grew from £25m to £36m and up to £52m in 2003. This led to the need for drastic measures and meant selling our inheritance."

Sandro Rosell was officially given the role of rebuilding the football structure of the club.

He was to oversee this department that included the responsibility for naming of the sports director and the coach. In contrast to the UK, in Spain there is a coach whose role is solely to look after the running of the team, while the sports director, on behalf of the board looks after the business of player contracts and transfers.

Having worked for Nike arranging sporting contracts he was ideally placed with the necessary contacts to build a formidable team.

The problem for him from the start was the jealousy from other board members and as importantly Johan Cruyff, lurking in the background. Cruyff turned down the chance of an official role on the board but he was a close confidante of Laporta and always had the ear of the president.

Cruyff also had many contacts within the game and it became a battle of egos between Rosell and him.

It was Cruyff who was instrumental in the decision to appoint Txiki Begiristain as sports director and Frank Rijkaard as coach. It was a major gamble as both lacked a proven track record but Cruyff knew them well from their playing days.

Begiristain was a member of the Dream Team and had shown signs that he had the communication skills and intelligence to master the role. Although Basque, he had managed to integrate effortlessly into Catalan life, learning the language he claims by listening to the radio on the way to training. He finished his career in Japan and was fluent in English, which was an important job pre-requisite.

Still, he had had no formal experience with clubs since retiring from football and had been commentating on Spanish television.

Cruyff had Guus Hiddink, Ronald Koeman and Frank Rijkaard in mind when he set out to find a replacement for Radomir Antic.

Hiddink was the only candidate with experience but he was under contract with PSV Eindhoven and ruled himself out, as did Koeman who was working with Ajax.

That left Rijkaard whose appointment would be the biggest step into the unknown and his very brief coaching career included a spell at Sparta Rotterdam where he led them to relegation.

The fledgling board though was also looking for a famous name that would boost their credibility and Rijkaard had this through his achievements as a player.

During the campaign, Laporta had promised to bring in a world-class player.

The link to David Beckham had proved to be merely a marketing ploy that worked perfectly but now they badly needed to find a reasonably priced star who would capture the imagination of the fans and this was no easy task.

Putting their thinking caps on there was one name that fitted these requirements and also could be enticed to Barça through Sandro Rosell. The vice-president had worked with Ronaldinho as a Nike representative in Brazil and had remained a friend of the player.

A more controversial element to the Laporta presidential campaign was to make the club a focal point for Catalan nationalism.

Laporta spelt out how he planned to make the club more closely identifiable with the Catalan fan base. It was a message that struck a chord due to the erosion of the Catalan heartbeat under Louis van Gaal and the introduction of so many Dutch players.

Nationalism being such an emotive subject in Catalonia meant that Laporta's stance was always going to raise strong opinions.

Since the death of Franco and the restoration of the Catalan local government, more and more rights have been given to the region but there is still a significant percentage looking for more independence. Only a minority, though, seek complete separation from Spain.

Some feel that Catalonia suffers at the hands of Madrid and that the region also receives less investment.

"The policy is to undermine Barcelona, they take advantage of the city in terms of industry and put little back. I do not see why Catalonia could not function perfectly well on its own with the size of the population and the industry here," said Marc, a Catalan.

"They even take water from us here and they give it to the south of Spain, to the extent we do not have enough."

Barcelona of course has always tied itself to the Catalan cause when able to, except under periods of dictatorship, but it had never aligned itself to the radical edge.

For many Catalans, Barça is their national team and they support the club even though they have no interest in football.

Returning to the rivalry with Espanyol on the national day of Catalonia, on September 11, both teams put flowers at the statue of Rafael Casanova, but when representatives of Espanyol do it, they receive whistles. To many they feel that Espanyol is against the Catalan team and interestingly even though Espanyol have taken active steps in recent years to promote Catalan, their fan base has not increased.

Barça is truly a club of the people, helped by the fact that fans elect the board, something that has become the envy of many others in a world where football has become a business. Even the club hymn is more frequently played and better known than the downbeat Catalonia anthem.

Barça, rather than football in general, is never far from discussion. It has centre stage in newspapers and local television while there is surprisingly little talk about other clubs.

When Barcelona were eliminated in the Champions League semi-finals by Manchester United in 2008 several of the non-sport newspapers the following day had their first five or six pages devoted to the coverage. When they won the following year against Manchester United to reach the Champions League Final there were even more column inches.

Local journalists discuss the comings and goings at the Nou Camp on a daily basis on all four Catalan channels while games not shown live are analysed to saturation point.

That is why, partly in jest, it is said that the most important job in Catalonia is the Barcelona president not the head of the local government.

Supporting Barça has a religious quality to it.

When Barcelona won their fourth league on the trot in 1994, thanks to the missed penalty by Deportivo la Coruña in the final minutes of their game against Valencia, supporters were describing it as a miracle.

"God exists and Cruyff is his prophet or messenger, or his colleague, or his envoy, his friend of course, only a close friend of someone superior to us can achieve four leagues like Barcelona have done. They were not owners of their own destiny but they survived everything," ran El Periodico the following day.

After that game there was a procession to the catholic pilgrimage site of Monserrat with fans arriving en masse in cars and scooters, with horns blaring, ready to pray and give thanks to God.

At the monastery the Barça board signed a book of honour and a plaque by the altar.

Then from Monserrat the crowd headed to Plaça Saint Jaume, the revered site of Catalan politics in the centre of the city that dates back to a time before mass media when the president of the local government would address the public directly from the balcony of the town hall.

This was the very location where Francesc Macià proclaimed the Catalan Republic and Lluís Companys declared the Catalan state of the Spanish Republic.

The players used to stand on the balcony to celebrate and it was where in 1999, Luis Figo, then a Barça hero, famously made fun of arch-rivals Real Madrid after winning the league title: "Blancos llorones felicita a las Campeones" (White cry babies congratulate the champions).

When Barcelona won the league in 2005 it was decided to move the celebrations from Plaça Saint Jaume to the Nou Camp because of its small size while at the stadium they could also stage more of a show with performances and fireworks.

As explained by the anthropologist JJ Pujadas i Dolors Comas there is nothing unusual in the way that Barcelona has become such an important force in everyday life.

"The idea of a community is a relationship with something defined, such as being Catalan, and this would include everything indistinguishable with that," he states. "It is stable in spite of adversity, is reborn at certain times and has a future without limits."

But the anthropology of the Barça fan base is far more complex than simply lying in the Catalan community. In other cities, teams represent specific communities, such as Celtic and Rangers in Glasgow or Livorno in Italy, which has a left-wing following.

Barcelona stands for many different ideals and has fans from other parts of Spain as well as from all over the world.

As Jordi Salvador Duch explained in his book Football, Metafora D'Una Guerra Freda, there is Barça versus Madrid, Barça as the forefront of Catalanism, Barça versus Catalanism, Barça and internationalism, which has evolved noticeably since the Olympic Games in 1992, and finally Barça as a name in the fight against centralism in all parts of Spain and around the world.

One of the most easily recognisable of these is Barcelona's fight against Madrid, which manifests itself in their football rivalry with their big enemy Real Madrid.

Everything else comes second to outdoing Real and a good example was how Louis van Gaal's achievement of winning the double in his first year at the club, in 1998, was entirely forgotten as Real Madrid won the Champions League.

Those players who leave and go to the enemy can expect never to be forgiven and have a torrid time when they return to the Nou Camp to play.

When Michael Laudrup came back there was a banner displayed showing the names of the Real Madrid players who had died in car crashes and it said that Laudrup would be next.

Laudrup said at the time that it was the most nerve-racking experience he had ever experienced but of course it was nothing compared to the reaction that Figo was to be subjected to.

Many years later when Laudrup returned as coach of Getafe he was still not allowed to forget his decision to go to Real Madrid with placards calling him a traitor.

An intriguing element to Barcelona is the support they receive from overseas with official fan groups around the world. Catalonia's fight for greater independence certainly has had an impact on this with the club having looked abroad long before it became common place in order to exploit other markets.

Barça have big fan bases in Portugal and Morocco where there also exists an element of anti-Spanish feeling.

"The reason why I came to Barcelona was because of the football team. I was a big fan before I left Morocco and I used to watch them play whenever I could with my brother," says Abdul.

"It is a club which represents a lot more than just football, it is what the club stands for, its values, that is why I support it so passionately."

In recent years the club has been able to build on this base with an effective marketing policy to boost the club's revenue.

Whereas Manchester United once led the way in the Far East with David Beckham the dream ticket with his good looks and clean-cut image they were unable to maintain this advantage after he left.

Barcelona now are at the forefront with thousands greeting the team as they turned out to train in a recent visit to Japan. Impressively the locals sang the Barça anthem in Catalan but in so doing also unwittingly backed everything else that the club stands for.

"Before it was really David Beckham who was the star and that was why Manchester United were so popular. When he left people looked elsewhere and now I would say Barça are the biggest team. People this time though are actually supporting the team rather than the a person so for example it didn't matter that Ronaldinho went as they just started to follow the next star," said Japanese journalist Ikuko Oda.

Up until 2003, while Barcelona sat comfortably at the centre of Catalan life, the leadership did not actively seek to push the nationalist cause. Joan Gaspart was a very passionate Catalan but as president he had not politicised the club but the problems that Barça were experiencing in 2003 opened the door for Laporta's extremism.

While many were happy to see Barça as a Catalan voice, there were many others who felt that in a time of democracy it was wrong to mix politics with football.

Laporta oversaw an exodus of foreign players including four from Holland: Michael Reiziger, Frank de Boer, Phillip Cocu and Patrick Kluivert; stalwarts of the Van Gaal era leaving.

It is true a couple of new Dutch players did arrive, though, with Giovanni van Bronckhorst signing from Arsenal and Edgar Davids coming on loan for six months from Juventus, on the behest of Frank Rijkaard.

"Having been at the club for a long time I wanted to stay and help win the league again but the reason I left was down to the pro-Catalan feeling, as they were given an advantage over the rest," admits Kluivert, who lasted just one season under the new regime before he too moved on.

"I was disappointed to go after six years and I thought that I could have offered still more to the club. I wasn't the only one to leave and I am sure that the coaching staff had pressure from above to make the decision.

"I will never forget Barcelona. When I have time I love to go back and I still have the nightclub there. I do feel that I was forced out but Laporta was the boss and if I hadn't gone then I wouldn't have been appreciated, so it was better to go."

Cruyff's influence on Laporta had seen the appointment of Rijkaard but the new coach quickly endeared himself to the fans by trying to integrate and communicating well in Spanish unlike Van Gaal before him.

A strong youth academy was central to the new board's planning. They looked to replicate the success enjoyed by Cruyff's Dream Team by bringing through young players and this had the added bonus of making the team more identifiable with its Catalan roots.

"After winning the elections we realised that the youth set-up was in a very bad state and without an overall director. We brought in Guillermo Amor and (Josep) Colomer to put together a better coordinated system," said Rosell.

"With youth development you are not going to get results overnight but we were putting together a long term project. We concentrated on bringing in kids younger than 14 so that if they were not from Europe when they reached the first team they would have no problem with the foreigners rule.

"It was like the situation with Leo Messi who was younger than 14 when he came and so has not filled up a foreigner's place in the team."

The board also discovered to their amazement that Gaspart's paranoia over losing players had spread to the youth team and big money deals had been made to tie youngsters like Nano Macedo and Haruna Babangida to the club. This pair like others hadn't even established themselves in the first team and in fact never would.

At the same time players with a bright future had been allowed to slip through the net. Arsenal and Manchester

United had successfully poached Cesc Fàbregas and Gerard Piqué respectively while the club was preoccupied by the presidential elections in 2003.

Feelings are divided about the players' decisions to move. For Rosell he felt that Piqué left because he could earn more money at United and that he should have shown more loyalty to the club, while he is more understanding of Cesc's motives as he was ready to make the move up and became an important player in his first season at Arsenal.

Arsenal manager Arsene Wenger had watched Cesc during the Under-17 World Championships in 2003 and pounced to prise him away from Barça before he signed a professional contract. He was not so lucky with Cesc's team-mate, Leo Messi, who he also tried but failed to capture.

Cesc became Arsenal's youngest ever player, debuting at 16, and is very grateful to Wenger for giving him his chance.

"I made the most of a fantastic opportunity but I would not say my style of football changed at Arsenal. I was at Barça for six years and I learned the concepts of playing the game as well as an all-round education," he said.

"At Arsenal the philosophy is similar to Barça and so you could say I continued my Barça education. I can say that I was given opportunities at Arsenal that I doubt I would have had at Barça. It is strange to think I have played in Champions League and FA Cup finals already."

Despite being an ex-director of Barça, Gerard Piqué's grandfather Amador Bernabéu, gave his blessing for him to move to United to further his development.

"It was an unforgettable day when he left but I don't know whether it was positive or negative. My dream was that he would stay at Barça and wear the shirt but this was his destiny," he said.

The fact that when he was talking with Manchester United, he was demoted from Barça's A youth team and actually spent two months without playing did little to encourage him to stay.

"I wasn't thinking about economics but things like what types of university are available so you can still study, which family I would be with while in Manchester and that sort of thing. You are looking at other cultures and other opportunities," said Piqué, shortly after moving to United.

Former-youth coach Guillermo Amor admits it was frustrating the way players left but he is also realistic.

"When we arrived, Cesc and Piqué were both in the process of going and everything had been arranged, but since then regularly there have been players leaving every year. (Fran) Merida went to Arsenal and (Dani) Pacheco also moved to Liverpool," says Amor.

"It is not easy to win a first-team place at Barça and so if a club comes along and says to a 15 or 16-year-old, if you sign for us then everything will be fine, you will get your chances in the first team and these clubs are like Manchester United and Arsenal, then they are going to be interested apart from the money.

"In terms of money, the family is going to see that economically it makes sense to go as it can provide more security."

Rijkaard was keen to bring through the youth talent but his task was made easier by the exceptional quality on offer as Amor explains.

"While the youth team has always been good at Barça, it is not often that you come across a complete team. Often you have maybe one or two who are going to make the grade but here we were talking about a whole squad of 20 and they were the best around," he said.

Andres Iniesta was given a regular first team place while Rijkaard also oversaw the gradual introduction of Leo Messi, Giovanni dos Santos and Bojan Krkic.

The idea of making a strong bond between the team and its fans is of course not unique to Barcelona in Spain. Athletic Bilbao who have been heavily influenced by Basque nationalists like Sabino Arana went a step further.

The idea at Athletic Bilbao was that they would generate a greater fighting spirit among the players if they prevented foreigners (including those from other parts of Spain) playing in their team. The club have been criticised in some quarters for what could be perceived as a xenophobic approach but there are no laws within the game to prevent this.

Chapter Eight

Ronaldinho and a new dawn

Sitting down with a coffee and a cigarette, Frank Rijkaard, was a picture of relaxation as he prepared for the interview. It was the summer of 2003 and Rijkaard had been appointed as the new Barcelona coach a few weeks earlier.

Many had felt that Radomir Antic deserved the chance to keep his position having finally led the team into Europe the season before, but instead the hopes of the club had been put in the hands of a coaching rookie.

His limited coaching experience which included death threats following the relegation of one of his sides hardly inspired confidence but even so Rijkaard if he did have any personal doubts, did not let it show, and was happy to talk.

He spoke calmly for an hour about his plans for Barça and how he understood the Catalan club and their sensitivities. His laid-back approach was to be the trademark of his five years as Barcelona coach, a memorable period for its success but then also for the dramatic collapse that followed.

Rijkaard is one of many successful Dutch players, like Ruud Gullit and Edgar Davids, who have Surinamese origins. His father played in the Dutch colony before moving to Holland in 1950 where he married a Dutch woman.

Born in Amsterdam, Frank Rijkaard was spotted by coach Leo Beenhakker and brought to Ajax at 13. He passed through the famous youth academy where his burgeoning talents were developed.

Rijkaard made his debut in the first team in 1980 and quickly dominated the midfield both physically and with his personality. In surprising contrast to his coaching style he was known for his volatile temper.

Rijkaard's ability and his reading of the game helped Ajax to win two domestic leagues and that was before Johan Cruyff took over in 1983. The mid-80s saw the rise of a golden generation at Ajax, which included Marco van Basten, Aron Winter, Richard Witschge, Stanley Menzo and John van Schip and culminated in the winning of the Cup Winners' Cup in 1987 against Lokomotiv Leipzig.

Cruyff had become a mentor for Rijkaard but a training ground bust-up in 1987 led to the player leaving the field and promising never to play under Cruyff again.

Neither were prepared to back down and Rijkaard ended up being loaned to Real Zaragoza with few takers for the 25-year-old who had been labeled as a troublemaker.

Holland coach, Rinus Michels, proved to be a saviour for Rijkaard though, as he appreciated the player's qualities along with his fighting spirit and played him alongside Ronald Koeman at centre-back in the 1988 European Championship winning side.

His success internationally opened the door to AC Milan and Rijkaard was able to play a part in Arrigo Sacchi's groundbreaking side that won virtually all before them.

With players of the quality of Roberto Donadoni, Franco Baresi, Paolo Maldini, Marco Van Basten, Ruud Gullit and of course Rijkaard, the team lifted two domestic leagues and two European Cups.

As he got older he moved from midfield to centre-half before returning to Ajax. In his farewell to Milan, Franco Baresi praised him as a real fighter, who battled most when the team was down. He had a close bond with the Milan fans who treated him with much affection and it is claimed that while at Barça he had a clause in his contract which would allow him to leave for AC Milan.

With Ajax he won the European Cup a third and final time in 1995 against AC Milan playing alongside another veteran Danny Blind at the back, and he set up the goal scored by Patrick Kluivert which won the Dutch the cup.

Rijkaard began his coaching career among the backroom staff at Ajax and then later was Guus Hiddink's assistant in the national team during the 1998 World Cup.

After a solid tournament in which they reached the quarterfinals, Rijkaard was the surprise choice to replace Hiddink but he proved his worth in the 2000 European Championships where the team was unlucky to go out on penalties against Italy.

However, he then took an ill-fated decision to become coach of Sparta Rotterdam and quickly experienced the flipside of being a manager as the team struggled and he had to contend with a vitriolic crowd.

The club was relegated and he received death threats before resigning.

Looking for a club that was ready to give him another chance, it was more than he could have hoped for that Barcelona would come calling.

Rijkaard had long since patched up his differences with Cruyff, which he now puts down to disagreements over tactics, and was perfectly placed to become part of Laporta's new project without any ties.

Rijkaard was given the vote of Cruyff after being praised by players and other coaches who had worked with him.

The new board acknowledged publicly the work done by Radomir Antic. The fact that he had stepped into the breach the previous season and led the team to the Uefa Cup but they said they wanted a clean break from the past.

Rijkaard gave no doubts in his presentation that he was ready for the challenge and would stand up for himself.

"I like the pressure here because it means that we have a team with good players. A team like Barça always looks to be the best and it has this obligation to its fans. It is one of the biggest teams in the world and I am very happy to be here, although I consider it to be a very big challenge," said Rijkaard.

"The club and I have the same football philosophy and that is very important. Now we have to work hard for the future."

Interestingly at his presentation, when he was asked about the prickly subject of the influence of Cruyff in the new board, sports director Txiki Begiristain attempted to answer the question for him but Rijkaard asserting his authority responded himself and in a more than adequate Spanish having preferred earlier to speak in English.

"Cruyff was a special footballer and it is good to have a close friend who is a supporter of the club but it is the people at this table (referring also to Begiristain and Laporta) who are responsible and no one else," he said.

Rijkaard continued the strong Dutch connection at the club becoming the fourth coach from the Netherlands after Rinus Michels, Johan Cruyff and Louis Van Gaal.

Attempting to build a team that would bring an end to the four-year drought without a trophy, Rijkaard also looked to Holland by bringing in the disciplinarian Henk Ten Cate, who had been the trainer of NAC Breda.

But he also realised the need for his coaching staff to include someone who knew the club environment and so he signed up Eusebio Sacristán, a former Dream Team player, who had been working with Valladolid when the Laporta board sounded him out for a coaching role.

"I finished my playing career with Valladolid and then did a coaching badge. After that, representatives from several Barça presidential candidates got in touch asking if I would be interested in working for the club, including Txiki, who asked if I fancied joining with Laporta and being assistant to Rijkaard. I didn't know Frank at the time but it was a great opportunity," said Sacristán.

"I found Rijkaard relaxed, open and intelligent enough to realise what each player could do. He worked hard and never really needed too much advice, even about other Spanish teams.

"The club had been in a negative run and there was an air of failure that we had to turn around and we all worked together in order to ensure this. We concentrated on the coaching side and tried to keep out of the politics as that was not our responsibility.

"We knew that change would not happen overnight and we would have to work slowly to bring back confidence. We did realise, though, that there were some players who had only ever experienced failure at Barça and so there was a lot of pressure on them."

Once the board had isolated the problems at the club, the question was about how much time and money they had available in order to solve them.

"The elections were in mid-June and so from that first day we set off to make a massive change to the team. What made it worse, on top of the fact that we had little money, was that it was already very late in terms of the market to look for players," said vice-president Ferran Soriano.

"We had to deal straight away with the fact that the club was badly organised and there was no time to make ourselves comfortable. We were all new to the job, I had just arrived, the sports vice-president had just arrived, the president had just arrived, but we needed to make an immediate impact.

"The structure which was in place at the club was anachronistic. People were against any change as they worried that it would affect them negatively and so this was another hurdle for us to overcome. Basically we had a couple of months before the season started to arrange everything."

With David Beckham having signed for Real Madrid the board, Ronaldinho was the perfect choice to fulfil the board's promise to the fans of signing a world-class player.

"The signing of Beckham would have been excellent in various aspects but the one which I was least clear on was the sporting side," said Rosell, in his book 'Welcome to the Real World.'

"When I thought of Beckham I was less sure as to what his role would be within the team but this was not the case with Ronaldinho because I knew what he was capable of doing."

Born in Porto Alegre, Brazil, in 1980, Ronaldinho was signed by Paris Saint Germain as a 21-year-old. He had only mixed success on the pitch and had established a reputation as a troublemaker after falling out with coach Luis Fernández.

However, his ability was never in debate and this was only reinforced by his performances in the 2002 World Cup where he helped the team to lift the trophy.

The Barça board decided that signing Ronaldinho would be a gamble worth taking but the next task would be to persuade him to come to the Nou Camp with Barcelona, significantly, unable to offer Champions League football.

The ace up their sleeve though was that Rosell had worked closely with him as a Nike representative and the two had remained in close contact.

With Ronaldinho receptive to a move to the warmer Mediterranean climate, the fear was how much they would have to pay PSG and the problems of constructing a new team if they spent everything on one player.

It ended up as an auction in which Manchester United and in particular the then chief executive, Peter Kenyon, lost out after refusing to send written confirmation after agreeing a fee with PSG.

They tried to squeeze the French club into accepting less but in the end Barça raised their bid to £20m plus a potential £2m, performance related, and PSG accepted the deal.

"It was incredible, it was like a Benny Hill comedy sketch going from one hotel in Lyon to another. We would give our bid to PSG and then come back and Manchester would make their bid, then we went back with another bid and it went on like this backwards and forwards during the day," explained Rosell, who was being informed by Barça's economic gurus Soriano and Ingla how much they could afford to pay.

For them, though, having to make the calculations on the spot was highly stressful.

"I remember working out the accounts with Marc, seeing whether we could raise the money. We decided that we could afford to make a bid of up to £20m for Ronaldinho and then after that whatever we offered would have to be staggered based on potential we had for making money. We were aware that we could make a dramatic increase in the amount of income we were making," said Soriano.

Sports director Txiki Begiristain agreed with Rosell that the incorporation of Ronaldinho instead of Beckham made a big difference to the building of the team.

"Beckham has a football style which is more limited. When we think of Beckham we think of a side with him on the wing and other players who would be fundamental to the team. Beckham was a very good player but we knew if we signed him we would have needed someone like Pablo Aimar in the team as well," he said.

"The arrival of Ronaldinho though transformed everything, we adapted the team and the style of play around him.

"We were still looking at other options right up to the point of putting pen to paper. We could not concentrate all our efforts around Ronaldinho, so we had to make enquiries about others like Aimar. The possibility of keeping Juan Román Riquelme as the creative player was another option."

Once the deal went through and the bulk of the new board's budget had been spent, Soriano and Ingla calculated that any other signings would have to be either cut price deals or loans.

Meanwhile, Barça's negotiating team led by Rosell, made it clear from the start that they would not throw money away unnecessarily on middle men.

"Barça had consistently paid large sums to intermediaries and from day one we said that we were not going to do this," said Rosell, "We were only going to deal with the players, the agents or the clubs. We would also only pay the commissions recommended by Fifa – that is five or ten per cent for agents."

The board and the coaching staff agreed that a major overhaul of the team was needed to inculcate a new winning spirit. This meant getting rid of nine players, some on big salaries, who were considered surplus to requirements.

"In 2003 we found ourselves with players who had suffered too many failures and so we all realised it was necessary to form a new squad so that they would be able to cope more easily with the situation," said Begiristain.

"Working with Frank was very easy as we were looking for the same kind of player. We shared the same philosophy, that on top of winning you also have to play quality football, and that was the case for all the members in the team from the centre-halves to the forwards."

In total, in the summer of 2003, Barça brought in Ronaldinho, Rustu Recber, Ricardo Quaresma, Luis Garcia, Rafael Marquez, Mario Alvarez and Gio van Bronckhorst. The cost of all the signings was £30m but this was less than half the amount that Gaspart spent in each of his years in charge.

Highly-rated defender Mario, who has never since lived up to his billing, moved on loan from Valladolid for a season and Van Bronkhorst came from Arsenal where he was having a bad run after returning from a serious knee injury.

Then Barça moved to buy Mexican defender Marquez and Portuguese winger Ricardo Quaresma cheaply for five and six million euros respectively. Luis Garcia arrived for just one million euros due to the fact that Atletico Madrid still owed the club 80 per cent of his transfer from a year earlier.

The Porto midfielder Deco was another player the board wanted to sign. Rosell had contacted him but after negotiations with his agent Jorge Mendes the grim reality was that there were not the funds to sign him, at least for the coming season.

Rosell began the job of breaking the news to those who had no future at Barcelona: Frank de Boer, Gaizka Mendieta, Juan Pablo Sorin, Philippe Christanval, Fabio Rochemback,

Giovanni and Nano Macedo; with most leaving on free transfers.

They also tried to get rid of Patrick Kluivert and Marc Overmars, who were coming towards the end of their contracts, by inviting them to look for other teams but they chose to remain for another season.

The most difficult cases were those of Javier Saviola and Riquelme who were considered foreigners as they had not yet been with Barça long enough to get Spanish nationality. With only three foreigners permitted and those places taken by Ronaldinho, Marquez and Rustu, there was no space for the highly paid Argentines.

In the end they decided to keep Saviola and loan out Riquelme to Villarreal.

The new board also looked to renegotiate player contracts that had been arranged under president Joan Gaspart. Although some, Saviola for instance, would not accept a pay cut, those that did were given incentives such as earning more if the team was successful.

"We aimed to build a team over three years. The idea was to make a few adjustments each season and this would mean bringing in players with a medium value and so no one else who would cost 20 or 25m pounds," said Soriano.

"To buy players who would maintain the level of the team at the top isn't easy and each year it gets harder as the best players are few and far between, and more and more concentrated in a small number of teams.

"We could say that there are 20 great players in the world and you would probably find they are in five or six clubs.

"As well as this, in general there are now no more new avenues for income in football and so we have reached a plateau. The amount of money in football has actually fallen and many clubs have not been able to maintain their level of spending.

"The television rights have been less than expected and a major divide has opened up between the amount that some clubs receive and others."

Barcelona's first match under the new Laporta regime was their traditional Joan Gamper season curtain raiser at the Nou Camp. Boca Juniors had been the team chosen to face the new look side and 90,000 fans gathered to see how they would fare on the pitch.

The unspectacular match ended in a 1-1 draw and it was followed by a penalty shootout won by Barça. It was far from an emphatic endorsement of the new regime, but considering the club's many problems, few supporters expected a miracle and they accepted Laporta's call to give them time.

The Spanish way of life may take some adjusting to with working days finishing about 8pm or 9pm and evening meals can be as late as 10pm or 11pm. Fabio Capello once said that he could never feel comfortable living in Spain because they eat so late.

Football games can also start later and there is always a televised match at 10pm on a Saturday night and another at 9pm on Sunday.

But even for Spain it was out of the ordinary when Barcelona arranged their first match of the 2003-04 season for a Tuesday at midnight.

It was yet another example of how Barcelona can be all things but never conventional, particularly with Laporta who liked to be the protagonist.

The board was making a stance against Sevilla who refused to bring forward the match before a round of international games. Rather than accepting the loss of a number of players, Barça arranged for the game to take place on the Wednesday but at 00.05. After the match the players would be able to go off to their respective international squads.

The new professional approach of the directors meant they still wanted to ensure a fine turnout in order to make the match economically viable and so they laid on entertainment and free gazpacho to entice the locals.

After all the talk and speculation over the summer this was the real moment of truth and fans turned up with their expectation tinged with apprehension over whether Laporta's promises had foundation.

Their fears of an opening day defeat were avoided by a moment of sublime skill from Ronaldinho. The Culés were brought to their feet as he stole the show with a breathtaking run and shot which grabbed the headlines the following day.

Picking up the ball on the half-way line he burst past three desperate challenges before firing in off the underside of the cross-bar from 30 yards.

It was just a brief indicator of how the Brazilian was to go on to steal the limelight over the coming seasons and become the inspiration for the team.

That strike against Sevilla is now savoured in the memories of fans similar to that of Ronaldo in 1997 against Compostela when he beat eight players to score.

Ronaldinho's goal also allowed fans to glaze over the fact that the team had only managed to draw and there was still a lot of work to be done. Sevilla had found it easy to create chances against Barça's defence with José Antonio Reyes running riot and providing the kind of performance that led Arsenal to buy him. It was Reyes who forced a rash challenge from Carles Puyol to win a penalty that led to Sevilla's goal.

The coming months were to be difficult for the board as Rijkaard showed uncertainty with his tactics and the team struggled to find its way. There appeared to be little sign of a turn around in the club's fortunes: the only difference was that Ronaldinho was on hand to rescue the team from defeat.

Marc Overmars continued to suffer from injury, Patrick Kluivert was more apparent than effective and new signing Ricardo Quaresma seemed always to go down blind alleys before running the ball out of play or shooting from impossible angles.

In defence, however, Rafael Marquez and Giovanni van Bronckhorst offered hope for the future.

One of the main causes for concern was that Rijkaard looked more the inexperienced coach who had been sacked by

Sparta Rotterdam, than the trainer who had led Holland to relative success at the 2000 European Championships.

He kept changing his formations and his line-ups, making it abundantly clear to the fans that he did not know the best. They were, though, prepared to give him some time to settle in and again Laporta was helpful in calming the expectations saying that success would not come overnight.

But as the months went by and there was no sign of improvement, frustration began to grow. Tellingly, Barça's performances were better away from the expectation of the Nou Camp.

The team went from bad to worse in the autumn with Ronaldinho out injured.

They crashed 5-1 to struggling Malaga with their only goal coming when defender Fernando Sanz put the ball through his own goal. It was a particularly bad day for the youngster Mario, who having been presented with his big chance by an injury to Carles Puyol, was given the runaround.

Pressure on the board to make a change was mounting with defeat at home to Real Madrid on December 7, the first loss at home for 20 years against their archrivals, and Rijkaard was criticised for being too defensive.

The team desperately needed the return of Ronaldinho and he came back in the nick of time.

He was instrumental in a bizarre victory over derby rivals Espanyol away at Montjuic. The referee lost control and three players from either side were sent off as Barça won 3-1 to earn Rijkaard some respite although in reality there was little improvement in the performance.

One specific concern was the goalkeeper. Rijkaard's choice, Victor Valdés, was proving raw and impulsive, and this had led him to concede a spate of penalties. His experienced alternative Rustu Recber was proving equally unreliable though and with little confidence he was far from the impressive figure he had been in goal for Turkey in the 2002 World Cup.

Communication for Rustu was a major problem as he was slow to pick up Spanish and knew no English. His comment: "football is like rock music you don't need to speak the same language" during a press conference also raised a few eyebrows.

Ironically, the progression of the team was more or less the same as the season before which had led to the sacking of Louis van Gaal. Halfway through the campaign they only had a point more than the year earlier, while they had scored just 23 goals and conceded 25.

Importantly for Rijkaard the fans took to his personality immediately and this was another reason why they were ready to stand by him.

As always at Barça success is measured in comparison with Real Madrid and the 'galacticos' had moved 18 points clear. There were signs of player unrest with the Mexican Rafael Márquez claiming that Rijkaard confused the players with his constant tactical changes.

Rijkaard's fate was becoming increasingly uncertain as rumours spread from the boardroom that vice-president Sandro Rosell planned to show him the door, replacing him with his original preferred choice, Felipe Scolari, who was at the time coach of Portugal.

This was when the first real friction began to engulf the relationship between Laporta and Rosell that had been simmering for a while with the vice-president unhappy with what he saw as Laporta's arrogant and autocratic style and the way he preferred to listen to Johan Cruyff.

As a Cruyff appointment, Laporta was prepared to stand by Rijkaard and this infuriated Rosell who, effectively being the head of football, felt the decision was his to make.

After the Christmas break, Barça lost away to Levante in the first-leg of the King's Cup, but then the team started to fight back with a win at home to Zaragoza.

The pieces of the jigsaw were finally coming together with Rijkaard finding the winning formula and with his new four-three-three line-up the team remained unbeaten until the end of the season.

Ronaldinho was in-form and was asserting his personality on the team that although still needing work in some areas was beginning to play the open, attacking football that the board had promised.

The extra aggression of the Dutch midfielder Edgar Davids had proved to be a crucial addition to the team in the winter transfer window. From a defensive aspect he was almost as valuable as Ronaldinho offering the cover to allow the Brazilian free license to concentrate on beating his opponents.

In January, when Davids was unveiled, his signing had caused consternation from the local press who saw the addition of the Dutchman on loan from Juventus as a continuation of the policy of bringing in second-rate foreign talent. Joan Laporta had to field questions in the press conference about why he had brought in yet another Dutch player when fans had made it clear they wanted a return to watching home grown talent at the Nou Camp.

While Ronaldinho took all the plaudits, Davids was a driving force in midfield, sweeping up behind the three forwards. He blended perfectly alongside Phillip Cocu and Xavi Hernández, while in defence the team had also found a solid partnership at centre-half with Puyol and Márquez.

The new regime had planned a long-term policy to give the team a stronger Catalan base and also make the foreign players aware of what Barça means to the local community but sports director Txiki Begiristain feels that this was rightly kept within limits. He followed the same approach as Cruyff and Rexach before him.

"It is important for the to be a Catalan heart, then there has always been a percentage of Spanish players and finally you have the foreign contingent. They should be the truly world class players who can offer something extra that the local players haven't got," he said.

"The Catalanism of the club should always be respected by any player as this is fundamental to Barça. While it is easier to buy players from your own country who understand this, they are more expensive and this has meant that the job of scouts finding young players is more important than ever."

However as mentioned before, Kluivert felt he and other foreign players were unfairly hounded out for being foreign and many Catalan players were given precedence.

"We knew it was better to have Catalans coming through the system and having a balance as they can be a reference for people arriving from outside and show them how the club is run," explained Rijkaard's assistant coach Eusebio Sacristán, who did not feel the environment was made uncomfortable for foreigners.

"For those players who did come from outside there was enough pressure on them already with the expectation from the fans and so we did not look to push the issue of Catalonia on them.

"It is not difficult for players who arrive here to realise the difference between Barca and other teams with their connection with the fans and the region. The fans are more a part of this club than many supporters at others: they own this land and for that reason they are right to demand and pressurise."

The turn around from Barça in the second half of the table was dramatic. After that victory against Zaragoza they then won five straight games, including a win against the champions Valencia. They then also showed their resolve as they hung on to a 3-2 win, after Thiago Motta had been sent-off, against Deportivo la Coruña.

In the Uefa Cup they crashed out at the hands of Celtic but the club was critical of the way the first leg was allowed to go ahead with Spain in turmoil after terrorists bombed the central train station in Madrid.

The events of March 11, 2004, had a dramatic impact on Spain. People were left shell-shocked as news slowly filtered through that morning that there had been a terrorist attack on four commuter trains heading to Madrid's Atocha station with 191 people killed.

In the aftermath, vast crowds took to the streets in protest and there were major political repercussions. In the final straight of election campaigning, the incumbent Partido Popular (PP) initially blamed the Basque separatist group ETA for the attack but this appeared to be a smoke screen for the real perpetrators Al Queda.

The PP were wary of a loss of support if it was established that it was an Al Queda led attack as it was they who had got the country involved in Middle-East politics after they had taken the decision to enter the war in Iraq against the wishes of many.

Voters felt this was the case and it proved crucial as the anti-war socialist party, the PSOE, was elected. Incidentally, a later court hearing into what took place in Madrid ruled out ETA involvement and accusations of underhand behaviour from the PP continue.

In this climate of grief and panic, Barcelona attempted to get their Uefa Cup match against Celtic postponed to a later date but the request was turned down by Fifa and Rijkaard's players were forced to take to the field.

They went on to blame their defeat at Celtic Park, which also saw Thiago Motta and Javier Saviola sent off, on not being focused for the game. In the replay at the Nou Camp they could only draw 0-0 and were knocked out.

In the league they continued their impressive form charging up to third in the table with only Real Madrid and Valencia ahead of them. Rijkaard's commitment to an attacking three-man forward line, whether home or away, began to receive rave reviews across Europe.

The negative impact for Barça was that teams set out their stall from the start to defend against them – as the Spanish say 'to park a bus in front of the goal' – and Rijkaard became more and more frustrated. He realised that in the summer they would need reinforcements who would offer more of a cutting edge than provided by Kluivert and Saviola.

Even so, Rijkaard's side was in record-breaking form although a draw against Villarreal prevented them matching the historic ten straight wins set by Barça in the 1956-57 season when Ladislao Kubala was the talisman. That record has only been bettered in Spain by Real Madrid in the 1960-61 season when they had 15 consecutive wins.

Barça had reduced the gap with Real Madrid to just six points when they travelled to the Bernabéu Stadium in April.

They were in confident mood and Kluivert equalised after the early set-back of a Santiago Solari goal for the home side. Xavi then won the game for the Catalan side, scoring after a one-two with Ronaldinho.

Barça's dramatic rise came at the same time as Real's free fall with the wheels well and truly coming off the galacticos' side. Florentino Peréz's system of 'Zidanes and Pavones', buying world-class players and bringing through youth team products, was foundering on the president's obsession with bringing in stars rather than players the team really needed.

David Beckham's arrival in 2003 coincided with the start of the downward spiral. Beckham was the perfect example of Peréz's desire to sign famous players who raise the image of the club around the world. The same summer Claude Makelele, a defensive midfielder, was allowed to move to Chelsea after failing to agree financial terms on a new contract.

While Zidane, Ronaldo and Figo had captured the imagination, Makelele had been also important as the engine of the team and yet Peréz did not value his contribution. His departure left a gaping hole with no satisfactory cover.

Figo and Beckham fought for right midfield position and in the end the Englishman played in the centre, taking on part of the role of Makelele, but he was unable to provide the necessary defensive cover.

Barça ended the season on something of an anticlimax losing against Celta Vigo and Zaragoza but the hard work had already been done and they finished in second place behind Valencia. This gave them an automatic place in the Champions

League without the need to first pass first through the preliminaries.

Joan Laporta could also be very satisfied with his part in the success. Rightly or wrongly he had listened to the advice of Johan Cruyff, ahead of board members. The appointment of Rijkaard had been a high risk but in the end he had proved to be the perfect man for the job.

Laporta also publicly backed him and the team when they were struggling, telling the fans to be patient.

As well as the pacifying approach to fans he showed a hard edge to the players privately. After the New Year he went down to the dressing room to speak to them warning: "before Rijkaard goes one of you will."

At the end of his first season Rijkaard received praise for the style of football Barça were playing, including from Arrigo Sacchi, his former coach at AC Milan.

Rijkaard had been brought up to be aware of the need for good technique and to play attacking football.

"I knew the size of the task I was facing at the club but in terms of pure football I had no problems because the style of football they like at Barça is similar to that at Ajax and the way I like to see the game played. I learnt a lot from all the coaches I worked under especially Cruyff and Sacchi but I have my own ideas too," said Rijkaard.

"I knew about Barça's importance to the Catalan people and the pressure that would be on the team. Van Gaal had problems integrating and this was something I felt was very important from the start and I made sure I learnt the language. I think it is right as well that when you move to a place that you accept their culture.

"There was a lot of work to do and it was especially tough during the first few months with the fans getting on the players backs. But they are entitled to complain if they do not like what they see.

"Everyone knows what Barça stands for around the world and so it was not a difficult choice to go there but at the time we did not have the money to immediately bring about a turnaround."

Rijkaard singled out Edgar Davids' strength of personality that made a difference to a team with a lack of self-confidence.

"As well as giving us better balance, Davids gave us more belief and we began to grow together and become stronger. At the start everything was new and we were finding our feet, experimenting with different tactics," said Rijkaard, who also began to play Xavi Hernández in a more attacking role.

"He started to play in a more advanced position closer to the penalty area and didn't have so many defensive duties. He could afford to make incisive passes whereas before he had to be more cautious, protecting the back line.

"Generally, we built the team with the system in mind so we looked at players and considered whether they would fit into it, rather than the other way round."

The coaching team also copied Cruyff's technique of pressuring in specific areas of the pitch.

"If you chase the ball on the wings then it means that you cut out the outlets for the opposition to build an attack. We tried to squeeze the other team so that even the midfielders come over from the other side of the pitch to leave less space. The forward is the first line of defence and his job is to force the ball out wide," said Begiristain, who was working closely with Rijkaard.

But what was special to Rijkaard's system was to have a centre-half style player in the midfield who was the defensive pivot and could provide cover for the back-line.

This position became a key aspect of the team and Thiago Motta, José Edmilson and Rafael Márquez all played this role. The extra line of defence has the advantage of allowing the full-backs to get down the line and attack.

But aside from the new tactics, the revelation of this re-born Barcelona was without doubt Ronaldinho.

He had almost single-handedly carried them for much of the season and restored belief in the new footballing structure. The team finished second at the end of the campaign but most importantly Ronaldinho demonstrated that he was able to deliver so much more still.

"In the first half of the season it was clear that there was a fear of playing at the Nou Camp. It is the only explanation because otherwise how was it possible that the results away from home were very good and yet at home it was the opposite," said Begiristain.

"It was a stadium in which the team had been losing for year upon year and at the end of the season if we had not lost those 20 or so points at home we would have won the title.

"Ronaldinho gradually took the pressure off the rest of the team and shouldered the burden.

"Expectation was high before he arrived but in reality he had only shown his best with Brazil as at PSG he was inconsistent. In France he was playing football in a city and a league which does not live and breathe football; it is a city where there is so much more.

"He is a player who in an environment where there is no great passion just does what he has to do. That was the doubt that we had before we signed him but we believed that the change of atmosphere would make the difference.

"A team is prepared to sacrifice itself more when they have an attacking player of the calibre of Ronaldinho. In my era it was the same with Romario, people said that he wasn't giving his all but the team worked hard. With Ronaldinho if he had to defend more it would limit his options in attack and that is the most important thing for him to do.

"He is someone who generates a lot of expectation and rises to the occasion. An added advantage was that his presence meant that players wanted to come to the club. Many asked before signing whether Ronaldinho would be continuing at the club."

That summer the board continued to work hard with the restricted money they had available to reinforce the squad.

They had told Juan Román Riquelme, Dani García, Alfonso Peréz, Roberto Bonano and Robert Enke at different points of the last season that they did not have a future.

Those who were not loaned out had trained separately from the full squad. In January, the injury plagued Patrick Andersson had agreed to end his contract and return to Sweden.

More of the Van Gaal old-guard were also shown the door. Phillip Cocu, Marc Overmars, Patrick Kluivert and Michael Reiziger all moved while Javier Saviola and Rustu Recber were both loaned out.

The Catalan, Luis García, had only played a bit part in the team but the coaching staff had been impressed with his contribution and wanted to keep him. However, the player was enticed by the opportunity to play in the Premiership with Liverpool.

Edgar Davids also left as the club would only offer him a one-year-deal rather than the two that he demanded.

The major signings were those of Deco and Samuel Eto'o while Jose Edmilson, Henrik Larsson, Juliano Belletti and Sylvinho all arrived on cut-price deals.

After a successful campaign and qualification for the Champions League, Barça were able financially to land Deco who had proved out of their reach a year earlier. Deco was also ready for a new challenge having won the Champions League with Porto.

It was still a major coup for Barça's negotiating team, led by Sandro Rosell, to persuade Deco to sign as Chelsea were also interested and had far more financial muscle. Also to Chelsea's advantage was the fact that Deco's mentor and previous coach Jose Mourinho had signed for the Stamford Bridge club.

The project that Barça offered and the style of Spanish football over its more physical English counterpart, led Deco to the Nou Camp, while Ricardo Quaresma was a makeweight in the deal, moving the other way.

The sale of Kluivert, freed up a large amount of money spent on his salary, and their search for a prolific goalscorer led Barça to the door of Mallorca and their striker Samuel Eto'o.

It was not an easy deal to make though as half the player's rights were owned by Real Madrid, where the player had started his Spanish career, and they would be reluctant to sell to their major rivals.

"Eto'o was the icing on the cake with the other transfers already made. We were all sure that he was the right player to bring in," said Rosell, "both Laporta and myself had meetings in Mallorca but the problem was Real."

The key to the Eto'o transfer was that Mallorca needed the money and had to force Real to sell the player.

"To be honest I feared that Real would not let him leave despite the great offer that was on the table. In the end though they eased off, but if Eto'o had been 50 per cent owned by Barça I would not have agreed to sell him to them," said Rosell.

"The acquisitions were based on looking for players for certain positions but we also considered their human qualities. We knew it was important to have a strong bond within the team and we did manage to create a great atmosphere in the dressing room.

"The key to a good sporting model is bringing in the right players and as we had a team which was functioning and had several others who were coming back from injury we did not need to make too many moves in the transfer market.

"We had managed to overtake Real Madrid in the league in our first season and as we did not have to make a lot of signings we were able to slowly pay off the debt."

Qualification for the Champions League also meant that there was less concern about other clubs attempting to entice away their most influential player, Ronaldinho.

In the summer Chelsea owner Roman Abramovich went to speak with Ronaldinho after Brazil played France, in Paris, and presented him with a Chelsea shirt with his name on the back, but the board were never tempted to sell.

"We rejected his approach without thinking about it because Ronaldinho was untouchable, his transfer would have been a hard blow for the fans and a mistake for us. I must say though that they put forward a salary a lot higher than we offered and this worried me as it would have been very difficult to improve his contract," said Rosell.

Chapter Nine

Friction in the Boardroom

While on the pitch Barcelona was going from strength to strength it was a different story in the boardroom where a battle of egos was beginning to undermine future progress.

Gradually it was becoming clear that there was a major rift between the two most important men on the board – the president Joan Laporta and his vice-president Sandro Rosell, who had been instrumental in bringing the top players back to the club. There was a clash of personalities but the heart of the unrest involved the role which Johan Cruyff played within the running of the club.

The board assembled in 2003 had come together with the aim of forging a new Barcelona but while all had worked together to win the elections following that success a more complicated picture unfolded with different opinions about the right way to take the club forward.

The relationship between Joan Laporta and Sandro Rosell was a typical example. The two had played football together 20 years earlier and had met each other from time to time through mutual friends since then, but that was as far as they knew each other.

Being both keen Barça fans and wanting to change the fortunes of the club was the key to how they came to work together but once on the board their differing personalities soon came to the fore.

Laporta became actively involved in the direction of Barcelona earlier than Rosell being a vociferous critic of Núñez and a spokesman for the Elefant Blau. A lawyer, he had his own firm Laporta & Arbos that boasted several high profile clients and it was through his professional work that he first got to know Johan Cruyff.

Laporta studied law at the University of Barcelona but he has many friends and professional contacts from the prestigious Barcelona business school ESADE. That was where Rosell studied before launching his career in marketing.

There was plenty of ground for antagonism between Laporta and Rosell. One was president but the other had a rich array of contacts throughout the game thanks to an impressive track record starting as an organiser for the 1992 Olympics in his home city and moving through to his career with Nike which took him to South America and Brazil.

His job in Brazil was to consolidate the image of the brand. There was a lot of work to be done at the time with the game in Brazil suffering from corruption and a lack of organisation.

The reputation of the Brazilian federation needed to be rebuilt as did Nike's relationship with them. Rosell was able to achieve this by becoming directly involved in the federation's operation, which in Brazil is made more complicated by the fact that with international games most of the players are plying their trade in foreign leagues.

Nike though helped to arrange trips and matches leading up to the 2002 World Cup.

"We took advantage of organising a Catalonia v Brazil game, the first between the two, which was a big success with the CBF (Brazilian football federation) and the Catalan federation both making one million euros," explained Rosell.

The Brazil coach Luis Felipe Scolari believed in a laid-back approach and wanted to take the pressure off the players

125

before the World Cup. During the build-up to the tournament Rosell helped organise an impromptu night out for the team at a nightclub, hiring a van and taking them there incognito.

Brazil went on to win the World Cup and Rosell celebrated with the players and staff before returning to Barcelona to consider his next step. It was then, witnessing the problems at the football club at first hand that he decided to get involved.

Looking back Rosell says that even from the start his relationship with Laporta was not always smooth but that it was not something that he dwelt upon, not expecting it to deteriorate to the extent it did.

He was worried though about the lack of openness between those involved in the election campaign.

"On a personal level there were signs that the future was not so bright for the medium to long term or at least it was not how we imagined it to be. There were examples to which we did not give as much attention as we should have done. One of those recently incorporated into the operation proposed to Barto (Josep Maria Bartomeu) that we forget the rest of the group and only work with Jan (Joan Laporta) until the point of putting an initiative into action. To put it another way to ignore them," explained Rosell, in his book 'Welcome to the Real World'

"Now I think it was an error on our behalf that we did not do something about this from the start. Barto, attempting to calm the situation down, organised a business lunch with six or seven colleagues to put them at ease. Barto recommended that they be patient, the key was to win the elections and then after that we could look into the situation."

After the elections Rosell became vice-president and theoretically took complete control of football matters with Txiki Begiristain, as sports director, the go-between the board and the coaching staff.

It should have been a position of considerable power as he was to be responsible for players coming and going and ultimately how the team performed. Rosell, though, was in the

126

unique position on the board as the only member with real knowledge of the football arena.

He found himself operating in the same world that he had been in with Nike; it was just that he was coming to the table from a different angle. Rosell was used to speaking to players, agents and clubs and so he was able to bring a wealth of experience and expertise. He had established a reputation as a skilled negotiator with Nike that was crucial in the first few months after the election due to the difficult circumstances of the club.

"Negotiation is not art but common sense. If a footballer is worth say ten million pounds you should go to the table ready to pay eight million pounds; what must never happen is that for one reason or another you pay 20m pounds - and this does occur. Studies have shown that you have to be very careful with your first offer because normally it has a correlation with the final outcome," says Rosell.

"There are always alternatives, in negotiations between clubs, an agent offers a player and tries to make you think that he is the only or at least the best alternative for you – if he really is the only option you are in a lot of trouble. If you have alternatives then you can be calmer and it allows you to be able to withdraw from the negotiations.

"It is easy to make a mistake with the pressure which is coming at you from all angles and it is important to remember that we all have a capacity to deal with pressure which is greater than we think.

"The capacity for pressure does not necessarily lie in intrinsic power; with very little power you can have a big pressure capacity if you play your game right.

"Negotiations are about people's perceptions. In a negotiation you must try to make the other person think as highly of you as possible. There opinion is something that can vary during negotiation so it is important to expect it.

"You should also be aware of the fuller picture and the future. I was negotiating for six hours with the president of Celta Vigo over 75,000 pounds and finally Horacio Gómez said to me, "Listen, we have just been relegated to the second division, that money is a lot more important to us than it is to Barça," and I accepted this and so we maintained a good relationship."

Rosell's knowledge of the game also meant that he knew how to cut down costs by getting rid of unnecessary people in player deals.

"The agent is good for everyone while the intermediary is not good for football, the intermediary goes from one club to another looking to raise the price of the player and earns from both sides," he says.

There was one element that perhaps Rosell had not expected before his arrival at the club and that was the competitive nature of the boardroom.

Laporta liked to wallow in the limelight as he showed soon after winning the elections by appearing regularly on television and in the media.

Even the day following his election he went to a gala concert to celebrate 20 years of Catalan public radio at the famous Liceu theatre, one of the most emblematic venues in Barcelona, and was photographed alongside the president of the local government.

While he could not compete with Rosell in terms of football experience he was able to fall back on the help of his confidante Johan Cruyff who was given the input that he craved without having to endure the responsibility.

Laporta also begrudged the fact that Rosell came from an influential Catalan family and that he had roots at the club through his father who was a former director.

After the elections Rosell, Laporta and other directors flew to New York and met up with Nike vice-president Ian Todd, who, of course, Rosell knew well from his time with the company. The reaction of his colleagues to this and other similar experiences led Rosell to realise that his contacts and influence were a cause of resentment.

A wedge was developing between Laporta and Cruyff who were on one side along with Begiristain and Rijkaard, and Rosell who was backed by his signings notably Ronaldinho.

It was Cruyff who brought in Rijkaard who was to lead the new team as coach and it was Rosell who brought in the flag-bearer of the new regime Ronaldinho.

The Laporta board has officially always been quick to downplay the role of Cruyff saying that he had no direct influence but was free to offer his opinion.

"Cruyff is a friend of mine and a world figure; he may mention something and I will either agree or not agree like any friends," says Laporta.

Cruyff's opinion is always respected among Barcelona fans and he has become almost a wise elder, though, he isn't of course Catalan himself. His impact as a player and then coach meant that his weekly column in a local newspaper is widely read.

At the same time there is of course a danger with someone unaccountable having so much power as he can undermine others in their jobs.

"Cruyff is part of Barça. The club is used to people saying what they think of the team especially as the fans have such an important part to play in what happens, but Cruyff is a step above that because he is almost like a symbol and everyone listens to him," said Rijkaard's assistant, Sacristán Eusebio.

"He is someone who you pay attention to as he knows what he is talking about and wants the best for Barcelona. I don't think it is a problem for the people running the club though because in the end you can make your own decisions."

Former president Joan Gaspart is also unconcerned about the presence of Cruyff despite the fact he was a major critic of his when he was president.

"I would give Cruyff ten out of ten as a footballer and as a trainer, while as a fan he can make his opinions known like anyone else; people should listen and respect his opinion because he knows a lot about this sport," he said.

"It is understandable that Cruyff would especially mean a lot to Laporta's age-group as they were brought up when the Dutchman was a hero for the Catalans as a player in the 1970s."

Rosell felt that Cruyff wanted to manage affairs from the backstage and tried to undermine his position.

Certainly, after the 2003 elections, Cruyff, in his weekly column in the Catalan paper La Vanguardia, said there was a "big risk" about giving the vice-president so much power. Then once the season got under way with the team doing badly he tried to deny any involvement in the signing of Rijkaard, which was untrue.

"I knew that before the elections of the Laporta, Cruyff, Rijkaard and Begiristain clique but I never had to give any consideration to it," said Rosell.

The question of Cruyff's influence never went away during the Laporta presidency and when the team played badly many resented that he was not made to account for his input.

The non-political director Javier Pérez Farguell, who was involved in the financial affairs of the club during the changeover to the Laporta regime, did not witness any trouble between Cruyff and Rosell but was well aware of the Dutchman's involvement.

"Cruyff was always there in the background and it is something that I saw as negative for the club," he said, "the truth, though, is that I did not see any special tension between Laporta and Rosell at the start, of course there are always disputes but I did not envisage them escalating.

"Rosell knew the football world very well and there were a lot of jealous people on the board so I suppose when you look at it this way you can see how it all started."

This envy among board members was evident when Rosell decided to go to the wedding of the daughter of the Real Madrid president Florentino Pérez. It was unpopular among other directors who said he shouldn't attend as Laporta was not invited.

Rosell described the position of Cruyff as like having the "sword of Damacles over the sporting side of the club, that is to say over my head." He also hit out at the director of communications Jordi Badia in his book 'Welcome to the Real World', another close friend of Laporta who he felt tried to ride roughshod over his position.

With Barça's poor start to their first season running the club, the situation deteriorated and the two parties fell further apart, to the point that Laporta and Rosell were barely on speaking terms although publicly they maintained a more amicable relationship.

By the end of 2003 the team had made no noticeable strides forward and Rosell, along with fans and journalists, was critical of Rijkaard's tactics.

He pointed out the cup match against Zaragoza when Rijkaard replaced key players, Ronaldinho and Davids, late into the game and Barca ended up conceding a late equaliser and went out of the competition.

Normally though Rosell preferred to bite his lip and stay silent in front of the media. He was angry at the way Laporta handled the future of Rijkaard but in public he has only made calculated comments.

"We discussed the future of Rijkaard for several long days and this was also being discussed by fans, journalists, directors, all the way to the president at the top - it was logical because things were not going well," he explained.

"Laporta asked me what was plan B as this was too much, but it was no surprise to me that he said one thing in public, and also to Rijkaard, that the board was ready to stay by him, and another in private. I said that we had to discuss the situation with Rijkaard before we could start looking for someone else but Laporta did not like the idea and preferred to avoid the confrontation.

"At the end of January 2004 we were up against the wall. Before the upcoming game against Sevilla there was a meeting with Laporta, Rijkaard, Txiki, Ten Cate and me. Although I felt for Rijkaard, I was prepared to play the bad guy. I know that Txiki prefers to tip-toe around these issues and that Laporta is like a two-sided piece of paper.

"I explained the situation as it was and that we could not continue as things were."

Whether true or not, Rosell claims that after this meeting it was Laporta who then mentioned the idea of bringing in Luiz Felipe Scolari who at the time was under contract as coach of the Portuguese national team and would not move. At the same time the situation put out to the press was that Laporta and Cruyff were standing by Rijkaard.

Rosell does admit that in the summer of 2003 he wanted to sign Scolari but knew that it was not possible due to his commitments with Portugal ahead of the 2004 European Championships.

Laporta manufactured a position, according to Rosell, whereby he was made out to be the enemy and wanted to see the back of Rijkaard.

"There was someone interested in the fact that our relationship wasn't good and he went behind people's backs and created something else; it is not difficult to imagine who that was," said Rosell.

The former agent Josep Maria Minguella believes the fallout was a result of a clash of egos.

"In football it is down to those in charge, everyone has the right to give their opinion but in the end there can only be one person who is taking decisions. If you have Rosell as director of football making one decision and Laporta with the board, or Cruyff, making another then you have problems, I am sure though that it was Laporta who was taking the decisions," he said.

"It is not logical among a group of successful young directors that there should be a difference of opinion of this magnitude, obviously you are going to have in-fighting but not to this extent.

"It is a question of power and in football it is more complicated because it is down to opinions. We are not dealing in precise terms, for example, in other businesses it could be whether we buy land and then the question would be is it good quality, a good price, etc. When you deal with coaches or footballers there is a lot of disagreement.

"Rosell I think was jealous of the influence of Cruyff and he was not prepared to accept it."

He also feels that it is logical that Cruyff had a strong influence on the Laporta board because they worked together in opposition until 2003.

"He was on the side of Laporta and the Elefant Blau against Núñez. Cruyff in one way or another supported this group and when Laporta won the elections it was natural that he would be involved in some way," he said.

"He would meet up casually with Laporta and it was a comfortable position for Cruyff as he gave his opinion but did not take decisions. He could say he liked one player or another but if they signed him and he didn't do well then he could say it wasn't his fault, and vice-versa, he could write in his newspaper column that they should have bought a player who went on to do well."

Despite the internal conflict, Laporta still headed a board that masterminded a remarkable recovery given such a short amount of time. Not solely in terms of sporting success but also by apparently turning around the club's finances, though, a lot of facts and figures were not made available as promised by Laporta in his election campaign based on transparency.

The club borrowed large amounts and the extent of the gamble will only really become apparent if the team suffers a long spell without success and the anticipated income drops.

Rosell claimed that Laporta kept the truth from the fans.

"He thinks he is God. When I look at the situation I see that he lied to everyone saying that he had paid off the debt and the figures he did give were to journalists not to accountants," he said.

"They borrowed money and because they couldn't borrow any more they tried to sell off the club's infrastructure.

"Laporta wants to be in charge of the government, the club, everything; and basically he just doesn't want to go back and be a lawyer again because he wasn't very good. He has obviously benefitted from being president because he has suddenly got a lot of money now.

"I went away with him many times on club business and I know how self-obsessed he is. One night we went to his room and he got out his laptop and put Laporta into the google search. I asked him what he was doing and he said he wanted to see how many people had searched his name. That sums him up."

There is no doubt that Laporta has made a lot of unnecessary enemies along the way and he appears to have used the club as a political vehicle on many occasions but his supporters would say he has shown himself able to withstand severe criticism to fight the Barça cause.

Laporta had graffiti sprayed on his house and received death threats as he suppressed the violent and unruly sections of the fan base notably the Boixos Nois group of ultras.

Laporta cracked down on the perks given the Boixos Nois under Núñez and Gaspart such as free tickets and an employee at the club, Manuel Santos, with links to the ultras was arrested for his part in the anti-Laporta campaign. There was even an attempt to attack Laporta after a basketball match.

Not being from the club establishment, the Laporta presidency was always a likely target for those from whom they had wrestled power.

Fear that they had enemies from within was shown soon after they took power, when it was discovered that the boardroom had been bugged and there were many other examples following that.

Laporta's personal computer was stolen from his office during the Champions League semi-final with Manchester United, at the Nou Camp in April, 2008, which clearly suggested it was someone who had regular access to the room.

Within the board, Rosell was becoming more and more dissatisfied at the way Laporta had his own clique, and he along with other directors were becoming isolated. On one occasion Laporta completely by-passed Rosell to speak with the agent of Ruud van Nistelrooy, then at Manchester United, about a move to Barça.

On another, Rosell was criticised among board members close to Laporta for saying in the press that it was his influence that had helped to bring Ronaldinho to the club.

"On May 6, 2004, I first thought of resigning as vice-president and director; it was a question of principle which I felt along with Josep Maria Bartomeu. The president was saying one thing and doing the other, he promised things behind your back and that of the whole board. We thought about standing down but in the end we decided that it could prejudice the team," he said.

Rosell's lack of involvement in the direction of the club deteriorated to the point where he was not consulted at all during Laporta's second year as president. He is keen to add that he had no part to play in the signings of Demetrio Albertini and Maxi López, in January 2005, neither of whom made a significant impact at the club.

"The differences with the president gradually got wider and wider and I was not ready to be a spectator and put a smile on the problems we had between us, and the fact that in reality there was a dictatorship," he said, "The internal communication did not function and we were part of decisions in which we had no input. Any observations that we made were considered to be just awkward, and the way the club was being run had nothing to do with the original plan.

"The poison from the centre of the club against me increased. The president was actively involved in this and the distance got wider between the nucleus of the president and directors close to him and the rest. The full board only ever met to vote."

The animosity between Laporta and Rosell by this stage had become clear publicly and it was threatening to damage the image of the club. In February, 2005, the pair agreed to meet at a well-known Barcelona restaurant in order to give a show of unity.

There was a blaze of publicity over the meeting with journalists and cameramen waiting outside.

"As in all human relationships there are differences of opinion, some of which have grown too much but now we have solved them," said Laporta afterwards.

In the weeks following it soon became clear that the get-together was merely a media sham and that the fundamental problems remained the same.

Rosell acknowledges that he had a poor relationship with Laporta but he denies it was the same with Rijkaard and claims that this image was pure propaganda on the behalf of the Laporta camp.

"Rijkaard lives his life for football and he has two important qualities for training Barça: he has the capability to work with the press and he knows how to deal with top players. His one failing though I would say is that he does not improvise enough," he stated.

However, Rijkaard's singular praise for Laporta after Barça did win the league in 2005, in the eyes of Rosell, explains the close relationship he had with the president and the lack of a bond with the rest of the directors.

If Rosell was close to standing down after the first season then a year later he was adamant that it was time for him to go.

The first person to resign from the board was the lawyer Toni Freixa who since December 2004 had stopped being part of the board meetings at the behest of the president. His differences with Laporta began over the Alejandro Etxevarria affair.

In a clearly emotive issue for Barcelona, Laporta denied that his brother-in-law and fellow director, Etxevarria, had connections with the Franco foundation, an organisation set up to honour the former dictator.

The father of Laporta's wife was a powerful businessman and a founder of the AP, later renamed the PP, the Partido Popular, the right-wing political group that was formed at the end of the Franco dictatorship as its democratic successor.

His past was very much Francoist and his son Alejandro, as has since been revealed, was a founder of the Francisco Franco Foundation.

"Laporta told the club's assembly that it was not true that Alejandro Echevarria was a member of the Franco Foundation and that people were telling lies. Later though it was demonstrated that not only was he a member but actually a founder, it was incredible," said journalist Miki Santos.

"He had been telling the Barcelona fans that it was false and then when it was actually proved he changed his story admitting that it was, but that Echevarria could offer the club a lot through his influence. In the end, though, this could not stop the tide of criticism and Echevarria had to resign."

Freixa's relationship then deteriorated over the question of whether elections according to the club law should take place in 2006 or 2007. Laporta, as explained in greater detail in chapter 11, wanted to hold them in 2007 but in the end due to a legal case brought forward by a club member, Oriol Giralt, the matter had to be resolved in the courts and a date was made for 2006.

Freixa though had not been consulted by Laporta despite the fact he was a lawyer and this was his area of expertise. He explained: "They never asked me about it and with the legal documents in my hands there is no way that I could say that the presidential term finished in 2007 and not 2006."

A week later Rosell along with Bartomeu and Jordi Mones also tendered their resignations.

Afterwards Laporta said it was a sad day for him personally and he had done all that he could to avoid the situation occurring. He claimed that the issue was with those four people who were a separate group within the board and did not integrate.

"Decisions are taken by the whole board while overall I am the person in charge, we either accept this or we don't. We tried to achieve harmony but this didn't happen and while I am sorry that they are leaving I thank them for the work they have done for Barça," Laporta told a press conference.

"The problem was a division on the question of role; Rosell said to me that he and I had to control the club and I did not accept this as it is down to the decisions of the majority. Within the sporting management there was conflict between Rosell on one side and Txiki and Rijkaard on the other, and finally the situation got out of hand which was strange as the club was doing so well.

"I haven't changed my way of working, it is Barça that has changed and is working in a modern way, very professional, and this means that it respects the influence of Cruyff although the board is free to take the decision it feels is right. In all of this Rosell has taken the stance of victim but I am glad to see that Rijkaard has remained above it all."

Rosell hit back saying: "He would have got rid of me if he could have done but he knew that with my public image there was no way he was able to justify it. He also lacked the guts to try it."

He took a further swipe at Laporta's style of leadership, criticising him for putting himself ahead of the club.

"It is true that football is not an exact science and you have to approach it with a general theory. People make mistakes but you go out with the intention of doing your best. You have to discuss things and debate because achieving a consensus is the way to get the best results. In battle the most important thing is not whether you get injured but that you do not damage the image of the society you represent," said Rosell.

"While problems are not always avoidable you do what you can to limit them and you also have to get rid of people but you do it in the least traumatic fashion. At Barcelona the decisions are not yours alone but those of thousands of members who have given you the responsibility, so your own particular quirks and feelings should be put to one side."

Journalist Miki Santos believes that Laporta altered after becoming president.

"Rosell left because Laporta changed and the people he consulted were different, he was becoming a little Napoleon," he said.

"Laporta is now more vain. You have to consider that a few weeks before he was elected he was nothing, he was a lawyer in Barcelona and then he became someone who could practically do anything he wants."

Vice-president Ferran Soriano, who failed to see eye-to-eye with Rosell on the board, said that he walked because the pressure got too much for him.

"Being in a boardroom at a club like Barça is very difficult because there are the challenges of the sport itself and then the challenges of the media. Nobody knows beforehand what will happen when you are in the papers everyday and vanity, egos and personality all come into this. You have to be very mature to do this job and serve the club," he said.

"In general terms we did well, the club was in good shape and we kept going but some of the people couldn't. They decided to leave and I don't blame them because it is difficult and actually it is better to leave if you can't cope with something. Sandro physically left at the end of the 2004-05 season but he actually left a lot earlier because in his last year he was just in the boardroom fighting with everyone all the time.

"He goes on about the influence of Johan Cruyff but to begin with you have to ask if he had any input at all in the boardroom and the answer is no. He may have had some influence on the coach and the sports director, as is logical because it is an area he knows about, but not among the board.

"I've spoken to Johan Cruyff only a few times and he gives his opinions about games and players but they are just conversations. Not all his points were listened to and to be honest he complained as well saying that we should have considered what he was telling us. These are just chats amongst friends and he was friendly with Txiki Begiristain and Frank Rijkaard but he had no official duty at the club or any unofficial duty."

Chapter Ten

The Glory of Paris

In December 2004 Ronaldinho followed in the footsteps of Barcelona's previous Brazilian stars Romario, Ronaldo and Rivaldo by lifting the 2004 Fifa World Player of the Year Award in Zurich. Beating Thierry Henry and Andrei Shevchenko into second and third places, there was no surprise in the voting after a remarkable season and a half for Ronaldinho that had seen him transform the fortunes of Barcelona.

Ronaldinho's approach to football is typically Brazilian, he plays the game with a smile on his face and he is there to enjoy himself. When he is receiving praise and the fans are cheering him he is amazing to behold: when he is not happy as, at times, at Paris Saint Germain and towards the end of his career at Barça he can appear average.

Born into a working class family with his father Joao a shipyard worker, the success of his older brother Roberto, who played for the Brazilian top-flight side Gremio, allowed the family to move to a more affluent area of Porto Alegre.

It was not an easy upbringing for Ronaldinho as he lost his father through a heart attack while swimming in the family pool. Roberto, though, continued to bring in the money through his playing career that took him to Mexico, Japan and France before injury forced him to retire. Since then he has helped guide Ronaldinho's career as his agent.

After coming through the youth ranks at Gremio he rejected the chance to sign professional forms there and instead looked to Europe. While Premiership clubs including Arsenal were eager to sign the burgeoning talent, work permit restrictions kept him away from England and he ended up signing for Paris Saint Germain.

It was far from plain sailing in the French capital for Ronaldinho who filled as many gossip as sports pages while developing a reputation for enjoying the nightlife and was regularly to be seen in bars and clubs around Paris.

During his two years at the club, PSG failed to win a trophy and he had a public falling out with the coach Luis Fernández.

"He was very young when he came to Paris, he wanted to learn and work, he wanted to make progress. He came with his family, with his brother and his mother and the first year went very well because he accepted what he had to do if he was going to develop," said Fernández.

"But the second year was different because by then he had become the champion of the world with Brazil. That can make a difference to the mind of a player. He was still young but he thought he had won everything.

"Before Ronaldinho, I had coached other stars like Rai, David Ginola and many other internationals and it's not hard to integrate players with talent when you know what you are doing. He had the ability and it should have been easy for him but it was just a case of him not applying himself."

There was no doubt about his capability and his success for Brazil, helping the Canarinha to win the 2002 World Cup, meant that he was still a prize asset. He attracted the interest of top sides in Europe but cash-strapped Barcelona, who could only offer him an annual salary of 2.3m pounds, were able to entice him to the Nou Camp.

Ronaldinho's first season alone was enough to leave an indelible mark in the history of Barcelona and it also catapulted him into the leading candidate for the world's best player.

After Barça's charge in the second half of the campaign, expectation was high as they prepared for the 2004-5 season.

They were quickly into their stride beating Racing Santander in their opening match with goals from debutantes Ludovic Giuly and Samuel Eto'o.

From the very start there was evidence that the club was not going to be so reliant on Ronaldinho, who missed the first few matches through injury.

Barça were looking a lot more complete. In their next game against Sevilla, the team won comfortably with another strike from Giuly and a goal from Henrik Larsson, who scored the first of many for the club. Deco, fresh from his success in the Champions League with Porto was demonstrating an effortless adaption into the team.

The concern after the Sevilla game was for Thiago Motta who was carried off after just a few minutes with a cruciate knee ligament injury.

From the stands the Culés were able to watch for the first time in years a side that was combining championship-winning form with technically strong, attractive football.

They began to ask themselves whether at last another Barça team had been built which could take over the mantle of Cruyff's Dream Team and enjoy a similar amount of success.

They ripped through Zaragoza 4-1 with Eto'o grabbing a brace and Giovanni van Bronckhorst and Xavi Hernandez also on the scoresheet but again the worry afterwards was the loss of two more players, Gabri Garcia and Sylvinho, both with knee injuries.

While Barcelona moved five points clear at the top of the table with a win over Osasuna and were still unbeaten after eight games, there was growing concern over the number of players in the treatment room. By the end of November,

Henrik Larsson had also joined them carrying yet another cruciate knee ligament injury.

In total there were five serious knee injuries in just three months of football and while the coaching and medical staff put it down to misfortune others began to question how well the players were being looked after.

Club doctor Jordi Ardevol came under attack by the press for the way the players prepared for matches especially their warm-ups but the club's then director of medical services Jordi Mones hit back claiming the critics had no idea of what they were talking about and it was merely a smear campaign against Ardevol.

Leading Spanish sports scientist Jesus Rico-Sanz was at the front of calls for changes to be made to the way training sessions were held. Rico-Sanz was a Real Madrid B player at the same time as Rafael Benitez and, similarly to the former-Liverpool manager, suffered a career ending injury. Instead of going into coaching, though, he went to the United States to study sports medicine. He claimed that the Spanish coaching tactics in general were well behind the times.

"When I watch training sessions it reminds me of something from the last century and the problem is that they are not open enough to change; I would say that tactics are far better in the UK, more up-to-date." he said, "It is proven that for training to be beneficial it has to replicate what you will be doing on the pitch and so running in a straight line for an hour serves no purpose as you will never do that in a game.

"They said that the number of injuries at Barça were just coincidence but for me there were far too many happening and especially just after players had started playing."

Before the 2004-05 season began, Rijkaard admitted that the team was short on players and with the large number of casualties it reached a critical level. At one stage they were left with a squad of just 14.

Even so, in the league they continued to win while rivals Real Madrid struggled.

José Antonio Camacho walked away from the Bernabéu after just a few games, not happy with the conditions he was working in, with the interference of president Florentino Peréz, and it was left to Mariano García Remon to take over the misfiring team.

And apart from Real there was no clear threat as challengers in recent years like Valencia and Deportivo la Coruña were going through difficult times.

In Europe the progress of the team over the past year was demonstrated as they swept aside Celtic in the Champions League with ex-Buoys favourite Henrik Larsson setting up the winner for Ludovic Giuly in Glasgow.

Also in their group they beat Shakhtar Donetsk and then given a real chance to test their pedigree against the eventual Champions League finalists AC Milan they came out all square having lost away and won at home.

In the first leg, Andriy Shevchenko gave Milan the victory in a close encounter that saw Andres Iniesta come closest for Barça, hitting the crossbar. In the return match Rijkaard's side were desperate to prove that they were capable of beating Milan, and were not content with what would have been a satisfactory draw after Samuel Eto'o cancelled out a goal from Shevchenko.

They continued to push forward and in the final minute they got their reward through a memorable goal from Ronaldinho. He controlled the ball on the edge of the area and powered a left-footed drive into the top left of goal.

In the league, Barcelona produced a routine away victory over city neighbours Espanyol that was notable for the debut of a 17-year-old Argentine, at the time the youngest ever player to debut for Barcelona in the league, Leo Messi.

His reputation had been spreading like wildfire since his arrival at the club aged 13, but he was to have just a bit part role to play during the season as he was introduced slowly to life in the first team.

(A demonstration of the commitment to youth was that Messi's record of being the youngest ever Barça player to make their league debut was beaten only a few seasons later by another prodigious talent Bojan Krkic).

Growing up in a disadvantaged district of Rosario in Argentina, Messi's talent was exploited to the fullest by his father Jorge, an ardent football fan, who even took over the training of his son's team when he was very young.

At seven he moved to the youth side of Newell's Old Boys where he continued to make giant strides and his coach at the time Enrique Dominguez was so amazed at his capabilities that he became one of the first to liken him to Maradona.

The low point in Messi's development came when at 11 he was spotted by River Plate scouts and was set to join the Buenos Aires team but his routine medical reported a hormonal deficiency which would require treatment costing 900 dollars a month, a bill which the club was not prepared to foot.

Messi's parents were able to raise funds to pay for the treatment but could not do so in the long term. They looked down other avenues and spoke to relatives in Catalonia about arranging a trial with Barça for him.

The Barcelona youth coach Carles Rexach who oversaw the trial took little time in being convinced and was so keen to have him that he famously signed a contract with his parents on a serviette.

Messi went on to play for four youth categories in one season as he made his mark.

"It was incredible how quickly he adapted, he was very strong and fast for 17 but also very brave," said another youth coach Guillermo Amor.

Rijkaard's side suffered their first defeat of the season away to Betis in November and with Real Madrid thrashing Albacete 6-1 the same weekend the gap at the top of the table was reduced to four points.

A comfortable victory against Real Madrid did help to restore confidence but they then lost to Villarreal and Atletico Madrid over the coming weeks. Importantly Laporta never gave up hope in the team despite their inconsistency and he confidently predicted that they would win the league.

Barça were forced to delve into the transfer market in January due to the number of injuries and they recruited Maxi Lopez from River Plate, a beanpole striker who had been talked up in the Argentine press, for £6.2m. Former AC Milan midfielder Demetrio Albertini in the twilight of his career, and a friend of Rijkaard also agreed to rescind his contract with Atalanta to play for Barça until the end of the season.

"If they had looked for big names, the problem was that they would probably have already played in the Champions League and so couldn't be fielded in the competition for Barça. Alternatively, going for someone experienced like myself, I could play in the Champions League and I knew a bit about Spanish football, so for a six-month period I could do a job for them, said Albertini.

"I also knew Rijkaard from when we were together at Milan and we used to talk about how they train in Italy and the differences at Barça. It was interesting for me as well to have a Dutch trainer who had a style different to most Italians, and also it was good to have the chance to go abroad again.

"The one thing that really struck me was Rijkaard's character in the changing room because he talked a lot and when he was at Milan he never said anything.

"Apart from that he has always tried to be very calm and transmit this in the dressing room and with journalists. That doesn't mean that he doesn't live for the game, he is a winner, you can see that by what he has achieved.

"His coaching style is more Dutch than Italian, I would say that he learnt some things from Arrigo Sacchi but his style is different and although I never played for Cruyff I would say it is nearer to him. The Italian aspect that he has learnt is the quality of the work that is done each week and his attitude which is something very important."

The number of injuries meant that Rafael Márquez became a regular in midfield and youth product Oleguer Presas was put in the heart of the defence alongside Carles Puyol. Apart from Leo Messi, Damià Abella also made his debut as a makeshift right-back.

It would be understandable with the lack of options for Rijkaard to rethink the style of football and play in a more defensive way but he persisted with the four-three-three system.

The key signings from the previous summer gelled immediately while the team's balance was unaffected by the number of departures. Deco had answered his critics who considered him to be too light and always looking for a free-kick.

He showed that his success for Porto was no flash in the pan and that he could adapt his style of play from Jose Mourinho's defensive approach to the more flamboyant Barça.

"At Porto he had a more attacking role and for that reason we were not sure about bringing him in straight away in 2003. While we were offered him we were unsure whether he could play along with Ronaldinho and we decided not to go for him. There was also the problem of money and we could not afford to buy the two of them anyway," said Rosell.

"Later when we watched Deco during the following season we realised that he was more versatile and with Porto still prepared to sell we decided to put in a bid. He really wanted to play for Barcelona to the point that he even said that he could play defensively if necessary.

"The rhythm at which he played, the speed at which he recovered the ball and set up attacks was extraordinary."

Deco also had battling qualities that helped take him to the summit of European football with Porto and Barcelona.

Playing in the Brazilian second division for Corinthians Alagoano he was given the chance by Benfica, aged 19, to move to Portugal. He was discarded though by the then Benfica coach Graeme Souness and loaned out to FC Alverca. Moving in one door and then out the other he was sold to Salgueiros, a small club in Porto, and there after playing just 12 games he caught the attention of FC Porto.

It took Deco a few years to really make his mark but he became instrumental in the club's success at home and abroad. Playing more deeply than a typical playmaker he improved his temperament under the guidance of coach Jose Mourinho, who made him the captain of the team and he was nicknamed 'El Magico' by the fans. He helped Porto to win the Uefa Cup in 2003 and then a year later the Champions League.

Chelsea were favourites to sign Deco with Mourinho moving to Stamford Bridge but the naturalised Portuguese chose to go his own way to demonstrate he didn't need his mentor anymore.

"I always wanted to go to Barcelona, they are a very big team in Brazil and I used to watch their games on the television and see all the Brazilians doing so well. Basically, I knew that if it was a choice between Barça or another team I would choose Barça," he said.

"It would have been easier for me to opt for Chelsea where the coach and I knew each other but it was a challenge for me to have a new start with another trainer and demonstrate my abilities. If I had gone to Chelsea some people may have thought that I was only playing because I was Mourinho's favourite.

"There is no doubt Mourinho is special because he is one of the few coaches who can change the mentality of players and personally he helped me a lot. He noticed me in the reserve team and then helped me to bring my abilities to the fore.

"He is very well organised, he knows what he wants and how to communicate it, which is important to the players as they then clearly know what they should be doing. He comes across as a hard man in the press but not to the team."

Deco, along with all the summer signings, quickly felt part of the team due to Rijkaard's easy-going style, while the Portuguese also fitted in perfectly with the attacking, one-touch football.

"Most importantly when the players arrived, they realised they had to work hard but that they were able to do so in a good atmosphere at the club. Teams will not win every game and they will not always perform at their best and so it is necessary to remember that and take away the pressure," Deco said.

He faced his former coach Mourinho in the quarter-finals of the 2005 Champions League in a tie which will be long remembered for its action on the pitch and also the behaviour of its protagonists, especially Mourinho, off it.

The Portuguese returned to Barcelona with the aim of proving himself to the Catalan people. As one journalist explained, Mourinho was one of them having worked as a translator and then assistant coach to both Bobby Robson and Louis van Gaal. He was not treated as a star and for that reason Mourinho was at his most provocative and his press conferences pure theatre.

For the first game at the Nou Camp in March, Mourinho kept his plans shrouded in mystery, training behind closed doors and preventing the players from speaking. He incorrectly gave the Chelsea line-up without Damian Duff who did play, while at the same time he had the audacity to name Frank Rijkaard's team.

Also in the charged atmosphere of the press conference before the game, Mourinho responded angrily to a question posed by a Catalan journalist, asking if he was surprised by the success that he had had since leaving Barça.

"Look at me, I have gone on and achieved things and done what I have wanted to do while, look at you all, you are still here doing the same things," was his stinging reply.

His approach, which also worked to take the pressure off his players, meant that he was in store for a heated reaction by the home fans but his touchline antics showed that he was in his element being the centre of attention.

During the game Barça were undeniably on top but the visitors went ahead with an own goal by Juliano Belletti.

After the break, Maxi Lopez came on to equalise with a well-taken goal and then Eto'o found the back of the net to earn the victory. Despite Maxi's dramatic start to his Barça career, the talk after the game was all about what took place in the tunnel at half-time.

Chelsea sent an official complaint to Uefa over Frank Rijkaard's discussion with referee Anders Frisk in the tunnel that continued to the official's office, which was out of bounds for Rijkaard.

It resulted in a confrontation between both sets of coaching staff in which Mourinho was kicked.

After the game Rijkaard said that Chelsea were inventing an incident, he had spoken to the referee but that was nothing out of the ordinary. His assistant, Ten Cate, was even more forceful the following day.

"It was pathetic for Chelsea to react in this way, they are just moaning about being beaten and that is all. Mourinho lied about the line-ups before the game and now he does this," he said.

However, he admitted there was an altercation in the tunnel.

"It was the fault of one of the Chelsea coaches, there was pushing and shoving but nothing serious," he said.

The events turned into a major saga centering on the layout of the Barça changing rooms and alleged views from the Chelsea camp. Suffice to say that once down the tunnel at the Nou Camp it is possible to go left or right to either dressing room. If you go on through a glass partition you come to a small area where you can still access either dressing room or you can go straight on to the referee's room.

Rijkaard went through the glass partition with Frisk, which was not allowed on Champions League nights, and then Chelsea claimed that he went into the referee's changing room.

The outcome was that Mourinho was given a two-match ban for making the allegations and referee Anders Frisk chose to stand down after saying that the stress and pressure he had been put under had become too much. The incident also came soon after he was hit by a coin in a Roma v Dynamo Kiev Champions League match.

All eyes were unsurprisingly on Barça's second leg against Chelsea and there was yet more controversy. The home side came out on top and qualified for the next round through a goal from John Terry that involved a push by Ricardo Carvalho on Barça keeper Victor Valdes.

In a thrilling game between arguably the two best sides in Europe, Barça went 3-0 down before Ronaldinho, as he so often did for Barça, clawed them back into the game but it was not enough with Terry's goal taking the English side through.

Barça were left with only the league to fight for but at least they could concentrate their efforts on a competition they had not won since 1999.

They got back to winning ways with a victory over Athletic Bilbao at home but a disappointing draw against Real Betis, after conceding two late goals, and then a 4-2 defeat by Real Madrid at the Bernabeu Stadium left the championship wide open.

Barça responded with a four-match winning run, which put them on the verge of the league title that they then secured with an away draw to struggling Levante, three games before the end of the season.

Being a Saturday night many people were out in the centre of Barcelona and over a million were recorded celebrating the victory of the team. Plaça Catalunya and Plaça de Canaletas, where traditionally celebrating Barça fans gather, were heaving with people including tourists who found themselves caught up in the emotion. Thousands also went to the airport to cheer the team as they returned.

As explained in Chapter 7, instead of going to the traditional Plaça Sant Jaume to lift the trophy from the balcony of the Town Hall, the club decided that they should celebrate at the Camp Nou, so that more fans would be able to attend.

Beforehand, they held a city bus ride that finished at the stadium where fireworks and entertainment were offered. Players individually paid tribute to the fans and even Rijkaard tried speaking in Catalan to thank the Culés.

When the microphone was passed to Samuel Eto'o, though, he shouted "Madrid cabron, saluda al campeon!" Which translates as "Madrid bastards, salute the champions!"

His comments received plenty of cheers from the fans but the next day he was forced to apologise to Real Madrid at an improvised press conference, saying it was something that had happened in the heat of the moment.

"I don't want to spit on the plate which feeds me and I didn't want to offend the team which first gave me the chance to play football in Europe," he explained.

In a demonstration of the speed of Spanish bureaucracy it took almost two years for him to receive a fine for his comments from the Spanish football federation.

With their target of league champions achieved a year early the pressure was taken off the board and with a winning formula in place they did not need to make many changes to the team, only minor adjustments.

After an injury plagued season it was almost as though they had reinforcements with the number of players returning. Even so, they brought in Mark van Bommel, from PSV Eindhoven and Santi Ezquerro, from Athletic Bilbao, both on free transfers.

Barça had a successful pre-season in Denmark before going on a tour of Japan and China. Returning to Spain they picked up their first trophy of the season with victory over the King's Cup winners Real Betis in the Spanish Super Cup.

The major talking point after the traditional curtain-raiser, the Joan Gamper, that year against Juventus, was the emergence of Leo Messi, a constant threat to the Italians, and it appeared that he was now ready to realise his potential.

In his first season he had played just six games being brought on as a late substitute and generally he struggled to make the step up. It was only against Albacete in the title run-in when he scored with a chip over the keeper that he offered evidence of what was to follow.

However, in the summer, playing in the Under-20 World Championships in Holland, he helped Argentina to victory and was the player of the tournament. It convinced the Barça board to offer him a professional contract instead of the youth deal he had before.

This, though, opened up a bureaucratic can of worms as by signing professional terms a technicality meant he was now considered a foreigner, and not an assimilated player as he had been before as a youth player.

With the three non-EU places already taken he had no place in the team.

A clear oversight by the board, it even led to Messi's father looking at other clubs with Inter Milan expressing strong interest, and there was the possibility of a loan deal until December.

In the end, Barça were able to rush through the papers to enable Messi to have Spanish nationality thanks largely to the role of board member Alejandro Echevarria, who had strong ties within the Spanish establishment.

While many wait years for the process to be completed, Messi had his Spanish passport within a month and he was cleared to play after a hearing of the Spanish Football Federation in September.

It did not stop protests from other clubs headed by Deportivo la Coruña and Alaves who said that Barça were breaking the rules by fielding him as his league subscription came after the August deadline, which meant he should not be eligible until December.

Smaller clubs claimed it was an example of the strength that Barça yielded, but their arguments were thrown out and Messi was able to play.

Barça had a slow start to the 2005-06 campaign with draws and a defeat against Atletico Madrid, but they hit form away to Real Betis with a 4-1 win which they managed even without the undoubted stars of the team Ronaldinho and Deco.

They began to show the best football of the Rijkaard era with a strong defence and a potent forward line. Ronaldinho's sublime skills continued to capture the attention of the world but now the team as a whole had more to offer.

The side had the experience of winning the league and the extra confidence that came with that, while Rijkaard had a replenished squad after the injury crisis the previous season.

This was perfectly demonstrated in the 3-0 destruction of Real Madrid at the Bernabéu stadium in November. Ronaldinho produced perhaps his finest performance in the intense atmosphere of the el clasico in which he took apart the Madrid side almost at ease and the Real fans were left applauding the Brazilian genius.

Barça had complete domination of the game against Real who appeared panic-stricken and although still early in the season it gave strong evidence of both sides' title credentials.

Ronaldinho showed why he was to be named Fifa World Player of the Year, again, scoring two goals. The first came when he slalomed past Sergio Ramos and Iván Helguera before slipping the ball home and for the second, he again came in from the left-wing, beat Ramos for pace and slotted past Iker Casillas.

"It was an unforgettable experience, I suppose I'm lucky that I play my best games in this kind of atmosphere. It was the same before in Brazil when I played for Gremio. It was a great team performance though and the defence played as much a role as the forwards," explained Ronaldinho after the game.

He remained down to earth and approachable despite his success. After winning his second Fifa World Player of the Year Award he was quick to praise those around him.

"Everyone was saying I was going to win but I had no idea until it was announced. I am very proud to have been given this award but it is the result of the hard work, not only that I have put in, but also my team-mates," he said.

"I am trying to make the most of my talent and give a good example to others. I am grateful to God for giving me this ability, we all have our strengths and mine is playing football.

Often footballers forget how lucky they are compared to other people out there who are really struggling.

"I know what it is like when life is not easy, how it is to suffer and that is why I would never turn down an opportunity to help. I often think that God is with me and helps me during matches.

"When I became a father it changed my outlook but my main priorities remain the same, my family and football which have given me all the success and allowed my child to have a good education.

"Again I have been credited with the success of this team but when I arrived there were a lot of changes with a new board and coach and we all played our part."

The el clasico also witnessed the emergence of Messi and the changing of the order as he was given a starting place for the first time ahead of Ludovic Giuly. Messi went on to set up the opener for Eto'o.

It was proving to be a one horse race for the championship and Barça fans were lapping up the problems at Real Madrid who appeared to have a revolving door to their coach's office.

In the Champions League they had a relatively straightforward passage to the quarter-finals where they were to meet their nemesis from the previous season, Jose Mourinho and his Chelsea side.

There was the usual pre-match build-up where Mourinho baited the opposition with "revenge is only for losers" but this time round it was Barça who were to come out on top with Rijkaard out-playing Mourinho.

The tie was decided at Stamford Bridge and the guilty party more than anyone else was Chelsea's Asier del Horno who was dismissed for a rash tackle on the man-of-the-match Messi.

Barça went on to win the game 2-1 and then a draw at the Nou Camp was enough to see them through to the next round where they faced the more modest challenge of Benfica.

"Those Champions League games between Chelsea and Barça were always high pressure occasions with lots of fireworks and controversy. Mourinho of course would always say his bit beforehand to liven the occasion and make it something to remember. I often watch recordings of the matches just to relive the atmosphere and also to watch the football which really was superb," says Eidur Gudjohnsen, who joined Barça from Chelsea in 2006.

Barça were playing well and accustomed to high-pressure European games where a single mistake could cause their elimination. They were prepared to wait for their chance against a defensive Benfica side coached by former-Dream Team player Ronald Koeman. This came in the second-leg at home and Barça secured a 2-0 win after a goalless draw in the Stadium of Light.

The emotive subject of racism had become a major talking point in Spain since the country played against England at the Bernabéu stadium in 2004. A month earlier the then Spain coach Luis Aragonés was picked up on television using racial abuse when talking about Thierry Henry with the player José Antonio Reyes.

Then in November, Spain played England and the black players in the England team were singled out for abuse from the crowd.

It led to plenty of debate in Spain about whether there was a higher level of racism than in other parts of Europe and if so how to combat it.

Most Spanish considered the issue was blown out of all proportion. They felt people in the country were not any more racist than elsewhere and that terms like "negro de mieda" (black shit) often were not intended to be offensive. Certainly swear words are more acceptable and used more frequently in Latin languages than English and they are by no means restricted to insults.

The intensity of the debate escalated with Barça's visit to Zaragoza in February, 2006, when Eto'o actually tried to leave the pitch after receiving racist taunts, before being persuaded to return by team-mates.

Afterwards he said the situation was out of control in Spain and that it would be impossible for Spain to have black referees like in England.

"If one was in charge here they would kill him; referees are all hated and seen in a bad light and if on top of this they were black then you can guess what would happen," said Eto'o, who was regularly on the receiving end of racial abuse.

In another game against Zaragoza he responded to the home fans chants by doing a monkey impression after scoring.

"People paid for their tickets and wanted to see a monkey and so I did it. I am a performer on the pitch and they paid to see it," he said.

Generally, though, less of a stand has been made against racism in Spain and players are more reticent to come forward and complain. High profile names such as the Brazilian Ronaldo even denied there was a problem and Barça's assistant coach Ten Cate tried to divert the issue.

"I remember what it was like in England with black players such as Viv Anderson. There are problems in all countries with racism and I don't think it is any worse in Spain than anywhere else," he said.

If anything the focus on racism led to a greater amount of abuse given out to players on the pitch. At most matches around Spain, chants could be heard against black players.

Meanwhile, Eto'o remained deadly in front of goal along with veteran Henrik Larsson and Barça practically killed off any possible comeback by Real Madrid in the title chase with a 1-1 draw at the Nou Camp.

Real in truth were already well beaten in the league and were struggling to the end of the season with a caretaker president since Florentino Pérez, the founder of the 'galacticos' resigned in February and in effect said that his policy of bringing in superstars and rearing youth players was a failure.

In the Champions League, fans were daring to believe that they had a team capable of matching the success of the side of '92 and become the best team in Europe.

Rijkaard's reputation was on a high as his personality and style of coaching had fitted in perfectly with what Barça needed. Not only were there player comparisons with the Dream Team but also between Johan Cruyff and Rijkaard.

Carles Rexach, former-assistant coach to Cruyff, feels Rijkaard's more relaxed approach was important.

"He was involved in a new era of football where the player is almost more important than the club and for that reason Rijkaard was a good coach for Barça. People talk about the lack of discipline but players are harder to manage now and if you are too strict they will stand up to you as they have power," he said.

Facing AC Milan away, although they did not put in one of their best performances, they did enough to get a 1-0 win with Ludovic Giuly scoring in the San Siro.

In the return match, Rijkaard realised it would be too dangerous to sit-back and so his team went out to take the game to Milan. Although they did not manage to find the back of the net, neither did the visitors, though Kaka saw a shot come back off the post and Andriy Shevchenko had a goal disallowed for an earlier foul.

The final whistle was greeted with a roar from the Nou Camp fans as they looked ahead to the prospect of playing in their third Champions League final, this time in Paris.

Barça mathematically secured the domestic championship with their nearest challenger Valencia losing away to Mallorca. In any case, Barça produced a professional job later the same day to beat Celta Vigo with a goal from Samuel Eto'o.

Henrik Larsson had made it clear that he would leave at the end of the season as he was keen to move back to Sweden with his family, he joked that he was worried that his children's first language was English with a Scottish accent. He did though have one last important event which was the Champions League Final against Arsenal in mid-May.

Tickets for the game in Paris were like gold dust as thousands planned the invasion of the French capital. Around

16,000 were made available to members and many others travelled just to soak up the atmosphere.

For millions watching on television it was the perfect final between two footballing sides.

Arsenal's key player, Thierry Henry, who had been strongly linked to a move to Barcelona with his contract running out, had a couple of excellent chances in the first few minutes but he failed to convert them.

At the other end keeper Jens Lehmann was also called into action with several important stops before crucially, after 18 minutes, he was dismissed for a foul on Eto'o just outside the area.

If the referee Terje Hauge, a replacement for Ole Hermann Borgan who was removed from the game after sporting a Barcelona shirt in a Norwegian paper, had allowed play to continue with Giuly scoring into an empty net, then it could have led to a more entertaining final but instead Arsenal were down to ten men.

Sol Campbell gave Arsenal the lead mid-way through the first-half and their fans began to hope they could hold out as the game wore on but Rijkaard's decision to bring Larssen into the fray changed the contest. He helped set-up two goals in the last 14 minutes first for Eto'o and then Juliano Belletti.

"It was amazing to be there and experience the crowd and the emotion," said Pau, a Catalan who had travelled from Barcelona with friends, "before the match the city was full of fans from both sides and we were all getting on fine there was no trouble at all.

"Inside the stadium we really felt the tension and it was a massive blow when they scored. I think that Rijkaard made mistakes with his line-up and should have played Iniesta from the start instead of Van Bommel but he changed that after half-time.

"Larsson was fantastic when he came on and showed he's more than just a finisher with the two passes for the goals. When Belletti scored it was amazing."

159

After the game Henry was furious with the referee and the Barça players, and a few days later chose to sign a new deal with Arsenal, turning down the beckoning call of the Champions League winners.

"I don't know if the referee was wearing a Barcelona shirt or not but I was kicked all over the place. If the referee did not want us to win he should have said so from the start. Some of the calls were strange, maybe next time I'll learn how to dive. I expect the referee to do his job but I don't think he did," he said.

On the final whistle in Barcelona people began a long carnival with thousands making their way to the centre with cars and scooters blowing their horns in triumph. Later in the week a fiesta was held in the Nou Camp.

It was a significant final for Sylvinho who was playing against the side that originally brought him to Europe.

"To play the match against Arsenal was amazing, everything about the occasion was a great experience and I would never have imagined that it would happen. It wasn't that I wanted to beat Arsenal, because I have great memories of the club and of Arsene Wenger, but it was about football," he said.

"I enjoyed my time at all the clubs that I have played for beginning with Corinthians of Sao Paolo. At Arsenal I was grateful for the discipline and work of Wenger and for all that he taught me. At Celta Vigo it was another good experience although a modest club and then I came to Barça.

"I arrived a year after the general change in 2003 and the club was already on a good run. There was a positive feeling in the dressing room with a lot of new players coming in. We felt a responsibility to bring the success back to the club."

In just three years the Laporta board had achieved what few had thought possible and Barça had returned to the summit of European football. It was thanks to a dynamic board of young people who had the confidence to carry it out.

"Looking back at what we did it was a bit crazy. The year before we came, the club had made big losses and to be able to run the club we had to put down a bank guarantee for 15 per cent of the budget which was 15m euros," said vice president Ferran Soriano.

"The club was losing 50m euros a year and we were not going to get paid, yet we put in 15m euros as a guarantee against making any more losses. I suppose you do these things driven by passion but we were also convinced that things could be done better.

"It was a big pledge but we put forward a three year business plan by the end of which we would have revenues of 150m euros a year and nobody believed us because it was too aggressive. Now it is easy to say because we not only went to 150m but to 200m euros.

"The secret was to have common sense and being bold and actually doing it. The revenue then climbed to over 250m euros, more than double what it was when we arrived. We achieved this by investing in the team.

"The product we sell is the players so you have to invest in them and we were brave enough to do so in the first two years by spending more than 75m euros mainly on three players, Ronaldinho, Deco and Eto'o.

"Then after that we managed the club very professionally. At the beginning they were just the directors who were running it. I was general manager for more than a year, before we hired professionals from the best places. The chief financial officer we brought in used to work for Mary Lynch in New York and the chief marketing officer was from Procter and Gamble.

"The challenge for all big clubs today is growth and globalisation and that is not easy for Barça, Manchester United or any of the big clubs because you need to choose your market, which business model you want and how you will sell the brand.

"Ronaldinho played a very important role. Back in 2003 we knew we needed a celebrity to attract the attention of the world, we tried to get David Beckham but we got Ronaldinho. After that, of course, this industry is all about winning, nothing would be like it is if we hadn't won two Spanish leagues and a Champions League.

"Ronaldinho helped in the first years and of course he attracted other players to come here as well. After that though it is no longer about one player, it was about the team. We should not forget about Ronaldinho, though, and that we were in the Uefa Cup when he arrived."

The question that was to be repeatedly posed in the summer of 2006 was what was the capability of this youthful team. The lynchpin of the side, Ronaldinho, was himself only 26 and Eto'o a year younger, while emerging was Leo Messi who for the first time appeared to be worthy of the 'new Maradona' title.

Certainly no one then would have thought that just two years later the president would have been forced to fire Rijkaard and tell fans that at least they should not forget the "glory of Paris".

Chapter Eleven

The Laporta dictatorship and the start of the collapse

It was Lord Acton who said: "power tends to corrupt, and absolute power corrupts absolutely. Great men are almost always bad men."

In Catalonia it is often said that the Barcelona presidency changes people and that the extent of the power turns people rapidly into dictators.

President Josep Núñez was famously criticised for his autocratic style of leadership and it led to fierce opposition in the 1990s with fans setting up the Elefant Blau to demand more openness.

Ten years later and one of those then calling for change, Joan Laporta, had become the president and fans were similarly unhappy at what they saw as a lack of democracy.

While many clubs have been derided for becoming businesses far from answerable to the fans, Barcelona's presidential elections help ensure that the supporters interests and values come first and foremost.

When the team is being run badly, fans are quick to demonstrate calling for the resignation of the president or for elections to be held.

On becoming president, Laporta became almost as high-profile as the players on the pitch. He was constantly in the media and incurred a lot of negative publicity over outbursts and petulance.

"For me the president should not be the protagonist and Laporta has been too forward, which has meant that a lot of people have tried to attack him. He has a lot of enemies, he would have been better only coming out into the open and speaking about five times a year. The more prominent you are, the quicker they are to finish you off," said former-coach Carles Rexach.

Laporta has always courted controversy and was never going to be a president ready to sit back and allow others the spotlight.

He was ardently anti-Núñez and his stance with the Elefant Blau, which the then president compared to being like a 'terrorist with a gun in the street', is something that Núñez has never forgotten.

Núñez fell out with Gaspart after the latter befriended Laporta and Núñez refused to take part in official Barça events as long as Laporta was president.

There was plenty of debate from Laporta's own group about his presidential credentials when he was put forward to represent the break from the past and many were worried that he was too conflictive to win over the support of the Núñez supporters.

During his presidency, despite much success on the pitch, he alienated many people and failed to deliver on important promises. Many journalists discovered only too quickly that the close ties that they had been able to forge with the media friendly Laporta campaign in 2003 had simply been an election ploy and that once in power the hierarchy had become even less approachable than under Núñez and Gaspart.

The Laporta policy of working with a few journalists and alienating the rest was put into effect by the head of communications Jordi Badia, a man very close to the president and someone critics said wielded far too much power.

A key theme of the election campaign had been the promise of a new age of openness at the club and Laporta vowed to pull back the carpet and reveal exactly what had been taking place during the Gaspart regime.

None of this happened and fans felt further let down by the way he put up ticket prices by 40 per cent, having said he would not raise the cost of membership.

In power he has made a number of high profile blunders that taint his legacy as president such as Alejandro Echevarria's involvement on the board and Laporta's denial that he was a Francoist and helped set up an organisation in the dictators memory.

There is no doubting the power that Echevarria holds within the bureaucracy of Spain and if Laporta had been honest about his past from the start then maybe he could have officially kept him on-board.

"When Laporta ended the relationship between the club and the ultras he enforced controls and took people to court. Echevarria was the man behind the scenes who was able to bring this about using his influence and he successfully got rid of any threat. In Barcelona the establishment still has a lot of power although not as much as in Italy and Latin America," explained the journalist Miki Santos.

"Spain is changing but the people who were in power 25 or 30 years ago were largely Francoists. Alejandro Echevarria has a lot of contacts that are still important today.

"There are lots of South Americans who have been waiting year after year for Spanish citizenship but Barça players like Márquez and Ronaldinho were able to get the papers arranged very quickly.

"When Echevarria stood down as a director he still had a lot of influence and was in charge of security."

The extent to which he had become carried away with his position was shown at Madrid's Barajas Airport in July, 2005, when he obviously felt he was above normal airport security procedures.

On a trip to Bosnia he was stopped three times by the bleeper as he attempted to pass through to the departure lounge.

Losing his cool he took his shoes off and threw them into the air and then proceeded to take off his trousers while making insulting comments to the security guards, which included homophobic connotations that they wanted to see him naked.

Later he apologised for the act but his behaviour was criticised by fans and it was a major embarrassment for the club.

On another occasion on a main road in Barcelona he kicked the chauffeur out of a club car and continued driving himself after becoming annoyed.

"Laporta probably became involved at Barça for good reasons because Núñez was really like a dictator and so he helped set up the Elefant Blau but Laporta then went down the same route," says Miki Santos.

"When Laporta was part of the opposition he hit out at a plan by Núñez, called Barça 2000, where he wanted to do more or less the same as Laporta tried to do himself with the restructuring of the Nou Camp and its surroundings. Then, though, Laporta said that Núñez was just trying to make money for himself."

The Barça 2000 plan was to enlarge the stadium and create a big avenue leading up to the ground with entertainments and shops. But people living in the area complained saying it was for Núñez's own private gain being a construction magnate, while the local government headed by Pasqual Maragall, who brought the Olympics to Barcelona in 1992, refused to give its backing.

Ten years later and the local government was in the process of considering a new proposal by the Laporta board.

They aimed to extend the Nou Camp with 8,000 more seats and put on a retractable roof, while also selling the mini-stadi and other training ground land. Sir Norman Foster, who designed the new Wembley, was commissioned to redesign the Nou Camp, the main feature being a second skin made up of illuminated panels wrapped around the stadium.

"Laporta was clever and he said that everything he was planning was for Barcelona and he was defending Catalonia, while Núñez was not a Catalan and was never really accepted into the social strata here. Núñez's plan also failed because he was politically to the right and it was a socialist local government," said Miki Santos.

Laporta's plan for the stadium caused concern over how the club would be able to pay for it, especially as invariably the cost of such work is greater than originally projected.

"The members were saying they are going to have to pay something in the end because Foster's project was very expensive. Barça would make money from the land they sell and the hotels and facilities they build but I don't know if that would have been enough," says Santos.

In the end Laporta was no more successful than Núñez as opposition and red tape meant the work had not started by the time he stood down in 2010.

The board appeared aloof and distant from the fans. An outcry at the way directors retained a significant number of tickets for the 2006 Champions League Final, to distribute private led to a belated admission from the club that the matter had been dealt with badly.

Of almost 20,000 tickets made available to fans, over 4,000 were kept by the directors. One agency was given 6,000 to distribute among members but 1,300 were never given out although this was denied originally.

Then Laporta completely disregarded club legislation and decided to hold elections a year late in 2007.

A presidential mandate as laid down by the club rules is for four years and in the case where one ends prematurely the period up until the end of the following June is considered a year. As the Laporta board started in office in mid-June it meant that the period up until the end of that month was a year and this was clearly stated.

One fan, Oriol Giralt, was not prepared to stand by any longer and was ready to take the case to the courts if necessary to force elections.

"The Laporta presidency offered the hope of change, he said he would do big things but he told lies. He claimed he would clarify everything that had been going on at the club before he arrived but he didn't and then after that he started to do things you don't expect from a president like at Madrid airport but there have been many other examples," said Giralt.

"You can't imagine how difficult it was for me, though, to take Barcelona to court over the elections and people tried to make out I was a Real Madrid fan only looking to destabilise Barcelona. It was the first time in the history of the club a judge had to call elections.

"The Barcelona presidency makes people go crazy as you are the second most important person in Catalonia and you have a lot of power. There are a lot of newspapers just about FC Barcelona, a lot of people read them and the president dictates to them.

"When I stood up to Laporta he claimed that I was the guilty person so I thought that the best way to tackle the situation was to attack first so I started to prepare the case.

"I was on my own and I won the case, I think basically because they had political support behind them and they did not see me as a big threat. They still delved into my background trying to find things out and they sent dossiers to the press. Barça belatedly took the battle to me but I think I'm a good lawyer and fought my case.

"The sad thing though is that Laporta is a lawyer and it was very clear what the legal situation was so there should have been no misunderstanding. Laporta knew the elections should be in 2006 because I told him in 2003.

"There has been a lot of fighting, a lot of people have died in order to have democracy and 35 years after the death of Franco the club should have been represented better.

"I never backed him for president because I knew he would not do a good job. The first time I came across him was when I was working for the Catalan government. He wanted a copy of the Barça rules there and then but I told him they would not be ready until the following day. He said I was dead, that I didn't know who I was dealing with and that in the afternoon he would return with television cameras. That's what happened but I told him the same thing.

"You could say that he started deceiving right from the start in his first election campaign when he said he would bring in Beckham. Those of us who knew it wasn't going to happen were told to keep quiet. Since then there have been constant lies and mistakes. We would be here all day if we discussed all of them."

He would have liked to see someone take on the board and force Laporta to resign over breaking club law although presidential rules meant he had to stand down anyway in 2010 at the end of his second mandate.

"Laporta was found to be guilty over the elections and it would have been interesting to see a member making the case against him for deliberately breaking club law. If it did happen he could have been finished within a few months and then the law states that he would have been banned from working in that position for two years," he said.

"I don't think that would have happened though as he has the media on his side and a lot of resources available to him. I wouldn't take him on again as last time they attacked me very strongly and I have a family to consider. Last time I worked without a break from October, 2005, all the way through to the summer of 2006.

"It would have needed someone who knew the rules and the system like I do as a lawyer. People offered me money to do it but it is not something I would do for financial gain."

169

When the elections were forced through in 2006 the team had just won the league and Champions League double. Laporta's position was secure and no rival candidate even had enough votes to stand against him.

Of course it did not mean people were happy with Laporta; trouble was brewing and could come to the surface when the team went into a lull, which would happen sooner or later.

"I would say Laporta was more dictatorial than Núñez ever was, the board was a lot tougher on the press and Laporta even went so far as to try to get rid of journalists from their jobs because they did not agree with him," said Josep Maria Minguella.

"The club offered gifts in order to do business with some of the media while with others they didn't make promotions or respond to letters or calls."

It is easy to build a smoke screen over the club if the board only works with favourable media.

"I can denounce it but little else. There were a lot of things going on which people did not know about but I can't at my age fight like Don Quijote. It was wrong that there was so little transparency for example over the plans for a new stadium," he said.

"They said it would cost £280m and yet the members weren't even consulted. You have to consult them when you consider the risks involved and the fact that they were looking to sell club land.

"Sport and El Mundo Deportivo (the two main Catalan sports papers) were with Laporta because they knew that if they weren't they would really struggle. It meant that no one denounced the deals made and no one asked how they are going to finance the work on the stadium?"

Possibly the most heavily criticised aspect of Laporta's leadership was the way he used the club to back his own personal views. As mentioned earlier, Laporta put the club at the centre of Catalan nationalism, despite the fact he was elected to represent fans of all political persuasions.

"There are three important political parties and Laporta's problem as president was that he was associated too much with one side while he should reflect generally the interests of all the members," said Carles Rexach. "Along with this the fact that he involved himself with just one group was another reason he got attacked so much."

In 2005, Barça had held an event to encourage the speaking of Catalan before a game, which the political party PP claimed was a clear example of 'Catalan expansionism' and compared it with something you would expect from Nazi Germany.

Throughout Laporta's presidency he denied any intention of moving into politics but his rhetoric gave the game away and his speeches sounded as though he was on a political rally.

In October, 2007, Catalonia were prevented from playing a friendly match against the United States by the Spanish football federation.

As a region of Spain there was an agreement in place that only allowed them to stage matches at Christmas during the season and the Catalan federation sought to have this overturned. Its president Jordi Roche claimed they were denied the match on political grounds because last time they played against the Basque Country they managed to draw a crowd of 56,000 people.

Laporta took the opportunity to criticise the Roche for not being more vociferous in his opposition and not using the support of Barcelona, with its extra weight, to help their cause.

"If the Catalan federation had been run properly then there would have been no question of the game not going ahead, the authorities would have had to allow it," he said.

"The political parties have to protest as well in order to get what they have promised – an official Catalan national team. They should not hide behind the clubs and should assume their responsibility. I do not agree when people say that Spain does not understand us, they do perfectly but they do not accept Catalonia as a nation.

"We are clearly a nation and as such we belong to the international community and have our sports rights. Spain systematically refuses to allow us to play official games and the best way to show the freedom of the state would be to allow them. It is an embarrassment and they are going too far in what they are doing."

Laporta wanted to see compensation to clubs for players injured while on international duty while adding that he thought Barça's Spanish players should only give their all for the Catalans.

"I would say that they should be aware that they are Barça players. Some will get injured when playing internationals and then cannot play for us, which should be fundamental because it is us who pay. The Barça players do not realise that they should hold back when playing for Spain," he said.

"It is ridiculous that players go to their international teams, play games and earn money and we don't receive anything. It is a question which should be discussed with Uefa and Fifa and if there is no solution then we will have to start thinking about not releasing the players."

However, Laporta had nothing to say when reserve goalkeeper, Albert Jorquera, was injured playing for Catalonia against Euskardi (the Basque Country side) which suggests it is a political issue.

Generally Laporta felt it right to use his position to champion the Catalan cause.

"I would like Barcelona to continue being a promoter of Catalan culture as it would mean that Catalonia would be known more and so that there would be no need to create the Catalan Republic of Barcelona," he said.

"Language isn't only an instrument for communication but a way of facing the world and living your life. For centuries Catalans have been speaking in this language."

In March, 2008, he gave a talk at the French Institute in Barcelona on the theme of 'More than a Club' and he explained that when he goes abroad he tries to talk about the grandeur of Catalonia and believes it has the right to be a country like France and Spain.

He also took the opportunity to defend the actions of Barça at a youth tournament in the Algarve when the club ordered players not to be on the pitch when the Spanish national anthem was playing. Laporta said he wanted the team to go out to the sound of the Barça anthem and denied it was an issue of politics but blamed the organisers for trying to make cheap publicity.

Towards the end of the 2007-08 season with the team struggling on the pitch and many fans angry at the way Laporta and his board were running the club, he created a furore at a meeting of penyas (supporters groups) by getting on to the podium and launching a diatribe against those who had criticised him. One local journalist described him as sounding like Fidel Castro.

"The situation is not as bad as some people want to make it appear; people should be aware of hypocrites who say they are for Barça but are not, they are putting their economic and personal interests ahead of the club," Laporta raged.

Responding to questions on the stage he swiped aside one member who suggested he was now behaving like former-president Núñez with the comment: "You've had your moment of glory now let's move onto something more interesting."

However, the following day the Catalan paper La Vanguardia published the speech along with an almost identical one made by Núñez in 1985.

Sidestepping Laporta's political involvement, then vice-president Ferran Soriano felt that it was important for the club to have a high-profile president.

"I think that at times when we needed a lot of media attention, for example, when we were going through a bad spell and we had to deliver a lot of messages to the fans he was the right person and did extremely well."

One of the successes of the Laporta board was to modernise the marketing side of the club and make the most of Barça as a brand.

During the elections in 2003, Laporta admitted that they would consider advertising on the club shirt, something that they had never done before, if it proved the best way to progress.

Finally, they decided it was a better idea to align themselves with world humanitarian causes and put the Unicef name on their shirts.

The club considered many attractive offers, such as from the betting company Betandwin, which would have given them the most lucrative shirt deal in Europe. They were also very close to agreeing terms with the Chinese government to sponsor the 2008 Olympics but they were not convinced about the public response to either offer.

A modern marketing strategy that has proved highly successful is to attract business through a humanitarian message and this is what the Barça board decided to do.

They turned down the opportunity to make money up front preferring to pay to have Unicef on their shirts and make greater money in the long run with more people attracted to the name.

"In discussion we started thinking about the brand; what does Barça mean? We came to the conclusion that our selling line is on two levels, the first being spectacular football. Most people will think of our attacking football as opposed to people who play only to win. They will mention Messi and Iniesta but they also remember Ronaldinho, Maradona, Johan Cruyff and Kubala for this reason," said Soriano.

"That, though, is only one column of support. The second is social commitment that sets us apart. We are owned by fans and not here to make money but to bring success to the team.

"The challenge was how to explain this not only to a teenager in Barcelona, or elsewhere in Europe but in China or Toronto.

"We decided to use our main asset which was our shirt and to put Unicef on it, so that instead of having a sponsor and taking 15m pounds we chose to donate £1m to Unicef. It's more related to the essence of who we are and it's more about our position in the world."

On the pitch the Barça team started the 2006-07 season after their double success in high spirits. With the additions of World Cup winner Gianluca Zambrotta from Juventus along with Lillian Thuram; and Eidur Gudjohnsen from Chelsea they looked like a side ready to dominate for many years to come.

Yet over the coming two seasons all the major trophies would escape them.

"I thought that the cycle for this team would have been longer as the players were very good. It was all about managing them well. If that had happened then the success would have gone on for a lot longer," said former-player Albert Ferrer.

"It has got to be down to internal problems. I do not believe it was because the players did not have the desire to win; if they had won four leagues on the trot then it is true that they may have got carried away.

"Here was a situation where the team had previously not won anything for five years and so I don't think it is true to say they relaxed after winning what they won under Rijkaard."

In the summer of 2006, Rijkaard lost his assistant coach Henk Ten Cate, who took over at Ajax. The pair had worked well together with Ten Cate in many ways complementing Rijkaard as the hard taskmaster.

After he went news began to filter through to the public more and more about player excesses and the level of indiscipline in the dressing room.

Ronaldinho, Deco and Rafael Márquez, headed the list of players known to make the most of the Barcelona nightlife and were slacking in training. It became a running joke that Ronaldinho was in the gym when he could not be seen with the others out on the practice pitches. It is claimed he missed more than two-thirds of the club's training sessions.

Ferrer explained: "Ten Cate was certainly more on top of the players, but they trained more or less the same way all the

175

way through. It is about how you work with the group and it's going to go wrong at some point if you have a couple of players who rest and never train."

The problems were only going to come to the surface when the team's form dipped.

"You should treat all the players the same. While the they were doing well and winning the league there is no fighting; that starts when they start dropping points and some are not working as hard as others," he added.

Icelandic international Eidur Gudjohnsen endured a frustrating time as he watched the club go backwards, unable to win a regular place in the team.

He feels that the team became too relaxed after the Champions League final in 2006.

"It was José Mourinho who helped me choose Barça after I decided following six years that it was time to leave Chelsea. I had not mentioned the club to him but he always talked about the way the Catalans support the team and how important it is to them," he says.

"It was a great experience but on the pitch I had a difficult start and I think it was because the team was beginning to think it was all a bit too easy. In my first season we started off winning comfortably and we built up a big gap at the top of the table. It hurts to say it, but then we became complacent and we lost the league rather than Real winning it," he said.

The 2006-07 season began with victory in the Spanish Super Cup against Espanyol, the winners of the King's Cup the season before, and then when the league got underway, as Gudjohnsen said, there was little indication of the stagnation which would effect the club after Christmas.

The team appeared ready to continue where they left off in Paris, the season before, but the problems began to surface in autumn and the victory against Mallorca was the last away win for the next four months.

The players gradually lost their competitive edge and the new signings failed to offer any fresh ideas. Zambrotta was out of sorts at left back; Thuram at 34 appeared well past his best; and Gudjohnsen, out of position, was also disappointing.

Barça struggled in front of goal without Samuel Eto'o. The Cameroon suffered a knee injury against Werder Bremen in September and missed the next five months. On his return from injury he then flew off to play in the African Nations Cup and missed a further month.

Ronaldinho was at the start of an amazing downward spiral and the only real hope was the emerging Leo Messi.

However, with Real Madrid struggling as Fabio Capello was forced to work with the remnants of the galacticos, Barça were able to head into the Christmas break as favourites for a third consecutive title.

The New Year saw the rising tensions in the dressing room really become apparent. The press had caught on to the fact that there was discontent and a battle of egos over a hierarchy, where it appeared acceptable for some players not to train and go out partying.

The volatile Eto'o, in particular, felt that his contribution was undervalued while Ronaldinho could do no wrong.

On Eto'o's return to the squad in February, against Racing Santander, he refused to go onto the pitch with eight minutes left. Having spoken to the coach, Eusebio Sacristán, he went back to his seat on the bench.

After the match Rijkaard told a press conference that Eto'o had not wanted to play and team-mate Ronaldinho said that at times players need to put the team before themselves.

A furious Eto'o responded on local radio saying that the coach was a "bad person" and that he always did what he had to do for the team. He hit back at Ronaldinho as well saying that he has always trained even when he had a knock, an attack on the Brazilian's poor attendance record.

In what became known as the 'Eto'o case' he then turned his attention to ex-vice-president Sandro Rosell. He said there was a split in the dressing room between the supporters of Rosell and Laporta and that he had to struggle in the middle, receiving attacks from both sides. Referring to Rosell he said if he wanted to criticise him he should "be brave enough to say it to my face, even when he was my boss he did not say hello and now behind my back he is putting the knife in."

Rosell attempting to smooth over the incident said that he always was courteous with Eto'o and that his comments had probably been made in the heat of the moment.

Later Eto'o tried to deny the comments that he had made against Rijkaard but he did not retract what he had said about Ronaldinho.

The friction between Eto'o and Ronaldinho had already been seen a month before when he was angry that Ronaldinho was made Fifa World Player of the Year ahead of him.

"I am not complaining but if I was called 'Etoodinho' then I would be 100 times better known. Having said that, when I see Samuel Eto'o is the third best player in the world according to Fifa, I think of myself as being first," he claimed.

"At the moment players from South America are more valued in terms of their quality and the titles they have won and they are put on a level above the rest; a European or an African would not be valued as much."

It is similar to many outbursts by Eto'o who on other occasions jealously claimed that it was goals that count and not fancy flicks.

Eto'o was never far from controversy at Barcelona and he was criticised for showing a lack of sensitivity when he refused to answer a question from a reporter speaking in Catalan. First of all he asked him to repeat it in Spanish and then he walked away.

This rapidly spiralled into a major issue with a call made for him to learn the language and a Catalan minister in the local government asked for an apology. Eto'o though denied he needed classes and said he fully respected the language.

Along with Eto'o, Barça were without Messi for several months after he picked up a foot injury in November.

He was rapidly becoming the key player that Ronaldinho had been previously. Ronaldinho now was more in the news for his off-the-field activities than for his skills with a football.

He was regularly seen out partying. On his birthday, in front of the media glare, he hired a nightclub and stayed out until 6am despite training being scheduled for the following morning.

Rijkaard, though, refused to take any action over his poor attendance and covered up for him on many occasions.

But there was no hiding his developing paunch, which became a talking point after he took off his top following a 2-1 home defeat in the Champions League by Liverpool.

While the press had turned a blind eye when the team was functioning, they were ready to turn the screw on Ronaldinho's lethargic attitude as they struggled.

They compared the photos of him then with three years before, demonstrating how much weight he had put on, seven kilos was the estimate in the local press.

Barça had failed to defend their Champions League title and went out weakly. Although they did win the return leg at Anfield thanks to a Gudjohnsen goal, the damage was done at home.

The problems started to build up in the league as well with the team conceding too many sloppy late goals.

They were losing away from the Nou Camp, coupled with too many draws at home; and then came the worst week of the season when they were eliminated from the King's Cup while Real Madrid moved ahead in the championship race.

Barça won the first leg of the cup tie against Getafe, 5-2, with a memorable goal from Leo Messi which was almost a carbon copy of that by Diego Maradona in the 1986 World Cup against England. Running from the half-way line he beat all in front of him before coolly slotting past the keeper.

But in the second-leg they fell apart losing 4-0 to Bernd Schuster's team.

The home fans were angry at an apparent lack of desire or professionalism and the situation further deteriorated with a disappointing home draw against Betis in which they conceded a late goal.

179

It led to white handkerchiefs being waved for the first time since Rijkaard was coach.

Real moved to the top of the table and the title was decided two-weeks later when another late goal from Raul Tamudo earned Espanyol a draw against Barça.

Afterwards, Rijkaard refused to be too downhearted but admitted the team lacked the necessary punch to deserve to win the league.

"We wasted too many chances but we did not give it away. How can you give something away you don't have? The most depressing moment in the season was after the defeat by Getafe in the cup and that really affected us. At other times we were lacking in different ways: we struggled to kill off games and we were not solid enough," he said.

Laporta held a press conference at the end of the season and was harder on the players complaining that they had allowed their level to drop off and said that it would not be allowed to happen again.

"There will be a rigorous application of the internal code of discipline, some people need to come out of the shadows while others haven't shown enough commitment and have relaxed too much. The board too has been guilty and they have relied too much on the coaching staff to enforce discipline," he said.

Laporta's 2003 presidential rival, Josep Maria Minguella, believes that the board's lack of experience shone through as they failed to react earlier when the level of performance initially dropped.

"The whole club seemed to develop tremendous confidence after winning the league again. They thought football was simple and it meant they ended up falling into a trap; the disaster which followed was because they did not take it seriously enough," he said.

"I would not say the problems started when Henk Ten Cate left because I think the reasons were more profound than that. You had a young board that had never been in football before and yet in three years had won two leagues and a Champions League. They then believed they could do anything. Along with this you had some players who were too arrogant and complacent.

"As a whole the board did not anticipate what was likely to happen; in football you can win today but it does not mean that you are going to win next weekend. Looking at the season after they won the Champions League, Barça did not just lose one trophy but five – the Intercontinental against largely second level teams, the Super Cup against Sevilla, the league, the Champions League and the King's Cup.

"Why? This is not normal if all the players remain the same and it was because there was a lack of attention to detail."

The split in the club between Laporta and Rosell meant that when the latter resigned, his signings especially Ronaldinho and Deco became isolated.

There was an attempt from the Laporta camp to rid the club of the influence of Rosell and this also had an impact on the pitch. The Laporta friendly press was quick to stick the knife in on Ronaldinho, while Johan Cruyff in his newspaper column rarely had a good word to say for him.

The extent to which this affected Ronaldinho is arguable as he was very much responsible for his own decline.

"Ronaldinho may have had a good relationship with Rosell but players always go out to play for their own reward," said Minguella.

"After many years involved in this game I would say that most players go out to win and if they don't it is because they can't."

However, Ronaldinho, has only ever produced his best football when he was happy and felt wanted among those around him.

Chapter Twelve

The End of a Cycle

White handkerchiefs and a crescendo of whistles filled Barcelona's Nou Camp stadium. Despite a spartan crowd they were determined to make the president Joan Laporta hear their discontent with his leadership as he walked into the directors' box to watch the final home game of the 2007-08 season against Mallorca.

Protesters carrying placards stating 'dimision' (resign) had rallied outside the stadium before the game. No longer were they just the fringe groups and ultras who were calling for a change of leadership but a cross-spectrum of Culés from the radicals through to the middle-aged men with their Ralph Lauren shirts and jumpers over their shoulders.

Just 39,000 bitter fans had turned up to make their dissatisfaction felt on the team and those responsible for assembling it. With a second consecutive season petering to an end it wasn't just the poor results that had stirred the angst of the crowd but the manner of the defeats and the nonchalant air that surrounded the club from the boardroom downwards.

On the evening of the game there were only two who escaped the wrath of the fans and they were Leo Messi, who had risen above the malaise of his team-mates during the season, and Frank Rijkaard, who was given warm applause.

Rijkaard's reception was because he had days earlier announced his resignation and it was an appreciation of the work he had done at the club over five seasons.

The scene was so different from the start of the campaign when there was plenty of optimism and the sense that the team was ready to step up a notch after a barren year.

The Champions League victory over Arsenal was then still relatively fresh in the memory and fans were ready to forgive and forget when players admitted they had allowed themselves become complacent. After all, they had started the season well enough and their form had only really dropped in the final months leading them to finish second on goal difference.

Still there was pressure in the summer of 2007 as although one poor campaign could be forgiven a second would be unacceptable. The board backed Rijkaard giving him the players he wanted and Gabriel Milito and Eric Abidal were incorporated along with the high-profile transfer of Thierry Henry from Arsenal.

As the start of the season approached Culés looked at the abundance of riches at the club's disposal and speculated on whether it would be possible to play the 'Fantastic Four' of Ronaldinho, Messi, Eto'o and Henry in the same team.

A year earlier Barça had made public their desire to bring in Henry who had finished his contract with Arsenal but despite their overtures he agreed to sign a new deal with the Gunners.

While he led people to believe his decision was made after the defeat in the Champions League final against Barça, when he criticised his opponents for a lack of sportsmanship and said he still had goals he wanted to achieve with Arsenal. But it could also have had something to do with the fact that he received a major payout upfront for signing a new contract.

An overwhelmed Henry quickly felt the backing of the Barça fans as 30,000 turning up for his presentation but it was always going to be a difficult first season for him.

On top of the fact that he cost the club £16m when he could have come free a year earlier, he had just endured an injury plagued campaign and would need time to get back to his best.

"It is great to get up here and train in the sun. London will always have a place in my heart, it is one of the best cities in the world and I will always miss it, but it is amazing here with the weather and the passion of the fans," said Henry.

"You really get the feeling that you are playing for a region, a country; they love Barça and make you feel it. In the stadium fans may not be happy if you play a bad game but afterwards in the street they still support you and show their belief in the club."

While many excited fans pondered how Henry was to fit in among the already impressive collection of talent some predicted trouble ahead.

The board had invested 25m euros in defenders Gabi Milito, from Zaragoza and Eric Abidal, from Lyon, but Laporta appeared to be following the disastrous approach of Florentino Pérez at Real Madrid a few years earlier with the Henry buy.

While the nickname of the galacticos for Pérez's team became a running joke as the policy of buying stars rather than players they needed badly backfired, Barça appeared to be going down the same road with the fantasticos team.

As the Real dressing room had become a battle of egos, placing Henry alongside the already strained relationships of Ronaldinho, Samuel Eto'o and Deco, suggested further trouble ahead.

The debate, however, was put off by an injury to Samuel Eto'o in the Joan Gamper trophy at the end of August against Inter Milan and the Cameroon was to miss the first half of the season.

Far from an explosive start, Barça stuttered in the opening matches, failing to score in two of the first three games and critics began to ask whether there was actually any change from the season before. The team lacked the zest of Rijkaard's first seasons in charge and despite the players promising they were ready to bounce back, they failed to show any real desire.

There had been speculation during the summer over the future of Deco after he lost his place in the team during pre-season matches but with the campaign under-way he was back playing although not at the same level as before.

The major talking point centred on attack and once again the contribution of Ronaldinho, in particular, although fans were too expecting a lot more from Henry, who was scoring regularly but was far from setting the world alight.

Rijkaard's answer to the problem was to give youth its chance with Giovani dos Santos and Bojan Krkic both given their debuts in September.

The gossip columns were constantly being fed stories of Ronaldinho's nightlife excesses.

While the football world is often considered an unscrupulous business beset by lurid scandals there are exceptions like Edmilson and Sylvinho. Both are 'Athletes of Christ', an organisation made up of sportsmen who meet up for prayer meetings and bible reading.

Edmilson is known for being a genuine and honest player and so in November when he said that there was a member of the team who was not pulling his weight his comments were taken seriously and not another example of the battle of egos.

He made the accusation following one of the most ineffective performances of the season when Barça lost away from home to Getafe, and Ronaldinho's apathetic display was heavily criticised.

"We are all working hard but there is a black sheep in the operation," said Edmilson. "I love Ronnie a lot, he is vital for Barça and Brazil but also I think that he is a player who is passing through a difficult moment.

"I don't know if he has some kind of personal problem but one thing for sure is that I would not leave him out of the team as his confidence would drop a lot further.

"He is weak and must not lack confidence. We can play with various different systems but if the player is not concentrated then we will win nothing."

He also rued the lack of sacrifice in the team which had been provided by the likes of Ludovic Giuly, who left for Roma after the Champions League win, believing his time was up with the emergence of Messi.

"In two years we won two leagues and a Champions League. I remember a game against AC Milan that we won 1-0 with a goal from Giuly. He was in attack all the time giving his all, he made 50 or more sprints of 60 metres and was dead in the end; we now have a lack of team and family spirit, " he said.

Rijkaard tried to put up a smokescreen by bizarrely suggesting that in the interview given to Spanish television, Edmilson had seen an advertisement with a black sheep and was drawn to the words without really meaning it.

With Ronaldinho having missed so many training sessions, fans wanted the club to be harder on him.

He had no escape from the limelight and there were regular newspaper reports like that which revealed he was out until 6am, 48 hours before a match against Osasuna.

In October he made the headlines with Robinho by going out in Rio de Janeiro following a Brazil match and he partied until catching a plane the following day.

They went to the famous Catwalk club in the city, where Robinho is rumoured to have ordered 40 condoms, and then they are believed to have carried on partying the following day in their hotel.

Ronaldinho returned late to Barcelona and consequently was not included in the following game against Villarreal but rather than realising the error of his ways, the next week he turned up to training unfit to take part after a night out.

While the club planned to fine him Rijkaard, vetoed this instead choosing to support the player rather than punish him.

Laporta had revealed there was an internal discipline code existed and it needed to be enforced more vigorously but this was not Rijkaard's approach.

In his languid style told press that he preferred to discuss problems with players and he admitted at the end of 2007 that no fines had been levied during that year.

"It's true that I am not someone who shouts a lot. I think it is better to have a harmonious team where we lose together and we win together. I am not going to change my way of coaching and it would not be credible to the players if I started behaving now in another way," he explained, while criticising the negative Ronaldinho coverage.

"Ronaldinho should be left in peace and it is only the nostalgia of the fans that is causing the problems. People just want to see the great Ronaldinho, he's given a lot of joy to this club at a difficult moment and was fundamental in the birth of the new FC Barcelona. He has the mentality to return to what he was but it is best not to analyse him daily."

Another player with a reputation for enjoying the nightlife in Barcelona, Patrick Kluivert, also sprang to the defence of Ronaldinho.

"In England it doesn't happen this way and people don't whistle when things start going badly. The players shouldn't have to put up with this bullshit, I have heard it all before, if they don't want him then he can go but respect the player, they have forgotten already when he was doing well," he said.

"It is another example of the press here and the way they influence what goes on at the club by writing sensationalist stories. I am sure, though, that when he returns to Barça in the future he will be treated like a god."

Rijkaard stubbornly stayed with his 4-3-3 formation through thick and thin despite the criticism. It was a system designed to bring out the best in Ronaldinho but with him becoming less important, a new approach appeared to suit players like Henry and at the very least make the team less predictable.

Fans were frustrated watching Barça neutralised by the opposition. Rijkaard argued though: "I like to open up the pitch and play faster football and try and find a way of breaking down the other team.

"It is fine to change the players but if you start messing about with the system it only causes confusion. It is easy to forget that we are playing against very good opposition who have quality players and it is not going to be easy to win."

Former-Dream Team defender Albert Ferrer watched another side reach its end before its time, this time even quicker than that built by Cruyff.

"I think that in football you have to evolve and Rijkaard never changed. The fact is that other teams work out the way that you are playing, so with Barça they filled the middle of the pitch, leaving the wings free and then sit back," he said.

"There was no plan B; you need to tinker with the team and change little things from time to time which he never did."

Ferrer is one of many who were disappointed with Henry's first season in Spain although he understands that it was a difficult transition for the Frenchman to make in his 30s.

"Henry didn't played well. At Arsenal he was the key player but here there was Ronnie, Eto'o, Messi, Iniesta etc, and he is just one more: mentally this is very difficult to deal with," he said.

"It is much harder for a striker in Spain. In England except for the top four teams they are not technically strong. Here there are around 18 teams who know what they are doing so it is a lot harder to find space.

"Then apart from the football he had personal problems."

Before departing for the Primera Division, Henry split up with his model girlfriend Claire Merry and was forced to leave behind his daughter Tea. While it was understood that he was struggling to come to terms with the separation, it was not until his close friend and former Arsenal team-mate Robert Pires, playing at Villarreal, blamed Henry's phlegmatic displays on his personal problems, that the issue really came to light.

Henry arrived with hopes sky high as fans expected him to deliver similar performances to those at Arsenal and they were left disappointed when it did not materialise.

Perhaps unrealistically they were anticipating the dashing displays that had terrorised Premiership defences for years and he became frustrated with the criticism.

Finally he hit out and blamed Rijkaard's system.

"It is impossible to look back at the way I played for Arsenal and to expect the same from me at Barcelona, I used to play up front alongside another striker and here I am doing a different job," he said.

"I now have to defend and do everything, it has been the decision of the coach to put me on the wing. This is not about me, my job is to do what the trainer likes and not what I like, but it has been eight or nine years though since I played on the wing."

The following day he arranged a press conference to smooth over his comments and to state that his words had been distorted by the press and reassured supporters that he was happy at Barcelona.

"It is me that has to adapt to the Barça style and not the other way round. At Arsenal we played a direct style and here we move the ball around more, there are more passes to the left and the right and I have to adapt to this which will take time," he said.

"The main differences I have found between England and Spain is that in England it is faster and in Spain they blow up when there is any contact.

"I want to end the discussion as to whether I will be as well now as I was when I was playing for Arsenal. I do not play for Arsenal any more but I am trying to fit in here and do my best for this team.

"I am not sorry about having left Arsenal and I remember that when I went there it took me nine games to score my first goal."

In the eyes of Ferrer he was unsuited to Spanish football.

"He said that he preferred to play as an out and out attacker but I don't understand what he meant because when I was playing at Chelsea he always played on the left wing. Maybe physically he doesn't feel he is the same as three or four years ago and now he wants to play closer to goal and where he will have more chances," he said.

"He likes to knock the ball in front of him and run on to it but in Spain there isn't the room. He is not like Messi and one on one he needs space and power to go past players."

Henry's public image suffered to begin with from his reluctance to speak in Spanish never mind Catalan. The club has had a history of players and coaches including Bobby Robson and Louis van Gaal who struggled through a lack of communication and were viewed as being distant and uninterested in adapting to the Catalan culture.

The Catalans appreciate the effort to adapt and for Henry it was made worse by the fact that when he did speak Spanish, he spoke it quite competently but preferred to speak in English in which he was more comfortable.

Spanish journalists complained that he was happy to talk to French and English reporters but rarely to them but Henry said they were making up problems and causing unrest in the dressing room.

On his personal issues he admitted that he was unhappy and that he found it difficult seeing so little of his daughter.

"A father who sees his daughter only five times in eight months cannot be happy, it has got nothing to do with football. When I am on the pitch I try to forget it and do my best but it is something that affects my life. If I could see my daughter more often it would help," he said.

In November, Barcelona witnessed a mass invasion of Scots as a reported 20,000 Rangers supporters came to watch their side at the Nou Camp or simply to soak up the atmosphere in the city.

Their behaviour led to widespread criticism from the authorities and members of the public.

With many Catalans aligning their plight against Madrid centralism with that of Irish and Scottish nationalists against British rule, there was considerably more antipathy among the press before the visit of Rangers (a team they saw as upholding the Union) than there would have been for a match against Celtic.

When they arrived, locals looked on disapprovingly as hoards gathered in the centre of the city drinking and urinating.

It has to be said, though, that while their conduct was poor it was not dissimilar to what happens at the yearly Mercè celebration in Barcelona, where due to the lack of toilet facilities any back street is used.

Some Rangers fans also let their club down by trying to force their way into the stadium without tickets. Several hundred were hanging around outside looking for the easiest gate to storm and it led to the ticket office having to close early. Barça claimed it lost out on 500,000 euros from the unsold seats.

Inside the ground and there were pro-Celtic and Ireland taunts, partly a response to similar anti-Catalan flags and chants at Ibrox.

On the pitch there was no contest as Barça won comfortably.

Rangers carried on celebrating nonetheless with many bars claiming to have sold more than 1,000 litres of beer over two days and a total of 140,000 litres was reported to have been drunk.

Catalan politicians hit out at the behaviour of fans afterwards and the leniency of police who did not hand out fines for drinking or urinating in the street.

"I can understand that they did not want to worsen the problems but the lack of respect for authority is not something we can tolerate and this has now reached the limit," said Xavier Trias, of the CiU party.

Another, Alberto Fernández Diaz, of the PP claimed: "This passivity towards drunken Rangers fans who have been camped out around the city without showing the normal respect for public order, is an example of the loutish tourism which is a major concern."

The authorities did successfully deal with this problem for matches later in the competition, including those against Schalke 04 and Manchester United, by providing a special zone for fans to gather where facilities were provided for them.

Barça struggled through the group stages of the Champions League and domestically they had difficulty especially away from home but in a bizarre title race they remained in the running with Real Madrid also failing to fire on all cylinders.

Rijkaard was loathe to leave out Ronaldinho but with protests from fans and from the boardroom it became impossible to keep giving him another chance especially as youngsters like Bojan Krkic were jumping at the chance to make an impact.

Rijkaard decided to drop Ronaldinho for the first time in his Barça career at the beginning of December away to Espanyol and then later that month against Valencia he wasn't even given a single minute on the field as substitute.

"Ronaldinho was the flagship of the team and after doing so well it is natural that the fans expect so much from him," said Ferrer.

"Ronaldinho stirred the emotions. Everyone saw his ability and he put the team at the focal point of world attention. The difficulty after once that has happened is to keep at the same level."

It is true that while Ronaldinho was receiving considerable criticism and speculation was rife over his future there was little effort by the Laporta regime to make life easier for him.

Cruyff in his weekly column in the newspaper El Periodico accused him of resting on his laurels.

"When you are young you can only be your best when you are physically at the same level as your rivals and so you have to train and sacrifice. Only if you train can you make a difference. The best of Ronaldinho is his running with the ball;

he is not someone who plays the ball first time and so not to be fit makes it more of a problem for him," he explained.

"If he adapted and played more one touch football then it would be easier as the opponents wouldn't be so close. It is more difficult if he always looks to beat someone.

"The problem is his own and those around him, there are a lot of people with influence, it is not always good to have intermediaries.

"I rate Ronaldinho highly but I have seen his weak points, I have seen that he doesn't speed up the play and that his play doesn't allow for the participation of other top players. He should play more with his head for his own benefit. If you play just for yourself then you are finished earlier.

"It is not true to say it is the end of a cycle, this is only a word, because if you change a person and his influence then the whole thing changes and you can start again differently."

Ronaldinho responded saying that it was not he that was living in the past but Cruyff.

Laporta promised that a greater boardroom influence would be brought to bear on team affairs by the appointment of a new director in charge of football who would fill the void left by Sandro Rosell.

The move turned flat when it was announced that the man to take up the role would be the existing vice-president Marc Ingla, who had up until then focused on marketing.

"Ingla will participate in the sporting decisions without interfering with the sports director Txiki Begiristain and he will work actively in the design of the sports policies of Barcelona," announced Laporta.

"Ingla has had a decisive role in the contracts with Nike, Mediapro and Unicef, he is a competent man with a great capacity for analysis. He has a cool head in difficult moments and is a passionate football fan."

It was a move with more than a sniff of desperation; a case of shuffling the board members in the hope of finding the answer. Ingla to most fans looked every bit the stereotypical economist: a slim man with a beard, a pin-stripe suit and braces, they doubted the empathy or respect he would have with players in his new position.

In the league everything was building towards the el clasico, the match that divides the country between fans of Real Madrid and Barcelona and of course the one game in which if Barça win then practically all other failures can be forgiven.

The club hierarchy was saying that a victory in the game would mean they could rein in Real and also give themselves a major psychological boost as they went into the winter break.

Real had won just once in the previous 24 years at the Nou Camp but the atmosphere was not as intense as when real hate figures like Luis Figo, Ronaldo and Roberto Carlos played for the visitors.

The game was seen as the perfect chance for Ronaldinho to win back his doubters along with Deco, who was struggling for form and fitness.

In the hype beforehand, Ronaldinho discussed his time at Barcelona and after so much talk about his problematic personal life he said that he was settled in Castelldefels, on the outskirts of Barcelona.

In September his three-year-old son, Joao, saw Ronaldinho play for the first time at the Nou Camp against Athletic Bilbao. Joao had moved to Spain to live with his father after having been brought up by his mother, a dancer in Rio de Janeiro.

"It was very emotional for me to have my son watch me playing football and I really wanted to do something special on the pitch. God willing, he will have the chance to stay here and it will be great to live with him in my house. It is a responsibility to be a father and it changes your life," said Ronnie.

"It is important for me to have my family around me. I have been fortunate that my brother had already passed through the world of football and explained how things worked. I just like to play and do my best; my home is the dressing room."

He explained how the constant media intrusion irritated him.

"It makes me angry to see so much written about my personal life because in all the time I have been at Barça I have always tried the same and behaved the same. I am unhappy which is normal but I understand the world is not always wonderful. I am content to concentrate on football and I respond on the pitch. The team is still hungry, we are aware that we have entered into history but we still want more."

"When I go out to play football now it is the same as it always was. Everyone knows what I am like, I do not try and hide and I will continue to behave the same way."

Ronaldinho was grateful for the support he had from Messi especially the way he celebrated goals by making the famous Ronaldinho hand gesture with his little finger and thumb.

"He is a fantastic player and the best thing is the way he shows so much confidence. It is very special for me to see him remember me when I am not playing and people are saying a lot of unfair things about me. It was emotional to see people worried about me," he said.

Rijkaard decided to give him and Deco a starting place against Real but the decision was to fall flat on its face as Ronaldinho, in particular, showed once again this time to the whole world, who had tuned in for the game, that he was badly out of condition.

Julio Baptista scored the only goal of the game as Real Madrid stretched their lead at the top.

After the Christmas break in a bizarre move, the club decided to separate Ronaldinho from the other players for a month and give him a training plan designed to make him match fit after a tendon injury.

The intention was to take him away from the public glare over his lack of fitness. Saying that he was still recovering from a niggling injury was also a way to help the club save face for allowing the player to get into that condition when Laporta had started the season saying they would be more disciplined.

Ronaldinho could be seen training during January using a special harness and climbing up stairways at the Nou Camp to build up his resistance until he was ready to return to the front line.

With so much focus put on Ronaldinho it went unnoticed by many that he was not the only person to blame. Without him the team remained unconvincing and by the end of January the board held a meeting to discuss a crisis as Real Madrid had managed to race into a nine-point lead.

They considered carefully the possibility of replacing Rijkaard with Jose Mourinho but in the end they decided not to tamper with the set-up and Begiristain reassured them that when Ronaldinho and Eto'o were back playing regularly they would guarantee 40 goals a season.

Publicly, Laporta gave a vote of confidence to the trainer and quashed rumours that Cruyff would return as a trainer. He said that he wanted to see Rijkaard stay until the end of his mandate in 2010.

"Frank has a contract until 2009 and I would like to see him stay until the end of my presidency as it gives stability to the team; he has been here five years and we have full confidence in him. He is a very capable person professionally and privately and the club appreciates his discretion and calmness," he said.

Asked about the role of Cruyff he added: "Cruyff and Rijkaard are big friends and have meetings every now and again, with sometimes Txiki included, where they give their opinions but that is as far as it goes."

The question of player indiscipline continued to hit the headlines with Deco and Rafael Marquez also flouting club rules.

On January 17, Deco lost his licence for drink driving and in a bid to clear his name said that he had drunk a third of a bottle of wine, which in many other European countries would not have been enough to be over the limit.

The fact that this came on the back of his telling the press that footballers should be able to party and enjoy themselves, further aggravated the situation.

"We are young and we have all the right in the world to go out. If someone begins work at 9am and arrives on time and he does his job well then he is not a bad professional. If I have a game on Sunday then I can go out Wednesday night," he said.

He hit back at question marks over his commitment by saying that people should concentrate on supporting the players rather than knocking them.

"It is important to remember that the team isn't the same as the one that won the league titles, there are new players and it is never good to live in the past," he said, while hitting back at Real Madrid's then sports director Predrag Mijatovic, who said that the Madrid dressing room was more controlled and that he did not rate Ronaldinho.

"For two years we were ahead of Real but we did not say anything about them, either the board or the players, and now they are talking about being better.

"Mijatovic cannot speak about our dressing room because he does not know it and he should also show more respect for players. He was a great player and he knows that what goes on in a dressing room should remain there. To say he would not sign Ronaldinho is ridiculous because he would never be sold to Madrid anyway.

"We need to be united, the public image of this dressing room is completely different to the reality, players are annoyed when we lose and we were also angry with Edmilson when he made his comment (about the black sheep) because you should not say this to the press.

"Ronaldinho will always be remembered as the best player to have been at Barcelona because he changed things when they were very bad."

The question of indiscipline refused to go away and Gianluca Zambrotta added fuel to the fire when asked about the question of players being professional.

He said that if they go out 48 hours before a game and know their limits then there is no problem. This, however, was against the club rules, which state they are not allowed to go out two days before a game.

A stand-off was developing between players and press over the negative coverage and few players would pass through the mixed zone after matches. One player even breached Uefa rules by refusing to go through the zone after a Champions League game.

"We won the leagues and the Champions League and then we started the following campaign well until our level dropped off. Since then the newspapers changed the way they are covering us; they are not interested in the good humour in the dressing room but after a bad result they talk instead about problems and this is taking advantage of their position," said Xavi.

The previous season Ronaldinho had taken off his shirt after a game against Athletic Bilbao to show to the world that he was not over-weight after pictures in a Spanish paper compared him to four years earlier and suggested he looked bulkier especially around the waistline.

"Do I weigh too much? I have gone out and people have said to me I shouldn't eat so much. This was painful for me because I would look in the mirror and I could not see a problem but this has all served as motivation for me," he said afterwards.

In January, 2008, when Laporta was asked about Ronaldinho's weight again, he said it was normal that a player put on a few pounds when injured.

The Brazilian responded by showing his stomach during a training session in a bid to demonstrate it wasn't true, and he was backed by Rijkaard, but fans were left little the wiser by his explanation as to what exactly was the matter with him and why he couldn't play.

"Ronnie is fine and in optimum condition, this is what the medical staff say but we still do not know when he will reappear. He is working well and a situation like this passed a year ago when he didn't have problems but we separated him from the group so that he could work to find his top level," said Rijkaard.

"Ronaldo (the Brazilian), yes, was fat but with all respect he is one of the best strikers that I know. I see Ronaldinho each day and he is fine."

The infighting was playing into the hands of Real Madrid who were far from their best but had a battling edge that Barça lacked.

"We are hurt but we are not going to let up, Real have an important advantage but we can still catch them. Ronaldinho is a key player for us, one of the best in the world, and can return to being the player that he was. It is not the case of just putting the pressure on one player but with him on the pitch everything is a lot easier," said Puyol, after a draw with Athletic Bilbao and he also advised his team-mates to read Michael Jordan's motivational book My Philosophy for Triumph which concentrated on compromise and team spirit.

"In all sports there are teams who have great players but have not achieved that much because they are not prepared to sacrifice," said the ex-basketball player. A statement that appeared very apt for the situation at the Nou Camp.

A further surprising move in the Ronaldinho saga was the publication of a medical report in March by club doctors that said that there was nothing wrong with him despite the player saying he was injured.

Coming a day after he had trained for just six minutes, jogged a couple of times up and down the pitch and then walked off, it was seen as a move by the club to wash their hands of the Brazilian.

While his agent complained, Laporta attempted to smooth it over by saying that it is possible that Ronaldinho felt some pain even though the tests showed nothing.

Fans increasingly felt that the wool was being pulled over their eyes and they were not prepared to sit back and hear more lame excuses for what was a clear lack of firmness by the club towards its stars.

Barcelona is not big enough for players to escape being seen and people could see with their own eyes players who were supposedly injured going out and enjoying themselves and yet the club would deny they were acting incorrectly.

The supporters were not prepared to turn a blind eye as the side was playing very badly and their star players like Ronaldinho and Deco were not even available. Then there was Rafael Marquez who appeared to be more often than not in Madrid with his model girlfriend Jaydy Michel.

The supporters were confused at why no one was being punished for their misdemeanours.

By April the club had already reported more than 50 injuries and the question was also being asked if players really had a problem or was this some sort of camouflage.

The team's problems were typified by a 3-2 loss away to Real Betis, where after having gone two goals to the good they apparently lacked the dedication to finish off the match.

Tellingly, afterwards another member of the coaching staff was overheard saying to Rijkaard that he 'shouldn't forget his parachute' and the Dutchman said he had two days to prove himself.

Coming before the first-leg of the clash with Schalke it meant that he needed a good result in the Champions League tie or he would be out.

Barça won the first-leg away and scraped home in the return to the Nou Camp, although the fans showed their disappointment with the season so far with whistles and handkerchiefs while one placard claimed Laporta was a mercenary.

Before the return leg club economist, Xavier Sala i Martin, had lifted the lid on the internal problems explaining there were players who had been separated from the team for disciplinary reasons and that there had been a cover-up, whereby they were described as being injured.

"There are some sportsmen that work hard as well as having money and women, and others that out of 60 training sessions only go to 22. We are not saying that all footballers at

Barça are lazy as this is not true but there are one, two or three Barça players who are out all the time and they are now separated from the rest of the team," he said.

The timing of the comments could have been better with the team playing that evening but the insinuation was clear coming from a board member very close to the president Laporta.

Sports director, Txiki Begiristain, tried to diffuse the situation by saying it was untrue while captain Carles Puyol, said it showed a lack of respect to suggest this.

The responsibility had been lumped mainly on the shoulders of Ronaldinho, Deco and Marquez but the problems were with the whole team.

As homegrown players, Xavi Hernandez and Andrés Iniesta were more protected against criticism but they were regulars in midfield and had to share their share of the blame.

They are both tidy midfield ball players and rarely give the ball away but in many games the team needed to be more direct. There would be matches in that the team would pass the ball around for 15 to 20 passes in midfield but without making any inroads into the opposition penalty area.

When Barça enjoyed their earlier league titles and 2006 Champions League success, it was normally a case of Xavi or Iniesta playing alongside Deco and a more defensive midfielder. Deco would provide the main attacking arm from the middle of the pitch and combine well with Ronaldinho.

Later when Pep Guardiola became coach, Iniesta was to have more success playing a more direct role or even as part of the three-pronged forward line. Generally though he still needed to score more goals.

Then there was Henry who had come with so much expectation on his shoulders but was neither able to produce his best football or look sufficiently interested for the Catalans' wishes.

He complained of personal problems but he could expect little sympathy playing for one of the biggest clubs in the world and receiving a massive salary.

Rijkaard chose to look at the qualities Henry brought to the team and that he was always ready to assist and advise the youngsters, especially Bojan.

"Even as a substitute he is very important as he is always ready to help. A player like him must be able to unite his talent, quality and experience. It is not a surprise to me that when he arrives at the dead ball line he looks to pass it: when you talk of leaders you must talk of people who are generous," he said.

Much hope had been placed on the return of Eto'o in February but he was unable to make a significant impact despite a healthy goal record.

The defence too was not free from criticism. Gianluca Zambrotta looked far from the star of Juventus and Italy, and Abidal, admitted himself that he had lost his form in the second half of the season and even asked the coach not to play him.

"A team which wins two leagues and a Champions League after such a long time without success builds up a level of demand and we felt this pressure more each day," said Sylvinho.

"We wanted to keep winning but the results did not come. We suffered a drop not just physically but psychologically and I don't mean physically in the way people will automatically think but a drop out of a lack of confidence."

As Edmilson explained, Barça had lost modest players like Giuly who were prepared to work hard and did not complain about being on the bench and had bought more stars with egos.

The one forward to consistently avoid complaint was Messi as he remained the biggest and most real threat for Barcelona although injuries threatened to derail him.

His ability to run defenders ragged with the ball tied to his left foot not only put him a cut above the rest but also among the all-time greats.

In 2005, Messi was named the best player in the U-20 World Cup played in Holland, after becoming top scorer for the competition winners Argentina. Back in 1979, Maradona helped Argentina to win the Youth World Championships and his team-mate in that side, Guillermo Hoyos, feels they are very alike.

"Leo on his own can change games, he is like Diego as they kick him, they kick him again but he continues until he is virtually on the floor. They almost have to kill him before he stops," he said.

Messi's goal against Getafe in 2007 was on a par with Maradona's second against England in the 1986 World Cup, but the most incredible aspect is how often he makes similar runs, beating two or three players with ease.

The fact he had played more than 100 times for the club by the time he was 20 showed how important he had become. His lack of pretension helped him to be one of the most popular players in the dressing room.

"I still have to improve a lot of things but most importantly I lack experience and with it I will be a lot better. Other areas in which I have to change are in dribbling less and in my vision of the game," he revealed.

"I felt very comfortable playing next to Ronaldinho and I accept that in the past I tried to play too much with him and looked for him rather than other players."

Messi's ability to let the pressure roll over him suggests at times that he doesn't really take it all on board. Off the pitch he appears shy and awkward when interviewed but playing football he carries on without an apparent care in the world.

Similarly the comparison with Maradona has left him unruffled.

"This is a waste of time and I just think about playing my games. Maradona has always given me good advice but I do not think about copying him," he said.

In the league it was a season where both frontrunners, Real Madrid and Barcelona, kept slipping-up and giving the advantage to the other.

If Madrid lost to Deportivo la Coruña then Barcelona would only draw with Almeria but moving into the final straight of the campaign it was the side from the capital which looked the more worthy winners as they again, like the season before, showed more tenacity and fighting spirit; and gradually they began to open up a gap at the top.

Barça looked to the cups for saving grace but they crashed out of the King's Cup at the hands of a woefully under-performing Valencia side coached by Ronald Koeman. The former-Dream Team defender oversaw Valencia move from Champions League contention to relegation material before being sacked.

Still Valencia did have enough to beat Barça and it meant that with mounting pressure, Rijkaard's last chance for success that season was to be the Champions League semi-final against Manchester United.

Speculation among journalists and fans was rife over the future of Rijkaard and players like Ronaldinho, Deco and Eto'o The latter two both said in the press they would consider moving if they did not win anything for a second consecutive season.

Catalan papers were full of information about Manchester United as the media sought a way for misfiring Barca to beat the Premier League champions.

Johan Cruyff tried to create a mood of confidence saying that United were not as strong as people thought. Eidur Gudjohnsen was optimistic as United played attacking football, which gave Barça a better chance than against the more defensive English sides Liverpool and Chelsea.

As the date approached, tickets were at a premium and being sold for over £500. Two Saudi Arabian businessmen, flying in for the game, walked into a bar asking ticket holders to name their price.

As so often happens, when the match was finally played it failed to live up to the hype, finishing 0-0 at the Nou Camp.

The Barça fans remained behind the team sparing them the now regular 'pañuelo' of white handkerchiefs that greeted their downward spiral in the league. They gave the players their most uplifting support for a couple of seasons.

Rijkaard gambled on bringing the injured Deco back into the team and apart from surviving an early penalty miss from Ronaldo, the team had plenty more energy and dynamism.

Twice winner of the Champions League, Deco showed his winning spirit by raising the tempo in the midfield. The United defence was often on the back foot but Barça lacked a cutting edge. Messi dodged and feinted down the right-wing but too often the final ball was missing and Eto'o was largely anonymous.

In the return leg at Old Trafford, Barça failed to maintain the level and a mistake by Zambrotta allowed in Paul Scholes for a fine 25-yard strike.

Laporta's public image took a further dive as he was shown remonstrating with a fan outside a Manchester hotel before the game and during the match the way he ranted and raved at the referee was considered unacceptable for a president.

There was more bad news for the club as tests revealed that Gabriel Milito had ruptured a cruciate knee ligament in the game and would be out of action for six months. Seven years earlier Real Madrid had chosen not to sign Milito because of a perceived weakness in the same right knee.

Fans were in an unforgiving mood, rounding on the players, but their real anger was reserved for Laporta.

A key moment in the title race was a battling comeback for Real Madrid away at Racing Santander while the same weekend Barça could only draw at home to Espanyol. This opened up a sizeable eleven-point gap.

Barça then imploded and defeat against Deportivo la Coruna followed by draws with Recreativo de Huelva and Getafe, meant they surrendered second spot to Villarreal.

With Barça still to play Real in the league they wanted to avoid what would be the biggest humiliation of having to form the traditional tunnel and applaud out the champions at the Bernabéu.

It became unavoidable after an immense performance from Real who came from a goal down to beat Osasuna away.

With Fabio Cannavaro dismissed and Gabriel Hienze off the pitch receiving treatment, they managed to turn the result around. Gonzalo Higuain was the hero scoring the winner in the final minutes.

It meant Real Madrid were champions and Barça would have to perform the 'pasillo' in their next game.

Lack of discipline raised its head again as Deco and Samuel Eto'o appeared to deliberately pick up yellow cards going into the clasico so that they would be suspended and not have to endure the embarrassment.

This time, though, Rijkaard finally snapped. Having backed his players to the hilt up until then, he told a press conference afterwards that the players were fully aware that they were one booking away from a ban.

In the end, the 'pasillo' was something of a non-event and the true embarrassment for Barça was the performance as they fell apart.

They were 2-0 down after just 25 minutes and Gudjohnsen was substituted after the second goal although he was no more to blame than anyone.

Barça went on to lose 4-0 and Xavi was dismissed in the final minutes for arguing with the referee. It was a desperate display lacking pride and it was clear on the   faces of the players that they wanted the ground to the swallow them up.

Their rain drenched coach Rijkaard on the touchline deserved a better finale to his Barça career: he already knew his time was up having been given the news in the hotel before the game by Begiristain.

After the game midfielder Toure Yaya said he felt embarrassed and ridiculed by what had happened and that he had never seen Rijkaard so angry.

On their return to Barcelona in the early hours of the morning they were greeted at the airport by angry fans and the following day's training session was closed to the press and fans.

None of the players were spared in the Catalan press with the front page of Sport completely black but for the title –

'tragic end – you have dishonoured the Barça shirt'. Analysing the game no one was given more than a three out of ten and many including Rafael Marquez, who chose to stay behind in Madrid afterwards to be with his girlfriend, was given just one.

For Laporta in the Real Madrid balcony, next to his contemporary Ramon Calderon, he had completed a full circle.

He won the 2003 elections as a bright new hope for the club, a president ready to take Barça into a new era after the debt-ridden club had lost its way and failed to qualify even for the Champions League.

In an astonishing turnaround, Barça had returned to the elite of the sport but now they were back in full crisis.

Laporta as he watched the bleak scene must have found it difficult to comprehend that just two years had passed since Ronaldinho had mesmerised the Real team and reduced their supporters to simply applauding him.

He was facing a full-scale revolt from club members who were no longer prepared to tolerate his arrogance. He had led a campaign against the aloofness of Núñez in the 1990s and now incredulous fans felt that he was actually worse than the man who was nicknamed Napoleon.

From the start other board members had been unhappy at his autocratic style with some like Rosell choosing to walk away.

It might be apt to quote former American president Lyndon B Johnson who said: "It is better to have him inside the tent urinating out than outside the tent urinating in."

Rosell was able to sit on the sidelines, orchestrating his revenge and waiting for the right time to launch an attack on Laporta. During the summer of 2008 he announced that he would stand for president at the next elections.

He had spoken little since he resigned as vice-president although he was always critical of the way his department, involved in the buying and selling of players, was run.

"Arsenal must have been laughing when Barça offered 16m pounds for Henry as a season before they could have had him for free. Previously Barça have never bought players for this kind of money who are around 30-years-old. You want players with ambition who are looking to prove themselves," he said.

"The problem when I was there was that Laporta preferred to listen to Cruyff than to the rest. Cruyff has done a lot of good for the club and a lot of bad. I would say that the only good that has come to the club with Laporta has been the results."

Laporta continued to defend his record and remained confident despite the fans backlash.

"I don't think in terms of it being the end for this team, it is more about the footballing system in place. I am very happy with what we have won and a strong structure is important for us to keep progressing. We have a worldwide project for the club. It is not easy to cope with personal criticism but I do my best," he said.

"I remember the good moments. I was sad Rosell left when he did and I thought it was unnecessary but it was his choice. Cruyff is a friend of mine and a world figure, he speaks and I listen but I either agree or don't with him."

As the debate centred on Laporta's leadership talk once again returned to his commitment and whether he was now gearing up for a move into the political arena.

"I have no intention of moving into politics and after my period of leadership ends I do not know yet what I will do. The world of politics is very complex and I have not used Barça as a platform for my interests," he said, attempting to diffuse the issue.

"In terms of who will replace me I think it is good to have a system to promote people from the existing board and make them the president. There are people from inside this group who are capable of taking over and doing a good job."

Laporta stated publicly Rijkaard would remain as his coach all the way through to 2010, even though behind the scenes the search had been on for a replacement for a long time.

"For me he is the perfect trainer. We can see that not only from the football he produces but also from the respect he has for those around him and his politeness and courtesy," said Laporta.

With the deteriorating situation on the pitch the board could not wait for a smooth changeover of coach in the summer and was forced into immediate action.

It was endemic of the problems at the club that a coach who had brought Barça's second Champions League success and two league titles, was to be ushered out of the back door in a messy debacle. Rijkaard's departure was made official two days after the Bernabéu debacle.

Speculation was growing over who would replace Rijkaard with Jose Mourinho the people's favourite alongside former-Barça players Pep Guardiola, who was Cruyff's choice.

A board meeting was held on May 8, where directors discussed for four hours the man to succeed him. Against the wishes of directors who wanted a candidate with more experience, as usual Laporta had his way and at a press conference later in the day revealed that it was to be Guardiola.

"We have decided to replace Frank Rijkaard with Pep Guardiola. He has done a great job, led a project that won the Champions League, two leagues and a couple of Super Cups. I know that this does not make up for the bad results but Frank made history and with time we will analyse the mistakes that we made," said Laporta.

"We believe in Pep Guardiola and we know that he will continue the football line that has taken this club to major success. He is confident, he knows the club and has the capability to lead the new project.

"The cycle has come to an end, we did not win the league in the last campaign and we told him he had to correct the mistakes. Unfortunately the results have not been good and we decided that we had to part with Rijkaard.

"I have to accept a big part of the blame for not having corrected the problems. We work so that things function well, no one can doubt this, but the plans failed despite the effort.

However, no one should forget that Rijkaard led the team to the Champions League success.

"The trainer is responsible for the dressing room and the players have not reached the level expected. We planned to have one of the best squads in the world and we thought of everything but when Begiristain goes down to the dressing room he is not in control there."

Guardiola had been appointed coach of Barcelona B a year before and was working well with the team of youngsters. He learnt of his new role as he was guiding them to promotion from the Segunda B.

He had had no previous coaching experience and to take on a job with as much pressure as the Barça trainer was a major gamble but in his favour was the high esteem he was held in by fellow Catalans. A star of Cruyff's Dream Team he was a home grown talent who epitomised the way the Culés like to see football played.

Cruyff himself once said: "The Dream Team ended with the departure of Guardiola, the brilliant and triumphalist past of Barça died in that instant."

Sunday, May 11, was supposed to be Frank Rijkaard's day as it was his last home match at the Nou Camp but no tribute was made as it would have been badly out of place.

It was a strange atmosphere in the stadium. Outside there had been protests before the Mallorca game as there had been for several previous matches, and inside a spartan crowd of less than 40,000 whistled and waved handkerchiefs, reaching a crescendo when Laporta took his place on the balcony.

The players ran out to jeers and the only pause was for the appearance of Rijkaard who was politely applauded. That day Catalan newspapers were dedicated to the respectful and educated way that the Dutchman had gone about his work.

During the game touches from Eto'o and Deco were greeted with whistles from the crowd as they were singled out for missing the clash with Real Madrid, days earlier. One placard read 'Eto'o, Deco cowards'. When Eto'o scored he further aggravated the crowd by telling them to be quiet.

Barcelona moved into a two-goal lead, but in the second half with Messi substituted the team capitulated, like their season, and they lost 3-2, conceding a final goal in injury time.

Rijkaard admitted that he was embarrassed by the attention, and was sheepish as he was greeted by applause every time he left the dugout to give instructions to the team.

In the final moments of the game as a hail of abuse was being hurled at the players and the presidential box, he stood alone with his thoughts on the pitch side. Then with the game ended, disconsolate and beaten he attempted to juggle a ball a couple of times before walking down the tunnel.

But in his post-match press conference he refused to criticise the players.

"I certainly did not expect so difficult an end to the season, as a sportsman I hoped for something more positive. The suffering in the final stage of the season has been almost unbearable, it has been hard, hard, hard and I speak for everyone," he said.

"It is not easy, we could not do any more, we could not change the dynamic and it is very difficult to go out and play when there are a lot of problems at the club.

"The attitude of the public, the way they whistled the players, has been sad. I expected it to be like that but I cannot be happy, it is sad to play in an atmosphere like that.

"It is a normal reaction to what has happened but I am sad for the players as it has not been easy for them. Especially it was unfortunate for Giovanni dos Santos who had his 19th birthday and did not deserve to be whistled in that way.

"Barça is a great team and the club should be winning trophies. The public has the right to show how it feels. The team has to be stronger than the circumstances in which it plays and often they are but today the circumstances were stronger than the team."

From the outside it was somewhat strange that despite the problems on the pitch the main focus for the criticism lay at the door of Laporta.

His presidency had fierce opponents who remained loyal to the old order but this was made worse by the directors' petulance and lack of accountability.

The extent to which the board had lost touch with the grass roots was shown at the end of the season when the director of football, Marc Ingla, and sports director, Txiki Begiristain, tried to apportion all the blame for the failure on Rijkaard and the players.

"We have reached the end of a cycle and several important players will be leaving like Deco, who announced several days ago that he plans to move on, and Ronaldinho, who has several options," said Beguiristain.

At the beginning of May, Laporta's arch-nemesis the lawyer Oriol Giralt returned to the limelight with a proposal for a 'vota de censura', a vote of no confidence, against Laporta and the board.

The man who had successfully taken the board to court and forced elections in 2006 hit out at Laporta's leadership and enforced Article 49 of the club's statute allowing for a vote of no confidence if five per cent of members support it.

While there were several attempts at a vote of no confidence during the Gaspart presidency, there had only ever been one successfully called and that was under Núñez in 1998 and that had failed.

This time Giralt and Christian Castellvi comfortably achieved the 5,882 votes necessary under club rules, and after a ten-day period to check their validity the day for the vote of no confidence was announced as June 6.

Giralt denied that he was being backed by a heavyweight opponent of Laporta such as Rosell or Minguella but claimed that he was being investigated as the club was trying to find something negative about him.

Whether or not Rosell did have any contact with Giralt a week before the vote of no confidence was held, Rosell decided to throw his hat into the ring and said if there were elections then he would stand.

"My family said I was crazy but after Laporta's speech at the convention of members I thought that was the limit and so I decided to do something," said Giralt.

"You could say my director of marketing, though, was Joan (Laporta) himself and he helped my cause a lot when he spoke.

"I have not been put under any pressure from the board but if they did anything then it would not have mattered as there are thousands of other people along with me who feel the same way.

"I like money but I prefer Barça. I prefer a hot dog and watching Barça than a good meal without football. People came here from all over to support the motion even one person from Japan."

Laporta counter-attacked, defending his period in power.

"The work over the last five years has been good and history will show that. I think that I deserve to complete my mandate and we have the desire, the strength and the capacity to keep running the club. We are proud to have modernised it using sound economics and returned it to a world level. People all over the world now know what values it represents," he told a press conference.

In a further occasion in what was derided as an attempt at garnering support, he apologised in tears to his fellow directors and said: "it is clear that the Giralt-Rosell tandem is providing the momentum for the vote of no confidence; for years they have been putting sticks in the spokes and now they have taken off their mask."

Giralt claimed though it was all pretence: "He has obviously been told to shed a tear so as to give a sweet image to the fans and for me it appears pathetic; each time Laporta has come out in the press recently he has given more reason to vote for the motion.

"I don't know whether I am doing a service to Barça but I am trying to stabilise the club. After the handkerchiefs and two years without direction, it is necessary to stop and take a decision. People should vote for the 'censura' so as to end this nightmare."

In the actual vote 60% voted against Laporta, but although a significant margin, it did not reach the two-thirds necessary to force him to resign. He decided to dig in saying that the motion had failed and it was no more than a vote against what had happened over the last two years.

Many on the board though did not see it that way and it led to eight resigning including most importantly the vice-presidents Albert Vicens, Ferran Soriano and Marc Ingla.

Laporta could also have been ousted if 75 per cent of the board wanted him out but with only eight ready to force him to stand down they were four short.

Ironically, Laporta was saved by earlier resignations during his presidency as he had followed these up by appointing directors faithful to him like Joan Franquesa, Albert Perrin and Rafael Yuste.

Some die-hard Laporta directors even tried to play down the loss of the eight. Soriano they claimed had been working for himself towards the end of the previous season and was looking to steal the protagonism away from Laporta.

In purely football terms there was little change as Laporta would continue to be backed by Cruyff and hopes lay on the shoulders of his recommendation: Pep Guardiola.

"In my opinion Guardiola has everything to be a coach of Barça as he represents the club and knows what fans want. He knows how the team plays, what it is like in the dressing room and what the atmosphere is like," said Cruyff, in his regular newspaper column.

"His downside is his youth and inexperience, but what is experience? Experience of the dressing room, of pressure in an important game and what steps to take but he has experienced this as a player. His experience is enormous.

"They said the same of Rijkaard and Van Basten when they arrived at the Dutch national team but not of Van Gaal. Yet the other two qualified Holland for the World Cup finals and the expert failed."

Cruyff also stood by Rijkaard.

"Now Barça have gone two years without winning anything and yet before that they won two leagues and a Champions League. Has everything gone wrong for Rijkaard because of two bad years?

"Rijkaard is the same as he was five years ago, he is the only one in the dressing room who has remained faithful to himself. A lot of the others cannot say the same, you only have to look at what they are doing now compared to three years ago. They have lost credit and respect - but Rijkaard, no."

The traces of Rosell's spell at the club continued to drift away as Deco and Ronaldinho left for Chelsea and AC Milan respectively. Despite his immense impact on the history of Barcelona, Ronaldinho left the club without so much as a goodbye. Deemed unfit he did not play the final games of the season and preferred to stay away rather than watch the matches in the stand.

Rijkaard decided to spend a year out of the game, keeping his house in Barcelona, rather than going straight back into football management.

"I have been for many years in football, a sport which is draining as it demands intensive effort and this type of professional work cannot take over my life. You need to know how to separate things," he explained.

"I look for hard work and the same commitment from players because it is a team sport. Talent is important but also those things harder to define which make a good atmosphere and these elements can make the difference between winning and losing.

"I think that each player maintained their own level but we did not as a team. Maybe there was too much individualism.

"It is important to speak with people in the team and the trainer must show unity. I am against a manager as a dictator who makes his decision and everyone else is quiet. I was the one who took the decisions. I have been through teams since I was 16 and so I am used to this system.

"Pressure is something which comes from outside but motivation and adrenaline also come from the tension.

"I think I know myself better than I did two years ago, I have always said that I am not worried about getting older because intelligence comes with age, perhaps the challenge of life is to get to the end understanding it better. I hope to be old and able to look in the mirror say I have done everything in my life in peace, calmness."

Guardiola is articulate and thoughtful in the vein of Rijkaard and similarly is an advocate of open, attacking football. A key difference perhaps is that he is far more of a disciplinarian. He prefers to have two training sessions a day and exerts more control over the players' day-to-day lives, including having meals at the club to ensure they are keeping to their diets.

There was plenty of debate in the summer of 2008 about the appointment of Guardiola, with the vast majority of opinions against it. They felt it was the last throw of the dice by an embattled president.

Whether this was the case, no one could have predicted what was in store.

Chapter Thirteen

The New Dream Team

It had been the initial nod by the godfather of the Laporta presidency, Johan Cruyff, in the spring of 2007, which had led to Guardiola taking over the running of Barça B who had been humiliatingly relegated to the Segunda B, the third tier of Spanish football.

There is no reserve league in Spain but instead many clubs have a B side which plays in the lower leagues. For Barça's second eleven to have dropped to local league level, where matches until recently were played on sand, was a cause for major embarrassment. It was a further blow to the morale at the club after the first team had been pipped to the title by Real Madrid.

Guardiola, 'the orchestral director' of the Dream Team, was approached by Cruyff asking him what his plans were for the future, and a few months later he was installed as the new coach of Barcelona B. His task was to gain promotion in his first season.

The board also considered another former Barça great, Luis Enrique, for the position but Cruyff was confident that Guardiola would be a success.

"Whatever I did as a player I am now starting again from zero as a trainer. It was not a case of receiving an offer and discussing a contract because I am very grateful to the club and it is a great privilege to train Barça B," Guardiola told a packed press conference at his presentation in June, 2007.

"I will do my best and get the team promoted whichever way possible, losing as little as possible as that is the best way to teach youngsters. More importantly than whether we will play with or without wingers or two central midfielders is that the team always asserts its style on the game.

"I believe that everyone in the team has their responsibility and the best way to manage is by consensus, but of course there are times when there are doubts and there has to be someone in charge to make decisions."

Guardiola had left Barcelona in the summer of 2001 believing the time was right to discover new cultures and face new challenges. During his time away he had enjoyed success but also endured plenty of difficult moments and these experiences helped him to become a more philosophical coach.

It had been a hard decision for Guardiola to move from a club where he was loved by fans as one of their own but having made up his mind to leave Spain there were many clubs interested in him and his favoured destination was Italy.

His agent Josep Maria Orobitg spoke first with Inter Milan and then Juventus who appealed more to Guardiola even though Massimo Moratti at Inter was prepared to pay 30% more.

In a covert operation Orobitg had been taken out under cover by Juventus officials from Barcelona and flown to Turin to discuss a deal. There he was driven to a secret destination on the outskirts of the city, in what resembled a mafia operation, where he met Juventus' sports director Luciano Moggi. A verbal agreement was made between Orobitg and the notorious Moggi, who would later be banned from football for corruption.

However, Guardiola was never to join Juventus as three months later the Italian club denied the meeting had ever taken place and said they were not interested in the player. Since the talks they had a new coach and with the transfer budget boosted following the sale of Zinedine Zidane, they had other targets.

By now it was mid-August and other top sides had already made their moves in the transfer market and were no longer interested in Guardiola. The serious error of not having any written agreement with Juve meant that it was going to be difficult to find a club for the Catalan.

In the end he signed for the mid-table side Brescia and was not ready to make his debut until the end of September. On the plus side, Guardiola found himself playing alongside the legendary Roberto Baggio and Italy striker Luca Toni, while the coach was the charismatic Carlo Mazzone.

He was shortly about to enter one of the darkest periods of his career, though, when in November, 2001, he tested positive for the banned drug nandralone against Piacenza and then again the following week against Lazio.

He was suspended for four months, returning in March the following year, but continued to fight his case, which included details of how nandralone can be produced naturally, until he was entirely absolved by the Italian judiciary.

Guardiola had been caught along with other foreigners like Jaap Stam, Fernando Couto and Edgar Davids, and rumours were rife that it was part of a xenophobic conspiracy.

In the summer of 2002, Guardiola looked to move on from Brescia and despite interest from bigger clubs including Juventus again, who he rejected on principle, he decided to join Roma.

Having been enticed to the Italian capital by the club president Franco Sensi, he bought a flat in the centre of Rome, from where he could walk around the ruins of the city and enjoy its food, especially at his favourite Il Pomodorino restaurant.

However, the move rapidly turned sour as although liked by Sensi, the coach Fabio Capello had other ideas and put him straight away on the bench with the excuse that he was not sufficiently fit after overcoming a knee injury several months before.

Mid-way through the season the contract between Roma and Guardiola was annulled and he returned to Brescia.

All this time he had remained abreast of the comings and goings at Barça and in the run-up to the 2003 presidential elections he was approached by the Lluís Bassat camp about becoming sports director. Evarist Murtra, who would have been vice-president if Bassat won, flew to Italy and spent the night talking to Guardiola and discussing the proposal.

Murtra explained that due to the financial problems at the club, they would not be able to offer him a competitive salary but that they wanted Guardiola on board with his close friend Juanma Lillo as coach.

Lillo is a colourful figure and seen as one of the football philosophers of the Latin game. He began coaching his own team-mates at the age of 16 and was in charge of a Spanish third division side by the time he was 20.

He moved around the lower divisions training several different clubs using a 4-2-3-1 formation, which he claimed he invented. His major breakthrough came at the helm of Salamanca, where he coached from 1992 to 1996.

In his first season the team finished runners-up but lost out on promotion to the second division in the play-offs. The following year the side went up as champions playing an open and attractive style, which put Lillo in the public limelight.

Lillo then enjoyed arguably his most successful year as he guided the modest side with a small budget into the Primera Division. Aged just 29, he became the youngest trainer ever in the top flight.

But from there he went from one club to another without any sustained achievement.

It was while he was with Oviedo in 1996 that he became friends with Guardiola. After a match against Barcelona,

Guardiola went to the Oviedo changing rooms and said he would like to meet Lillo to talk about football.

"We got on well and since then we have had a good relationship and we discuss football as well as other things. My style of training has always been eclectic," said Lillo.

"Initially I wanted to be a footballer and while I was playing I was always listening and learning, and so when success did not come to me as a player, I started to train. I do not have a specific system, I would say my system is about the evolution of play and adaptation."

The pair also shared interests away from football especially literature and philosophy. Guardiola met Carlos Menotti, who had been a good friend of Lillo's since the 1980s when he was coach of Atletico Madrid, and he also became acquainted with other members of the curious band of Argentine football thinkers like Jorge Valdano and Marcelo Bielsa.

"I went to visit Pep many times when he was in Italy with Brescia and Roma, and I saw how difficult it was for him when he was accused of taking drugs. Then in 2003 I was offered the job of being trainer at Barcelona and Pep, the director of football, if Bassat won the elections," added Lillo.

While Guardiola agreed to the proposal from the Bassat camp, defeat in the elections by Laporta, saw him continue with his original intention of moving to Qatar and exploring another new culture.

After two years, he came back to Spain and completed a coaching course but still felt that he had one year left in him as a footballer. He considered a few offers in Europe including one from Manchester City and was close to signing for River Plate in Argentina before the offer fell through. In the end he was persuaded by Lillo to join him at Dorados de Culican in the Mexican league.

Guardiola's final season as a player was again plagued by injury and he missed half the games of a campaign that was a disaster and ended in relegation.

Lillo was also sacked and returned to Europe having caused controversy in Mexico by suggesting that the league was corrupt and that their rivals for the drop had survived after money had changed hands.

On retiring, Guardiola took the opportunity to travel to Argentina where he was able to talk football with Menotti and Bielsa. Menotti described him as one of the last football rebels for his football style that expressed his own personality. He also noticed that Guardiola was anxious not only to become a coach himself but also make a lasting impression.

Guardiola had paid particular attention to Bielsa since the 2002 World Cup when as coach of Argentina he employed a 3-4-3 formation to dominate the opposition. The tactic did not bring success but the coach remained satisfied that it was still the right system to have employed.

The Spaniard realised that Bielsa had very similar ideas to Louis van Gaal's theory of strong discipline mixed with flexibility on the pitch. Guardiola had spent long spells talking with Van Gaal in his office when he was the Barça coach and they would discuss tactics often over a bottle of wine.

Also while in Argentina, Guardiola met up with a fan group who had set up an internet blog to discuss his creative style of football. They presented him with a biography of Bielsa, 'Lo Suficientemente Loco' (The Sufficiently Mad) by Ariel Senosian.

"I went abroad to consider different outlooks and I was particularly interested in Mexico because I have always liked their style of football. It was the same for Pep and that was why he went to South America," said Lillo.

On the pitch Guardiola had always been a thinker, his great strength was knowing where his team-mates were on the pitch and making the right pass. As he grew up he spent his life studying the game and Cruyff was a major influence on him. There is no doubt that if he had not known the Dutchman his career would have turned out differently.

Cruyff taught him the importance of the environment surrounding the team from the physios to public relations and how long to spend giving interviews to the press. It was Carles Rexach, Cruyff's assistant, who said that a coach only spends only 30 per cent of his time on training his players and the rest on off-the-field matters.

"Guardiola has always stated that his main influence has been Cruyff and then me," said Lillo, "After that you have other trainers like Menotti and Bielsa but the fact is that he has not copied anyone, football is not a concept but a construction and he has his own approach. Most coaches are ex-footballers who take up the position afterwards but Guardiola was a coach as a player and so it was natural that he went on to do the job.

"He has a wider outlook than just football and this also helps you in the game as you are prepared for the challenges it creates."

Guardiola's upbringing meant he was a standard bearer for Catalans and he was the centre of attention even in his early 20s with a television programme made portraying him as a Barça symbol.

His interests from literature and poetry to fashion design set him apart from typical footballers and even led to a gay slur, but married with children he has always brushed off the remarks.

Moving in the Catalan art circles he became good friends with the singer Lluís Llach and through him the poet Miquel Marti i Pol. A fan of Marti i Pol's work, he asked Llach, in the early 1990s, to introduce him and he visited him and his family several times a year. The poet suffered badly from multiple sclerosis and was unable to speak but this did not stop them from discussing football and many other topics. When Marti i Pol died in 2003, Guardiola flew back from Qatar to pay his respects to his family.

Guardiola jumped at the chance to return to Barça in 2007 as coach of the B team and Laporta even claimed he was ready to do the job unpaid.

His first game at the helm saw the team only draw 0-0 with Premia but it was clear that Guardiola would benefit from plenty of support as despite the modest surroundings among the on-lookers were Laporta and other directors including Evarist Murtra, the man who had run as Bassat's vice-president in the 2003 elections and was now a close friend of the coach. The only person missing from a complete Barça turnout was Frank Rijkaard who was working with the first team.

After the game a realistic Guardiola assessed: "the ball bobbed up and down like a rabbit. We knew it was going to be an end to end game with the ball in the air but we looked like a team."

Using a 4-3-3 formation similar to the first team, Guardiola was satisfied with the quality of the players, telling them from the start that he accepted everyone could have an off day but he would not tolerate a lack of effort. He was in his element working on the technique of the youngsters who had the same desire as he did at that age.

Having dropped down a category with relegation, the players had to contend with a more physical, kick and rush style of football. Their opponents were generally older and technically weaker, which meant they often attempted to intimidate them, but even so Guardiola achieved his aim of promotion in his first season with a play-off victory over fellow Catalan side Europa.

Guardiola had demonstrated his burgeoning talent as a coach with the team an organised and disciplined outfit but it also had plenty of talent starting in defence with Marc Valiente and Victor Sánchez. In midfield there was Victor Vázquez and Sergio Busquets and the potent attack consisted of Jeffrén Suárez, Emilio Guerra, Pedro Rodríguez and Gai Assulin.

Only a few months into his appointment the board was already considering him as a possible replacement to Rijkaard. Begiristain realised that Guardiola had installed in the B side the professionalism that was lacking in the senior squad.

It was after watching Barcelona draw against Lyon in France at the end of November 2007 that the head of football, Marc Ingla and Begiristain felt that they had to up their bid for a successor to Rijkaard.

Cruyff as ever was sounded out and he went for lunch with Guardiola to see whether he was ready for the task and he returned with a positive response. Many others were considered but as the search continued it was narrowed down to Ernesto Valverde, a former player who was coach of Espanyol, the former-Chelsea manager Jose Mourinho and Guardiola.

Many on the board, headed by the then vice-president Ferran Soriano, felt that Mourinho was the best man for the job as he had built up a global appeal which would boost the club's exposure. Mourinho was also the fans favourite by a sizeable margin but, importantly, Begiristain and Cruyff were against Mourinho.

They feared he would try to take over. The Portuguese had made it clear that he wanted full control over the running of the team, which would largely make Begiristain's job redundant and Cruyff's influence would be greatly reduced. As a result, they did what they could to keep his candidacy out of the news, as if there became a public push for Mourinho then the momentum would be difficult to stop.

A meeting was held with Guardiola, which Laporta attended, and it was put to him that if Rijkaard did not continue then how would he feel about replacing him.

While the previso given for Rijkaard remaining was qualification for the Champions League, from February onwards Begiristain and Guardiola discussed potential changes to the first team and transfers.

When the situation finally became untenable for Rijkaard, Guardiola signed a two-year deal to replace him but showed his professionalism by seeing out his job with the B team until the end of the season and then after that having his presentation in front of the media.

He accepted that he would not have been given the job had it not been for his past as a player for the club but that despite being only 37, he had no fear of the position.

Guardiola was presented alongside Laporta and Begiristain and the real pressure was on their shoulders. They had weathered the storm at the end of the season with the poor state of the club and the vote of no confidence, and refused to resign. Now they had put their trust in someone with no experience of top flight coaching and the bets were on whether he would last until Christmas.

Laporta spent the summer months clinging on to power and the majority of fans and the media saw the appointment of Guardiola as simply a blatant attempt to curry favour by bringing in a man who was an emblematic footballer for the club.

Guardiola distanced himself from the politics claiming that it would not effect his running of the team. He also asserted his personality on the club from the start, showing a harder edge than Rijkaard by handing out two 500 euro fines for players turning up to training just two minutes late.

In other ways Guardiola was more liberal and he arranged for the team to travel on the same day for away trips. He felt that it could be negative for players to spend too much time in hotels and that they would be better at home with their families.

Influenced by his spell in Italy, Guardiola was very precise and scientific in his approach to training, paying particular attention to physical and dietary requirements to ensure optimum performance. He always filled his time watching and studying football, but as coach of Barça he also had a team around him that researched the opposition and drew up reports.

Guardiola moved the training to the new complex at Sant Joan Despi which as well as being state of the art, is also more secluded and out of the media spotlight.

He is far less accessible for the media than Barcelona coaches before him copying Marcelo Bielsa, although he is far less extreme than the Argentine, who refused to even look journalists in the face saying that they would try and read something into his expression.

While he understands the rights of journalists and that they should be respected, Guardiola says that he does not have time to make individual interviews although he will answer all the questions during press conferences.

Building the squad for the new season, Ronaldinho and Deco were on their way out and Guardiola would have preferred Samuel Eto'o to leave with them. A suitable transfer though was never made and Guardiola accepted that he was a player he could work with even if at times their relationship was going to be strained.

Thierry Henry's attitude had caused concern during his first season but Guardiola felt that if he could be more positive he would be an important asset to the team especially with his experience and the way he looked after the younger players.

Loyal to his principles, Guardiola refused to get carried away with his new position and like his mentor Cruyff he looked to promote youth players who had learned the Barça way to play football. He had the added advantage of having spent a year in charge of Barça B and so knew the players who were ready to make a step up.

Many were surprised to see a list of youngsters drafted into the first team squad for pre-season training to join the new signings of Dani Alves, Martin Caceres and Gerard Piqué, in defence, and Seydou Keita and Alexandr Hleb further up the pitch.

The acquisition of Piqué from Manchester United saw the return of a youth team player lost as part of the fall-out from the club's crisis in 2003. Piqué had struggled to adapt to the English game, rarely given a chance under Sir Alex Ferguson, but Guardiola saw the potential of the cultured defender.

While he had left under a cloud both the player and the club were keen to patch up their differences and Barça ended up paying a figure in the region of four million pounds for a home-grown prospect who had chosen to walk away.

However, Piqué still maintains that he made the right decision to leave based on how difficult it would have been to break into the first-team squad.

"It is always very hard to move up as all the players have a lot of ability. If you look at those who have succeeded, Valdés is one of the best keepers in the world; Xavi and Iniesta are leaders of the team in midfield; and Puyol is the heartbeat of

227

the side at the back, and if he went it would be a major loss. Then you have Messi, who I first knew from the youth team and he is the best player in the world," said Piqué.

"A lot of people said I went for money but they are wrong. At 17 you look to have a good sports career and if I had stayed at Barça for the next few seasons I would probably have been fighting for a place in the youth team which was playing in the lower leagues.

"It was the same for Cesc at Arsenal, to get into the first team here he had Iniesta, Xavi and Deco ahead of him, while at Arsenal he was able to play regularly."

Piqué had less of an impact in English football than Cesc and spent one season on-loan at Zaragoza before returning to the peripheries at Old Trafford. His signing was a gamble for Guardiola.

A debate over whether Leo Messi would be available for pre-season training and the Champions League qualifying matches threatened to derail the preparation of the team.

The Argentine Football Association wanted him to play in the Olympics but it was decided by arbitration that they could not force Barcelona to release the player.

While Messi was desperate to go to Beijing it appeared at one stage that his club would force him to remain behind. He was finally allowed to go, partly thanks to the intervention of Guardiola, who understood how important it was for the player to join his national team and the resentment that could later build up if he was prevented from going.

Barça arranged a deal whereby Messi would go but the Argentine federation would cover his insurance while he was there and he would not play in any other international friendlies during the season.

Barça had a successful pre-season build-up winning seven out of eight friendlies and passed through the preliminary stage of the Champions League without any hiccups. In the traditional Gamper Trophy curtain raiser they failed to impress but beat Boca Juniors none-the-less.

The team then went on to make their worst start to a campaign since 1973 causing plenty of anxiety in the boardroom.

In Barça's opening match, a Dani Alves mistake gave modest Numancia a 1-0 victory and then they could only draw against Racing Santander. From there though they began to find their feet beating Sporting Gijon 6-1, with Guardiola sticking by midfielder Sergio Busquets, who had made his league debut the week before.

By the end of the year, with the team inform, the comparisons with the side built by Cruyff were inevitable.

A 6-1 victory over Atletico Madrid followed by other high scoring matches sent the pulses of the Culés racing but the real calibre of the team was shown by four straight victories against their championship rivals, including Real Madrid.

Guardiola kept his feet on the ground saying that his side would never match that of Cruyff's and that their performances had been exaggerated by big wins.

He added: "all the teams in Spain have good players and trainers and I keep telling them in the dressing room that only by dedication and sacrifice can they expect to win trophies."

A 5-0 victory over Deportivo la Coruña saw Barça reach a record 50 points at the mid-way stage of the season, while they also scored 59 goals.

Guardiola attributed a 4-1 win over Numancia to the confidence in the team and the way they had been able to bond since the beginning of the season.

Remarkably, despite the quality of football on offer, Barça were still struggling to fill the stadium with the average attendance dropping below 60,000. Local newspapers appealed to fans to turn up and get behind the players.

The positive results were leading to a calmer season in the boardroom where Laporta had also generally adhered to advice telling him to try and stay out of the limelight. There were times when he could not help himself, for example, when he basked in the success of youth products Busquets, Victor

Sanchez and Pedro Rodriguez who had moved into the first team.

Laporta did admit that the success of Guardiola had been the equivalent to winning the lottery and that he had never expected things to work so well.

The one criticism labelled at the team was that once again they were over-dependent on Messi.

While Samuel Eto'o was as reliable as ever in front of goal and Thierry Henry was enjoying a far improved second season, it was Messi who was instrumental in lifting the team to victories such as those against Osasuna, Sevilla and Deportivo la Coruña.

Guardiola had wanted to rest the Argentine but was forced to field him for whole games or bring him on as Barça sought a win.

These claims surfaced as Barça hit their second blip of the season during the end of February and early March when they saw their lead tumble from 12 points down to four in just three weeks. They failed to record a win while Real Madrid, now under Juande Ramos after Bernd Schuster was sacked in December, kept rolling out the victories.

Guardiola refused to be flustered, and supported by the president, who pronounced confidently that they would win the league, the team bounced back with the quick passing of Xavi and Iniesta becoming a crucial cog.

Guardiola, Xavi and Iniesta are all footballers cut from the same cloth, graduating from the Barça academy with distinctions. They have gone on to make an important impact at the club as technically strong midfielders while at the same time they have tried to keep their personal lives out of the media spotlight.

It has become a myth that while still playing for Barça, Guardiola told Xavi that he would force him to retire but at the same time looking at the next generation, he said Iniesta would also make Xavi hang up his boots.

Xavi, has been a more understated player than Guardiola, who was an emblem for Catalans, but nonetheless has been an essential part of team under all the coaches he has played for beginning with Louis van Gaal in 1998. It was under Rijkaard that he was given a more attacking role, which brought out another dimension to his game.

Iniesta suffered a season in and out of the treatment room, with four different injuries, the most serious of which in November caused him to miss two months. His value to the team, though, whether as an attacking midfielder or deployed as one of the three forwards, was becoming more and more apparent and he began to steal the protagonism away from Messi in the final months of the season.

Albacete born Iniesta was 12 when he moved to the Masia and looked to follow in the footsteps of his heroes Guardiola and Michael Laudrup.

"I cried every day when I arrived but I was lucky to grow and watch the Dream Team and while I had lots of doubts, I really wanted to be able to emulate them," said Iniesta, whose eagerness to succeed is shown by how he still talks of the disappointment he felt at missing the 2001 European Youth Championships through injury, when he was 16.

"The last few seasons have been amazing for me but I still look to improve. It is very tough to be a regular in a team like Barça and you have to work hard because if you drop a level then you can find yourself forgotten.

"My style of football means that I can adapt well to different roles but I still think that the most important thing is to be on the pitch. It doesn't make it easy when you move around because each position demands something different, but I am used to it and the fact that you play shows the coach has confidence in you. My favourite position is in attack.

"I have benefitted from the facilities here and the philosophy; every trainer has taught me something from Van Gaal onwards. I know how to play to my strengths and to channel my frustration if someone tries to wind me up. While it's true I am naturally a quiet person, I do get angry at times on the pitch but I just try to control it."

The emergence of Busquets in midfield was one of the revelations of the season and a result of Guardiola's belief in youth.

When Sergio, the son of Carlos Busquets, a Barcelona goalkeeper in the 1990s, was given his debut against Racing Santander after Barça lost their opener, doubts were raised about Guardiola's astuteness but Busquets, timid off the pitch, showed no nerves and demonstrated a great tactical sense from the start.

Busquets involvement grew as the season progressed and he staked a claim for the third midfield berth along with the other contenders Yaya Toure and Keita. While Guardiola told Eidur Gudjohnsen that he had a role to play in the side, he enjoyed few opportunities and these were further marginalised by the emergence of Busquets.

By early March, Barça were firing on all cylinders and after beating Athletic Bilbao they went on a seven match winning streak which included memorable 6-0 and 4-0 victories over Malaga and Sevilla respectively.

The feeling was growing that the team was moving towards something special and talk began to spread of a possible treble with the club still going strong on all fronts but Guardiola was quick to rubbish this as impossible.

The fortnight at the end of April and the beginning of May was going to be crucial in Barça's fortunes as they played their Champions League semi-final against Chelsea either side of the top of the table clash with Real Madrid.

While Barça's displays had captured the attention of the world the question still remained that although aesthetically pleasing on the eye could they measure up to the challenge set by the top English sides who were dominating Europe.

They had shown their credentials with 5-2 and 4-0 home victories over Lyon and Bayern Munich, respectively, earlier on in the competition but now found themselves in the semi-finals along with Arsenal, Manchester United and Chelsea.

Barcelona fans felt that their opponents Chelsea would pose the toughest challenge of the three because of their physical approach that would look to stifle the Catalan side's attacking football. They were confident, however, that their own brand of football would win the day.

Chelsea's visit to the Nou Camp had less of the drama attached to the occasions when Jose Mourinho returned to the Catalan capital and the now incumbent Guus Hiddink focused on his side producing a cool and efficient performance.

He told the press beforehand that Chelsea were going to come out and attack but few were fooled. Hiddink had done his homework well and the Chelsea midfield refused to give Iniesta and Xavi time on the ball while the defence snuffed out the threat from the forwards. The result was a 0-0 draw with all to play for in the second leg at Stamford Bridge.

For Barça there was no respite and they had to turn their attention immediately to the el clasico against Real Madrid.

While all the attention in Europe remained on the Champions League return leg, the Real game had lost none of its importance domestically and was being billed as the 'game of the century'.

Real were still breathing heavily down Barça's necks and the fear in Catalonia was that defeat could put their bitter rivals in the driving seat for the title.

Barça had won the first classico of the season at the Nou Camp but were coming into the game with defensive doubts after a 2-2 draw with Valencia while Real had reduced the gap to just four points with seven straight wins.

In the event, the match proved to be more than Barça fans could ever have hoped for as they relentlessly tore the home side's defence apart after having conceded an early goal.

They stormed back to lead 3-1 at half-time, with Leo Messi playing through the middle and Samuel Eto'o out wide, and the match finished 6-2. There were braces from Thierry Henry and Messi along with goals from defenders Carles Puyol and Gerard Piqué.

It was Real's biggest home defeat since the 1950s and for Barça it brought back memories of their biggest ever victory at the Bernabéu, the 5-0 Cruyff inspired win in 1974. The rout also brought up Barcelona's 100th league goal of the season.

Real coach Ramos admitted that despite their good form in the league, they had been found wanting when they had come up against top sides in Europe.

While Barça fans were celebrating the team being on the verge of winning the league, Guardiola respectfully praised Real's fine run and pointed out that in any other season Barça would have already won the title a month and a half before.

Barcelona had entered the crucial stage of the season in form and the Catalan press began to dream of the treble, counting down the matches ahead of them.

The dramatic events in store at Stamford Bridge only fueled the belief that Barça were heading for a special finale.

As in the first leg, Guardiola chose to field Yaya Toure in the heart of the defence to combat the threat from the powerful Didier Drogba, while in midfield the inexperienced Sergio Busquets was given the job of supporting Xavi and Iniesta.

The game began badly for Barça as Michael Essien scored a sensational volley from a distance as Chelsea dominated. Crucially the home side failed to build on their lead and with the referee also turning down a number of penalty claims, Barça remained in with a chance with an away goal sufficient to take them through.

The dismissal of Eric Abidal added to Barça's woes but as the game drifted into the final moments and the game appeared beyond them, there was still time for a moment of inspiration from Iniesta to score a goal that will linger long in the memory.

Chelsea were slow to close him down on the edge of the area as the clock ticked into stoppage time and Iniesta, maintaining a cool head shot with the outside of his right boot into the top corner leading to pandemonium as players, coaches and fans celebrated.

The final whistle was greeted with fury from the Chelsea players after so many penalty calls had been waived away, and an incensed Didier Drogba was shown a red card.

Barça were in the final of the Champions League for the second time in four years but before they turned their attention to the final with Manchester United on May 27th they still had the league and cup to consider.

The first chance of silverware came in the final of the Copa del Rey against Athletic Bilbao at Valencia's Mestalla stadium. The match brought back memories of the last time the teams met in the final of the competition in 1984, which had led to victory for Bilbao and disgrace for Diego Maradona who had sparked a mass brawl at the end of the game.

Barça got their revenge 25 years later in a less controversial encounter in which the Catalan side asserted their authority and ran out 4-1 winners without even fielding several first choice players including Thierry Henry and Andres Iniesta.

The following weekend they were also crowned league champions. With Real's morale on the floor they went on to lose their remaining matches, which also proved the death knell for Ramos, and Barça found themselves winners before taking to the field against Mallorca on May 17.

In what had become a historic season, Barça were to finish the campaign with a 105 goals just two short of the record in Spain set by Real Madrid at the end of the 1980s.

Despite being a rookie, Guardiola had remained composed and eloquent throughout and even as the tension built towards the Champions League final his understated, thoughtful approach prevailed.

But he did have passion as had been demonstrated with nine dismissals as a player and now three already as a trainer.

He had painstakingly assembled a coaching team around him who worked on a day-to-day basis with the players and he took a more overall approach. Generally he would not enter the changing room except for post match talks.

"I think that the difference under Guardiola is that we are now battling for each other more. He ensures that the players know what they are doing and if we win or lose then it is down to us. Afterwards we look back at what happened during the game and analyse it," said defender Dani Alves.

"He has made it clear to us the benefits of working together. If we run five or ten metres to help a player it is better for the team and we enjoy the football more. There are no real secrets to our success, we all just have a great desire to win and we have three forwards who can make the difference. Messi is the best attacking player in the world but he would be nothing without ten players around him."

True to his word Guardiola had given press conferences in which he had answered all questions before and after all but two games.

On the media day ahead of the Champions League final he spent an hour and half in front of the press to take care of their needs and his language skills helped him to respond to questions in English and Italian.

Modestly he said how his team had been fortunate to beat Chelsea in the semi-final and that now it was a great honour for him to face Sir Alex Ferguson.

Guardiola tried out different techniques to get the best out of players. A fan of the band Coldplay, he would put on the track Viva la Vida before matches and on coach rides to help them relax and it became an emblematic song as the season drew to an end.

The final against Manchester United had extra significance for Gerard Piqué, having left Old Trafford the season before. He had made great strides on returning to his hometown club having become a fixture in the starting eleven by the end of the season. He even kept club captain Carles Puyol out of the side in the Champions League semi-final against Chelsea at the Nou Camp.

"I was very young when I went to Manchester, it was a fantastic experience even though I didn't play very much and I stayed at home and missed my family. I have no regrets about going there, I learnt to play football because there wasn't anything else to do, just play football," said Piqué.

"Ferguson was more like a father than a trainer, it was almost as though he was the owner of the club. He does what he wants and as he did not normally run the training I saw

(Carlos) Quieroz more as the coach. Ferguson controlled everything including your private life.

"The big difference between the dressing rooms is that there was more of a hierarchy at United that was imposed by Gary Neville, Ryan Giggs, Paul Scholes etc. and they respect the veterans. It is something normal there which is fine. I can see how respect is vital but at the same time this can lead to a less comfortable environment. At Barça with Puyol or Xavi you have respect but you can also joke with them."

Guardiola saw Piqué's experience of English football as important for the final and he played him alongside Toure in a towering partnership with both players well over six foot. He had to make other changes with Alves and Abidal ruled out through injury, but he was relieved to hear that Iniesta would be fit after missing almost three weeks with a hamstring injury.

Admitting that United would win in a battle of strength Guardiola claimed it was imperative that his side maintained possession and Iniesta would be crucial for this. After the final, Iniesta revealed that Guardiola told him not to shoot with his right foot as it could have aggravated the injury.

Guardiola had a final trick up his sleeve to motivate his players just before they ran out for the final at the Olympic Stadium in Rome.

"We went back into the dressing room after warming up and we saw a big screen. We wondered what was going on and then we heard the sound track to the film the Gladiator and some of the players in the clips. It was very emotive, perhaps too much as we began to feel quite tense. Guardiola then just told us to go out and win," explained Piqué. Guardiola had worked with local Catalan television to make a montage of the Barça players comparing the Champions League final to a gladiatorial clash in imperial Rome.

When the game finally kicked off, Barça began slowly and United dominated the early stages before Guardiola's side took a grip and scored through Samuel Eto'o with virtually their first attack.

Although the majority of the game was ahead of them, United never looked likely to equalise and Barça toyed with them in the midfield.

The contest was decided when an inch perfect cross from Xavi was headed home by Messi, one of the smallest players on the pitch.

The celebrations in the stadium were mirrored back home in Catalonia where the festivities carried on for several weeks.

Perhaps the coolest head remained that of Guardiola. After the match he made a point of dedicating the victory to Paolo Maldini, the great AC Milan defender who had recently announced his retirement.

Typically, Laporta was far from understated in his assessment of Guardiola and the team's performance.

"This is the glory we deserve, this trophy has returned prestige to the club and we are proud of the Cruyff based principles of football. The effort has been made worthwhile by winning the treble and this is a side to believe in as they are a Dream Team," he said.

"It has been a glorious path, it is not just enough to play attractive football as you have to win titles. We now have eight in six years and when we have not won the league we have finished second, level on points, with the winners. In the Champions League when we lost in the semi-final it was to the winners Manchester United. I want to praise the players, Frank Rijkaard, Pep as well as Txiki, who has been one of the keys to these triumphs.

"This is the best team in history and this title has given us the standing that we deserve. We have kept loyal to our principles, playing seven in the final who came from the youth team. Guardiola has surpassed all our expectations; when he arrived we thought he would do well but this has been our best season ever.

"The success has been that of the whole board, you can make mistakes but you need to be able to correct them. I enjoy being president but there are difficult moments as well and during those times you must be strong."

Barcelona became the first club in Spain to win the treble and their achievement is all the more remarkable considering the crisis they were in a season before and the changes that had to be made with the firing of the coach and the transfer of Ronaldinho, their most charismatic figure.

"I can't really explain how we won the trophies. A lot of time was spent coaching and talking but it is the players who achieve success and they did it using the Dream Team principles of letting the ball do the work and having an organised defence," Guardiola explained.

"During the first ten minutes of the final we were not there and Cristiano Ronaldo could have scored on several occasions. My only thought was to get three or four passes together so as to change the dynamic of the game. We did that and on top we had the luck to score. It is a lot easier to get three or four passes with Iniesta or Xavi as they never lose the ball."

In retrospect the appointment of Guardiola can be considered as either desperation or genius but the result returned Barça to the summit of European football. A player who was Cruyff's leader on the pitch in the original Dream Team had become the coach of an even greater side.

"This team is far better player for player than the original Dream Team and also in the results. Cruyff's side enjoyed luck while Guardiola's Barça were comfortably winning matches," said journalist and close friend of Guardiola, Jordi Basté.

"People say that Guardiola has inherited Cruyff's philosophy but while they both like to play good football there are differences in their approaches. Cruyff was happier to win 4-3 than 1-0 but Guardiola does put more emphasis on defence and trying to stop his opponent."

While the success on the pitch had taken some of the focus off the boardroom, Laporta and his directors were still no more popular. The resignations en masse during the summer of 2008 led to a more united approach from the remaining directors but it is debatable whether a poor campaign would have still seen Laporta in charge by the end.

Long term enemy Oriol Giralt who forced elections and then a vote of no confidence against Laporta remained as vehemently opposed to the president as ever.

"Before the season there were many fans who felt that we had the best team in the world and that the board was destroying it. The vote of no confidence put a lot of things in their place, like forcing the president into a secondary tier, creating a barrier between the board and the dressing room and so giving the coach full reign," he said.

"Laporta believed that his work won the treble while in reality the success came in spite of his leadership. I would have asked him not to try to be the star like, for example, getting off the bus first and looking to sign autographs. From a sporting perspective the club improved but I am not sure about the economic situation or how healthy was the state of affairs in the boardroom. His old flaws remained. He continued to say that the 80,000 who did not vote against him in the vote of no confidence would have voted for him and he allowed the kids of directors and friends to play on the Nou Camp after games. Laporta treated the club like a business."

New club rules, which stated that no president could stay in power for longer than two terms, meant there was plenty of discussion about who was to follow Laporta at the end of the 2009-10 season when he would have to stand down.

With Soriano out of the board along with other likely candidates such as Sandro Rosell, the current directors had to choose among themselves who would be the continuity candidate.

Guardiola is not easily carried away and approached the start of the 2009-10 season with the same meticulous approach.

"He has many interests in life and he is very aware about how fickle football can be. He knows Barça inside out and what he can achieve. I expect him to stay there for a while and then choose the right time to move and face a new challenge; he is able to put football in perspective. I can say that more important to him than any football success was to have his name cleared over taking drugs," said Basté.

The club made few changes in the summer with the main transaction being the sale of Samuel Eto'o to Inter Milan and Zlatan Ibrahimovic coming the other way.

Eto'o's confrontational attitude was never to the liking of Guardiola but his pace and eye for goal made him the focal point of the attack. While he wasn't technically as strong as some of the players around him, his direct approach and confidence made him crucial to their success.

Guardiola was confident that the arrival of Ibrahimovic and the maturing Bojan Krkic and Pedro Rodriguez could make up for his loss.

Either way "I don't know" was the frank reply when Guardiola was asked how his side could improve on the 2008-09 treble winning side.

Chapter Fourteen

The Six Cups and the End of Laporta

Barcelona had made history as the first Spanish team to complete the treble and were toasting their success but behind their celebrations there was certain trepidation at the news from Real Madrid that Florentino Pérez was returning to the presidency.

Whereas Barcelona finished the season with a flurry, Real had been left to seethe as they stuttered to the end.

President Ramón Calderón finally stood down in January after a controversial period in office when it was revealed that ten of his supporters who were not members had voted in a club assembly meeting.

Calderón, who took charge in 2006, had been reduced to ridicule long before that meeting in December 2008 and this was the final straw.

The way that he was taken in by a Nicolas Cage look alike at the Bernabéu stadium and presented the impostor with a Real Madrid shirt did little for his public image; and then he only made it worse by claiming afterwards he was aware but went along with the joke.

Although he did oversee two Spanish league titles, it was failure in the Champions League and poor signings that proved crucial.

Days before he resigned in January he had told press it would be "easy to stand down and walk away but this would be for cowards."

He was replaced by Vicente Boluda who became interim president until elections at the end of the season.

Real had done well under coach Juande Ramos but the 6-2 destruction by Barça was crucial in losing out to them in the title race and his six-month contract was not extended at the end of the season.

The merengues, the Real fans, were not used to being second best and with Barça looking unbeatable they put their trust in a man who could seemingly make the impossible happen.

In 2000, nobody believed that Pérez would be able to bring in Luis Figo from Barcelona and he had proved them wrong. He then built a side with the best players in the world and although it ended in failure it brought the glamour to the club that now they badly sought.

Pérez claimed he was wrong to resign in 2006 and that the problems at the club persuaded him to return.

"Real Madrid needs a real revolution to bring back the joy to the fans. I want the supporters to be watching spectacular football with great players," he said.

Pérez went on to win the elections unopposed and his return was met with fear from Barça who knew his capabilities and there were rumours that he was trying to lure Leo Messi.

But Real's 300m euro plan for rebuilding their team centred on the signing of Messi's rival for the title of the best player in the world, Cristiano Ronaldo, of Manchester United.

The Portuguese had made it clear his desire to play for Real and United appeared resigned to losing him after successfully holding onto him the summer before.

Eventually he moved to Real for 80m pounds, while Kaka (56m pounds from AC Milan), Karim Benzema (35m pounds from Lyon) and Raúl Albiol (13m pounds from Valencia) were the other main incorporations.

Real's ability to buy players regardless of their cost captured the imagination of the world and to the incredulity of Barcelona stole the limelight from their all-conquering side.

The first question on everyone's lips was where this money originated. The reply from Barcelona was adamant, that the Madrid club was once again receiving an unfair advantage.

"I do not know where the 300m euros that Florentino Pérez has borrowed for signings will actually come from. He says that he will recover it by selling replica shirts but that means he will have to sell 30m of them which is impossible," said Barcelona's economic director Xavier Sala i Martin.

Real were lent a large percentage of the money through bank loans notably from Caja Madrid and Sala i Martin was equally surprised by this.

"How is it that a football club can be given so much money when you consider the current economic situation and the restrictions that have been put on banks," he said.

"We would never spend 65m euros for a player you can be sure, for that amount of money you could have bought the whole of the side which won the Champions League in Rome.

"Someone is giving him the money and it would be good to know who."

Laporta was scathing at the way Real were looking to buy their way to success.

"There are two distinct models. One is based on hard work, talent and planning; all of which are part of a business project. The other is imperialist and arrogant which has its origins in opportunism," he said.

"I am pleased to promote a serious model which is based on hard work and talent, and importantly is successful. We will make some adjustments to the team in the summer but everything will be judged by common sense.

"We will look to maintain our sustainable growth and not take unnecessary risks. Real have distorted the market paying these kinds of sums. They are buying compulsively as a response to our winning the treble."

Of course, Sala i Martin and Laporta were made to eat their words when the following month Barça unveiled the signing of Zlatan Ibrahimovic from Inter Milan. They paid around 65m euros for him and Samuel Eto'o went the other way for a figure in the region of 20m euros. It was Barcelona's most expensive purchase in their history and it made a mockery of their high and mighty stance over not needing to buy players to bring success.

The signing raised eyebrows not only at the way that Guardiola got rid of Eto'o, who had been a vital cog in the team, but also the way that so much money was spent on a player who did not obviously fit into the Barça system and had question marks over his character.

Eto'o's confrontational approach had irked Guardiola but the man he had chosen to replace him was also outspoken and had a reputation as a individualist who didn't work hard for the team.

The tall Swede had been described by the then Inter coach Jose Mourinho as the best player in the world and while Ibrahimovic was undoubtedly talented his languid approach conflicted with the way Barça liked to attack at speed.

Then a further 25m euros was spent on the relatively unknown defender Dmytro Chygrynskiy from Shakhtar Donetsk. The longhaired Ukrainian was a personal request from Guardiola who said it was difficult to find defenders in his mould who are comfortable in possession of the ball.

The Brazilian full-back Maxwell was the other addition from Inter Milan for four and half million euros.

Barça went into the season having captured their fourth and fifth trophies of the year after beating Athletic Bilbao and Shakhtar Donetsk to lift the domestic Super Cup and the European Super Cup, respectively.

They started their league defence with a comfortable victory over Sporting Gijon in which Ibrahimovic made up for an indifferent performance with his first goal for the club.

Guardiola remained as organised and focused as ever, which helped the players to maintain their motivation. Barça tore Atletico Madrid apart 5-2 as they won their first six matches and Ibrahimovic scored in his first five games.

With the team involved in so many competitions, Guardiola rotated his squad with Pedro and Bojan given opportunities in attack and Thierry Henry found himself more and more often on the bench.

Despite the victories there was still criticism that the team was not playing as well as in the previous season and this intensified as Barça struggled to live up to expectations in the Champions League. Defeat at the Nou Camp by un-fancied Rubin Kazan at the end of October followed by a draw against them away in Russia put them on the ropes but a key home win against Inter Milan eased them through to the next round.

At the end of November they went into the first el clasico of the season a point behind leaders Real Madrid, who were still finding their feet under Pellegrini. Their lofty position was more down to moments of inspiration from players who were not yet functioning as a team.

Lower league Alcorcon had made a farce of Florentino Pérez's grandiose designs as they astonishingly ripped the expensively assembled team apart 4-0 in the first leg of their King's Cup clash in October. In the return match, Real could only win 1-0 and question marks grew yet further over Pellegrini's capabilities as he did not play a more obvious attacking formation in a game where his side needed at least four goals.

It was a tense battle at the Nou Camp and keeper Victor Valdés kept Barça in the game, saving well from Cristiano Ronaldo and Kaka. A cautious Barça got the victory though when Ibrahimovic, who was returning from injury, came on for an ineffectual Henry, and slotted home.

In mid-December, Guardiola's team headed off to the World Club Championships looking to complete an amazing clean-sweep of all major trophies.

Facing a mix of champions from around the world in Abu Dhabi, Barça reached the final against Argentine side Estudiantes, and then once again showed their battling qualities to come from behind to beat the South Americans.

In dramatic fashion Pedro equalised Estudiantes' opener in the 89th minute and then in extra time Messi scored the winner.

The result reduced Guardiola to tears while for Pedro his goal was all the more significant because he became the first player to score in all six competitions in one year.

"I was the most surprised to find out that I had done it. This will be an amazing memory and something to be proud about but other players will do it in the future and probably from this club," said Pedro, whose successes helped him shrug off the diminutive Pedrito, which is more often used for children.

Tenerife born Pedro was picked up by Barcelona in a youth tournament in 2004 and since then passed through the youth ranks, winning the third division title under Pep Guardiola in 2008, before the coach moved up to the first team.

"If it wasn't for Guardiola I would probably have been sold to another club or maybe even studying for a degree now," said Pedro. "I didn't find it difficult to step up a level from the youth team because all the players in Barça B know the system and how Guardiola trained and prepared to face the opposition."

After the match in Abu Dhabi, Guardiola was reflective about the feat achieved by his team.

"We have managed something very important but I am just somebody who is extremely happy and tired. It has been fantastic to win all these trophies and I would like to praise the players not just for today, but for the last six months," he said.

"We have had a lot of support and that is also down to the institution. We are different because we have Unicef on out shirts and we pay instead of earning money.

"Given time we will fully appreciate what has happened this year which has been the best in the history of the club."

Days later Messi fought off competition from Cristiano Ronaldo to claim his first Fifa World Player of the Year Award, having already been named European Player of the Year.

While all was well on the pitch the situation was a lot less smooth in the boardroom as the battle heated up among the directors over who would be put forward to replace Laporta in the presidential elections the following summer.

Perhaps it was an indication of the domineering approach from Laporta that there was no obvious choice as most of the directors with the personality and the characteristics to lead had resigned.

Laporta obviously wanted his successor to be someone who would allow him to maintain an influence at the club and so was careful who he put forward.

Many on the board felt Xavier Sala i Martin had been made a director in April, 2009, as Laporta's personal choice. The favourite among the board members had been Jaume Ferrer, head of marketing and media, and they were unhappy at what they saw as Laporta attempting to derail his bid.

Sala i Martin, an eminent economist who had a penchant for wearing flashy jackets and was a close friend of Laporta's, was not a popular candidate among fans.

As the atmosphere in the boardroom deteriorated, the Laporta presidency was stuttering to its conclusion. The relationship between Laporta and Ferrer had reached the point that they were barely on speaking terms, while other directors who had been close to the president felt that Laporta was more distant and putting his trust in Sala i Martin who had been on the board for relatively little time.

What had really sparked uproar was the revelation in September, 2009, that several months earlier a detective agency had been contracted by the club's director general Joan Oliver to investigate four of the five vice-presidents.

Oliver argued that these investigations into the private lives of the directors were to vet them for future presidency with the only vice-president not included, Alfons Godall, at that stage having shown no interest in standing.

It was not the first case of espionage involving Barça as Laporta's nemesis Sandro Rosell, another likely election candidate had claimed that he had been investigated as did club member Oriol Giralt, who brought the vote of no confidence against Laporta.

The irony was that on coming to power in 2003, Laporta had complained of spying and how for example the boardroom had been bugged, and now club employees with or without his knowledge were doing the same. It was felt by many that the aim was to uncover information damaging to the reputations of rivals to Sala i Martin.

While the president said that he knew nothing about the espionage, the club stood by Oliver for ordering the investigations, which had cost 56,000 euros.

Laporta said that it was not important whether he knew or not about what had been going on and the question of why the espionage was necessary was never answered.

Instead the president launched another attack on what he called the Madrid biased press.

"These stories come from people who do not think like I do; that are intolerant and will not accept me. We only have to look at some sports and non-sports newspapers to see that these people are not happy at the way that Barça are playing great football and have an international project," he said.

His comments were a further example of how politics was interwoven with football. The way Barcelona had splashed out so much money on Ibrahimovic was seen as a show of force to centralist Madrid that they too had the money to spend in the transfer market if they wanted.

Although still denying his intention to move into politics when he stood down from being president of Barça, Laporta was mixing football with Catalan independence more than ever.

On September 11, the national day of Catalonia, he represented the club at the traditional ceremony but then later joined an independence rally whose slogan read: 'we are a nation, we want our own state'.

He explained: "freedom of expression is a right and I have the right to march. I have come to express my national conscience.

"The time has arrived to recognise that Spain is a project which is politically finished and where the aspirations of the Catalan people are not included."

Laporta's aggressive stance was causing constant conflict. According to the president of the Cantabria region of Spain, Miguel Ángel Revilla, Laporta told him ahead of a game between Racing Santander and Barça: "You are imposing yourself on Catalonia."

Revilla responded: "The Catalan people are wonderful and you cannot generalise but this person is causing a lot of damage to his team."

The president of the Extremadura region, Guillermo Fernández Vara, a Barcelona fan, wrote a newspaper article politely stating that Laporta was representative of all 'Barcelonistas' not just those in Catalonia.

Laporta reacted by phoning him up and calling him an imbecile ten times as well as using other profanities. He finished the conversation by threatening him that he had better never say anything about him again.

The president of Sevilla, José Maria Del Nido, claimed that Laporta had belittled his own club and made them introspective while the sports director of Real Madrid Jorge Valdano said: "Barcelona are inward looking while Real Madrid reach out from Spain internationally."

Away from political statements, Laporta also continued to court controversy. After Barcelona's victory over Real Madrid in the autumn, Laporta went to celebrate in a well-known disco and pictures were taken of him drunk on the dance floor. He was covered in Champagne and dancing with a bottle.

Again Laporta tried to blame a Madrid biased press. "They cannot stand the fact that we are leaders and we beat Madrid. Look at the way they have taken these photos to try and embarrass us. They are always trying to damage the image of Barcelona, something they have been doing for a long time, long before we arrived, but they are not going to succeed." Laporta also had to fight a legal case involving an alleged lover Flavia Massoli, who claimed unfair dismissal after being given a job at the club by Laporta.

The president's 20-year marriage to Constanza Echevarria came to an end in 2007 and after that Laporta was linked to several women. He met Massoli in 2006, who was working as a waitress, and gave the Brazilian a job working in the club offices.

When Laporta found himself fighting a vote of no confidence in 2008 it was alleged by Massoli that she was forced into resigning as her appointment had been criticised and Laporta was looking to improve his image.

After returning from the Christmas break, Guardiola was under no illusions about the expectation that would now be on the team after winning the six cups and he urged the players to forget about what they had achieved and concentrate on the future.

However, Barça did start slowly, drawing their first match against Villarreal and then tumbled out of the King's Cup against Sevilla. The damage was done in the first leg at the Nou Camp when Guardiola put out an experimental side including Dymtro Chygrynskiy and Gabi Milito at centre half.

The Ukrainian was turning into a major disappointment as he struggled to find his feet at the club and it was his penalty that helped Sevilla to a 2-1 win. A 1-0 win away at Sevilla meant that Barça went out on goal difference.

"I don't feel like the players have lost their form. A lot of the time it is good to lose so that you are more down to earth. We achieved something amazing with the six cups but now we have to start winning again and quickly," said Guardiola.

"We have to accept what people say. The praises before were exaggerated and out of proportion. When we were winning we still made mistakes but now when we lose there is the same lack of proportion.

"The teams that have won nothing have less pressure on them and for us right now we are not given the slightest margin for error."

Barça did find their feet and maintained their place at the top of the table although they were becoming more and more reliant on Messi. Among the forwards, Andres Iniesta was suffering an injury-plagued campaign, while Thierry Henry and Zlatan Ibrahimovic were not at their best.

Henry, as in his first season, appeared to lack desire and Pedro was usurping his position; while there was plenty of pressure on the shoulders of Ibrahimovic as after a steady start the goals were drying up and he was losing confidence.

In the Champions League, Ibrahimovic did find the back of the net when Barcelona were lucky to come away with a 1-1 draw against Stuttgart and then a four-goal demolition in the second leg saw them comfortably through to the quarter-finals.

Generally though Barça were scraping through games rather than winning emphatically and Messi was the key.

He scored the winner against Malaga then a week later struck twice in a 2-2 draw with Almeria and followed that with a hat-trick in a 3-0 victory over Valencia. Next up came Zaragoza and he scored another hat-trick in a 4-2 win and could have had four had he not given the ball to Ibrahimovic, after he himself was felled.

The argument about how Messi compared to Maradona gathered fuel after his display against Arsenal to knock them out of the Champions League.

With the score 2-2 from the first leg and Nicolas Bendtner having given Arsenal the lead at the Nou Camp, Messi fired in four goals.

But no matter what feat he achieved he remained understated and Guardiola explained: "the best thing about him is that tomorrow he will get up and be the same person as always, one more player in the team."

April was a key month for Barça as they faced Real Madrid and then Inter Milan in the Champions League where they were fighting for a place in the final. It was set to be a highly charged occasion with the return of the Catalan hate figure, José Mourinho, as Inter coach, and Barça had extra motivation to reach the final as it was staged at Real Madrid's Bernabéu stadium.

First up was the el clasico at the Bernabéu and with the teams tied on 77 points, whoever won would be on the verge of lifting the title.

Although they had been rolling out the victories, Barça still remained neck and neck with Real who were equally indomitable and were having an excellent season despite the criticism that was levelled at coach Manuel Pellegrini especially over the early cup exits.

It was a similar scene to a year before when Barça had come away 6-2 winners but this time they produced a more workmanlike 2-0 victory.

In an even contest it was the individual skill of Messi that made the difference as he opened the scoring and then Pedro continued his knack of hitting important goals by netting the second after the break.

As Barça turned their attention to the Champions League they were in confident mood with Chelsea their main concern having been knocked out by Inter.

Guardiola's side had beaten Inter 2-0 at home the previous autumn in the group stages and gloating fans sang: "Mourinho go to the theatre."

The Catalan side didn't have the perfect preparation though as they had to travel for 14 hours by bus due to an ash cloud, caused by a volcanic eruption in Iceland. Fear that the ash could damage plane engines led to many flights being cancelled across Europe.

While the general mood was optimistic, Guardiola offered caution: "Inter are a very good team and have probably the

253

best trainer in the world, above all for his versatility in terms of tactics. They are now playing a bit differently from when we played them in the group stages, with three forwards and a player behind them."

Guardiola was right to be wary as having undeservedly gone a goal behind they stormed back to win 3-1 in an incident packed game.

The sight of Ibrahimovic and Eto'o playing against their former clubs added to the anticipation ahead of kick-off but neither had a large part to play in the result of the game which was a victory for Mourinho's policy of taking the game to Barça.

It was the first time that season Barça had conceded two goals and there were recriminations afterwards with the normally calm Xavi Hernández arguing with Mourinho in the tunnel. He was suggesting the Portuguese referee, a supposed friend of his compatriot Mourinho, had been biased. The Catalans were angry that a penalty had not been given for them and claimed that Diego Milito's goal was off-side but Inter also had their grievances with the referee.

Afterwards Mourinho stirred up the atmosphere for the second leg saying: "I don't think the referee influenced the result of the game. It is a shame that people have such short memories as last year Barça were more than happy with the referee against Chelsea and now look at them with this referee who has not influenced the game.

"I don't know why Barcelona are not capable of behaving like champions and accepting that the opposition played better."

Mourinho was also fully aware of how difficult it would still be at the Nou Camp.

"In Barcelona anything can happen. Losing 2-1 would be a bigger achievement than winning 3-1 here tonight. There is a 50 per cent chance for both teams," he said, while adding provocatively: "I have seen things from the opposition at the end of the game which you would not expect from a team at this level and so you can only imagine what will happen at the Nou Camp."

In the lead up to the return leg, Guardiola did not want to raise tensions and played down comments from defender Gerard Pique that "for 90 minutes the Inter players will hate their profession."

Mourinho though once again took centre stage. Firstly on arriving in Barcelona he threatened to break Fifa rules by holding Inter's press conferences at their hotel, and then when they did take place at the stadium, he strolled into the pressroom while his player Thiago Motta was speaking in order to distract attention.

The Portuguese strategy of seeking the limelight so as to take the pressure off the players worked perfectly as his carefully planned press conference succeeded in hitting a raw nerve with the Catalan press.

"To play the final at the Bernabéu is a dream for us while for Barcelona it is an obsession. I know what it is like because I already experienced it when we played the cup final there against Betis in 1997. I was a translator but I understood exactly what that match meant and to fly the 'senyera' (the Catalan flag) at the Bernabéu while hearing the Barça hymn was an incredible moment," he said.

"Barcelona achieved their dream in Paris and Rome, while now it would be a dream for Inter. I have already won the Champions League with Porto and so although it would be good to win it again, this generation of Interistas have never won it."

He finished off by adding mischievously: "the best team in world has to come back from 3-1 down, where is the drama with that? There is no war, there is no need for any of that."

In the game itself Barcelona threw everything at Inter but struggled to find a way through even after Motta was harshly dismissed for a flailing arm that made light contact with Sergio Busquets.

The centre-half pairing of Lucio and Walter Samuels were imperious and entirely nullified the threat from Ibrahimovic, while the midfielders were like terriers, snapping at the heels of Messi, Iniesta and Xavi.

Piqué did score a goal late on but it was not enough and a delighted Mourinho went racing onto the pitch to celebrate on the final whistle.

Eto'o summed up the feeling after the game: "We defended the best we could in order to classify for the final. Now we can congratulate Barça as they are the best team in the world."

Inter won the Champions League final against Bayern Munich but Barcelona still practically had their hands on their second consecutive league title.

They went on to win their final four games of the season with the only scare coming in the 3-2 win over Sevilla when they conceded two second half goals with the game apparently over.

For many, Barcelona's championship success was a victory for nurturing and building a team over the more mercenary approach of Real who had spent vast sums the previous summer.

Guardiola remained as respectful and considered in his second season whether it was against the taunts from Mourinho or the threat from Real.

With three matches to go and with Barcelona leading the table, Guardiola had stated: "Madrid also deserve to win the league. Whatever happens, all of us should go away happy with our work this season. Madrid have some very good players and a very strong mentality."

It was the first season that Barça had won the league while possessing the top goal scorer with Messi and the keeper who had conceded the fewest goals in Victor Valdés.

The season had started with a debate over who was the better player, Cristiano Ronaldo or Leo Messi but at the end there was no question about who had made the biggest impact.

For president Joan Laporta, he was bowing out after Barcelona's most successful spell in their history. In seven years Barça had won 12 titles including two Champions

Leagues and four domestic leagues but even so many were glad to see the back of him.

Talking to the fans during celebrations on the pitch after Barça won the league against Valladolid, Guardiola's first words were to thank Laporta for his work but rumours persisted that he had a poor relationship with the president.

Guardiola denied there was any ill-feeling saying: "he has given me what I need and it is easy to make assumptions. He offered me the chance to train here and it has been a pleasure working with him."

Laporta dedicated the league success to his former wife and the mother of his children, while saying back in 2003 he would never have believed what was about to happen at the club.

"Now Barcelonismo is in a very strong state and it makes me very emotional to see it. When you take decisions you hope that everything will go okay but the results have far exceeded the expectations. Now we can say the decisions were correct because the facts speak for themselves," he said.

"It has always been an honour to be president of FC Barcelona. It has been an immense challenge and an incredible experience. We are a club and a Catalan institution, which is open to a world that realise what we stand for.

"The basis of football is in the emotion and the feelings, if not how could we explain why Barça makes millions of people happy when they win and the opposite when things go badly.

"We achieved what we set out to do. Our plan was to put Barça at the cutting edge of sport, make it modern and an innovator. The club had to be made more professional while my own aim also was to recover its Catalan identity and make it more in tune with the motto 'more than a club'.

"Now Barcelona has more than 170,00 members around the world and we are the club with the most fans on the planet. We responded to the challenge of globalisation with ingenuity whilst at the same time being loyal to our values."

Despite this, Laporta will also be remembered for his autocratic leadership and arrogance. He courted the spotlight often for negative reasons, for example, the way he behaved at Madrid airport when he took off his trousers after an argument with a member of security or when he spoke to fans like a dictator at a meeting of members. His political stance distanced him from many who realised the danger of involving the club too firmly in Catalan nationalism.

The battle to replace him had been heating up for several months ahead of the elections, which were finally called for June 14th and Sandro Rosell was the clear favourite.

The choice of who was going to be the 'continuity' candidate that would maintain the existing mandate had turned into a shambles.

The decision by Laporta to bring onto the board, Xavier Sala i Martin and push him as the presidential candidate failed, as he was unable to generate support from other directors.

Vice-president Jaume Ferrer continued to be the favoured choice among the other board members and so Laporta then turned to Alfons Godall and convinced him to stand but his bid soon fell apart.

Godall began unofficial talks with former vice-president Ferran Soriano, who Laporta had fallen out with over the vote of no confidence in 2008. Mainly because Godall really did not want the position of president, he appeared ready to join forces with Soriano and this led Laporta to withdraw his support.

Faced with no alternative, Laporta was forced to put his backing behind Ferrer in the run-up to the election despite their strained relationship, as his biggest fear was for Rosell to win.

The former vice-president resigned in 2005 and his autobiography was published a year later in which he was scathing of Laporta for his dictatorial manner and the way he only listened to his confidante Johan Cruyff.

Since then, though, he had remained quietly in opposition and was respected for the way he rarely made public criticism of the board. Instead he dedicated his time to his sports marketing company and carefully planned his bid for president.

Rosell's contacts in the football world were well known and he was remembered fondly for the way he had been able to entice Ronaldinho to Barcelona in 2003.

Many of those who supported Rosell were anti-Laporta and his presidential style.

One of Laporta's promises on becoming president was to lift the carpet on the finances of the previous boards but this never happened.

Rosell now assured that he would make the board more transparent and would arrange for several club audits. One investigation would be into where the 23m euros had gone for the purchases of Henrique and Keirrison who had never actually played for Barcelona. They had been bought and then immediately loaned out.

Rosell was extremely critical of the deal struck between Barcelona and Bunyodkor of Uzbekistan in 2008 which involved forming ties between the clubs and playing two matches.

Uzbekistan is known for its very poor human rights record and the company behind Bunyodkor is closely bonded to the state. Rosell could see the inconsistency of a team, which carries the name Unicef on its shirts, having such an arrangement.

If all the engagements were fulfilled then Barça were to make around eight million euros from the deal and there were allegations that Laporta was given a financial incentive.

A member of Rosell's team, Xavier Faus, whose expertise was in economics, claimed that the existing board had run into debts of 489m euros "that could rise to 550m euros if you count the signings of Ibrahimovic, Villa and Chygrynskiy."

This was a debt significantly higher than in 2003 but Faus said that Rosell's project would be capable of raising the club's income to 600m euros annually within a six-year period.

Along with Rosell and Ferrer, Marc Ingla and Agusti Benedito were the only other two who received sufficient votes to go into the final ballot.

Ingla was the former economics vice president who had resigned in 2008 due to the strength of opposition to the board in the vote of no confidence. He had the heavyweight backing of Ferran Soriano and also Alfonso Godall, who chose to back him rather than Ferrer.

Benedito was the surprise candidate. The relaxed style of the Catalan businessman appealed to voters, while having never been in the previous board he was free from much of the criticism.

With Rosell's commanding majority in the polls, he was the focus of attack from the other candidates but more often than not he refused to rise to the bait.

In a series of televised debates Ingla in particular came off badly as he appeared ill prepared for the role of president. In one programme he vitriolically lambasted Rosell constantly and was hammered in the press afterwards. Then in the next show, having clearly read the comments, he appeared much more laid back.

Rosell responded to accusations from Ingla claiming he was involved in corruption in Brazil by taking legal action as he did similarly with Laporta who alleged in his book 'Un Sueño para mis Hijos' (A Dream for my Children) that Rosell had set up a deal with Chelsea where he would have been given money to sell Ronaldinho.

His policy of generally appearing above the accusations and recriminations of the other candidates was working well.

"I expected there to be insinuations, rumours and claims being made, while the talk was about sporting matters but instead I have found people have dedicated time to investigate others and try and dig up information. This is something that never passed through my head," he said.

Rosell was pronounced president after receiving 61 percent of the votes, in the biggest ever turnout.

"Before you is a delighted man who since he was a young child shown the way by his father started as a ballboy at the Nou Camp and now I have the maximum honour that any Culé could have, which is to be president," he told a packed auditorium.

"It is a dream come true and now the aim is to make a Catalan Barça which is open to all Barcelonistas outside of Catalonia. I want to form a transparent and winning Barça which is also integrated with the country and good causes."

Rosell was quick to address the issues of making Barcelona more welcoming to non-Catalans and having a more open and accessible board.

The main surprise about the election results was that the continuity candidate, Jaume Ferrer, whose support in many ways endorsed the previous regime, only polled ten per cent of the vote. It was a clear statement that while the team had been successful, the fans were not happy with the leadership of Laporta.

An arranged embrace in front of the cameras between Rosell and Laporta on the night of the results masked the real animosity that lay between the two but they both claimed they would work together until the end of June when Laporta's presidential term would officially come to an end.

The following day Rosell met with Guardiola.

"We had a friendly meeting where we discussed the success of the club and I made it clear to Pep that I wanted him to sign a long-term deal," said Rosell afterwards.

"More than being like the Ferguson of Barcelona, I hope that he is the Beckenbauer, who was a player, coach and then president. Would he be a good president for the club in six years? We will work for the next six years, as that the members have decided, and then see."

He added that he wanted to break down the divisions at the club but there were no bridges being built between Cruyff and him.

One of the final acts that Laporta performed as president was to name Cruyff in a new role as honorary president of the club. It was a way of trying to ensure Cruyff's influence no matter who took over, but Rosell was having none of it and said the decision would be made at a meeting of members.

After five years watching from the sidelines, Rosell finally had the power he had sought all along and he was eager to make his own legacy.

Chapter Fifteen

The World Cup

No sooner had the Barcelona players finished celebrating their league triumph than they had to meet up with the rest of the Spain squad at the end of May in preparation for the World Cup.

Predictably, there was less excitement in Catalonia than in other areas of Spain where the anticipation had been growing for several months. Still it did not mean there wasn't plenty of enthusiasm in Barcelona as the rich blend of different nationalities living in the city meant the kick-off on the 11th of June was eagerly awaited.

Out-going president Joan Laporta was one of those who had only a passive interest in Spain's fortunes.

"I will be following all those teams that have players from Barcelona," he said.

With the recent incorporation of David Villa, Barcelona had eight players in Spain coach Vicente del Bosque's final 23 to travel to South Africa. Apart from that, Leo Messi was going with Argentina, Toure Yaya was in the Ivory Coast team, France had Eric Abidal and Rafa Márquez was in the Mexico team.

"Spain are one of the favourites to win because they have the stamp of Barça with eight players represented and the Spain national team plays the Barça system of football, it is easy to recognise that," he said.

"I actually think they have nine players with the Barça stamp because when I see Cesc Fábregas play you can tell he was from here."

Laporta explained his stance once again: "as the Catalan nation doesn't have a state or a national team that can compete then Barcelona has to take on this function. The club is the best representation of Catalonia in the world and its mission is to represent our culture.

"When Spain won the 2008 European Championships I did have feelings about it although it was not pleasure because they stop my country from taking part. I was happy for the players and above all Xavi and my great friend Ángel Maria Villar (president of the Spanish football federation)."

Pedro Rodriquez was a surprise last minute choice to play in attack after scoring some crucial goals for Barça in his fledgling career, while keeper Victor Váldes, so often overlooked had actually gone away on holiday convinced he had no chance of being selected, when he received the call.

Spain went into the competition as joint favourites with Brazil to lift the World Cup trophy in Johannesburg on the 11th July due to the quality in depth they possessed and the fact that they had gone some way to shrugging off their under-achievers tag with victory in the 2008 European Championships.

It is a surprise that a traditional European powerhouse like Spain had done so badly down the years and in fact had never managed to go further than the World Cup quarter-finals since 1950. Their record in the European Championships was also disappointing with the team having won the competition just once in 1964 before the 2008 competition.

Even with the 1982 World Cup in Spain they were unable to get past the second round, and until 2008, for many their greatest moment was a 5-1 thrashing of a fine Denmark team led by Michael Laudrup, in the 1986 World Cup. Even then they were still knocked out in the quarter-finals by Belgium on penalties.

Instead, in recent years Spain's World Cup involvement is more remembered for an elbow by Mauro Tassotti on Luis Enrique, which broke the Spaniard's nose but was not seen by the referee as Italy knocked them out of the 1994 competition. There was more controversy in 2002 when Spain had two goals ruled out by the referee before losing on penalties to South Korea.

In the build-up to the 2008 European Championships, held jointly in Austria and Switzerland, there was little optimism in Spain despite the quality at the disposal of coach Luis Aragonés as fans had tired of building their hopes up only to see them dashed.

There have been many debates about why Spain have not done better and some put it down to regionalism which has led to only moderate support for the national team in areas of the country, for example, in Catalonia or the Basque Country. Others argued that the top players in Spanish football were too often foreigners.

However, the 2008 Spain team saw a golden generation come through to fruition. Real Madrid's veteran striker Raúl González, a talisman for club and country, was left out in a brave move from Aragonés, who put his trust in the younger generation.

The backbone of the team still had plenty of experience with Iker Casillas, arguably the best keeper in the world for several years, behind Carles Puyol and Carlos Marchena; and then in midfield were Marcos Senna, and Xavi Hernández.

This was mixed with younger players who had matured into world-class players like Andres Iniesta and Fernando Torres.

Spain went on to win the tournament in style with victories in all their matches, not achieved since France in 1984. In the final, a single first-half strike from Torres proved enough as

265

Spain's quick one-touch football undid the German's organised defence.

Aragonés found success by bolstering the midfield and Xavi was the star of the competition as the often under-rated playmaker's incisive passing cut through the opposition.

The veteran coach stood down after the championships and Vicente del Bosque took his place. He had a tough act to follow, but at the same time he came with an impressive managerial pedigree.

Closely bonded to Real Madrid he won the league five times as a midfielder at the Bernabéu stadium but he is best remembered for leading the 'galacticos' as a coach. He was twice in charge on a caretaker basis before being given the role full-time in 1999 and in a successful spell led the club to two Champions Leagues and two league titles. Del Bosque's self-effacing approach proved ideal to rule a dressing room full of world famous players that had been brought in by president Florentino Pérez.

Incredibly Del Bosque's reward was to be fired in 2003 as the club sought a more colourful coach.

After a disappointing time at the helm of Besiktas in Turkey, he was ready to mount Spain's World Cup bid.

He initially toyed with using more width in midfield before returning to the system used by Aragonés and Spain were unstoppable during qualification with a 100 per cent record which included some big wins such as a 5-0 demolition of Belgium.

The personnel were more-or-less the same but gradually a greater Barcelona influence reflected the success under Guardiola.

Gerard Pique became the regular partner for Puyol at centre-half, while impressive campaigns from Sergio Busquets and Pedro Rodriguez saw them make the final cut.

Ahead of flying out to South Africa, Spain played three friendly matches against Saudi Arabia, South Korea and Poland. They only scraped past the first two sides before they cruised to a 6-0 win over a poor Poland team.

There were a few doubts going into the competition with some critics saying that Spain had too many similar players that could do the same job and that the coach kept chopping and changing them. The players had looked jaded after a long season and Iniesta, who had been in and out of the treatment room for the previous year, picked up a thigh strain in the Poland game but was past fit to travel.

After a ten-hour journey from Madrid to Johannesburg the expedition took a short flight to the university city of Potchefstroom that was to be their base for the competition. Their accommodation was a rugby and cricket club and the austere facilities soon led it to be nicknamed the convent by the players.

On paper Spain had a relatively simple task of progressing to the next round from Group H, which also included Switzerland, Chile and Honduras. The main threat appeared to come from Chile, coached by Argentine Marcelo 'El Loco' Bielsa, who had enjoyed an impressive qualifying campaign where they won more matches than any other South American team.

First up was Switzerland on June 16 and Spain were assiduous in their preparation with Del Bosque holding the final training session behind closed doors to give no clues away. The good news was that Andres Iniesta was fit.

"The first game is going to be fundamental as if we can get a victory it will set us up well and improve the team spirit and confidence," said defender Sergio Ramos.

It wasn't that Spain had taken the first game for granted but the fact that they appeared tired while Switzerland coach, the wily Ottmar Hitzfeld, had done his homework well and stifled the threat from Xavi. With Iniesta and Fernando Torres both not at their best after injury lay-offs, the team struggled going forward and ended up losing 1-0.

The ball was almost entirely with Spain and Switzerland created little danger but scored when a mix-up between Piqué and Casillas allowed in Gelson Fernandes to slot home.

267

Afterwards Del Bosque claimed it had simply not been Spain's day but recriminations were quick to arrive.

Ex-coach Aragonés did not waste time in criticising Del Bosque for Spain not making the most of their possession and not pushing forward enough.

"We lacked speed with the ball, players looking for space and also the conviction to take the game by the scruff of the neck from the start of the match," he complained.

"We are not playing well and we need to improve. Xavi did not play in his normal position as his job is to link up the team from the defence as he thinks very quickly, more so than Xabi Alonso and Busquets. He is the one who thinks quickest and for me Cesc is the second choice to play in this position. Against Switzerland, Xavi played too far forward."

Others wondered why when Jesús Navas was brought on and made a countless number of crosses from the right wing, that Fernando Llorente was not introduced so that Spain could take advantage of his height.

Even Iker Casillas' girlfriend was blamed for what went wrong. The Spanish television reporter was standing only feet from Casillas, on the touchline and it was said that she was distracting him.

The defeat meant that Spain would need to win their remaining two matches in order to be sure of qualifying which they managed to do and in the process they began to find their feet although they had by no means hit form.

Perhaps they were lucky that after Switzerland they played Honduras, who had only qualified for the competition through the play-offs and were footballing minnows. Spain won 2-0 through two goals from David Villa but the scoreline could have been much greater with Villa himself missing a penalty.

It gave little comfort to fans of 'la roja' as defeat for Spain against Honduras had been considered practically inconceivable and there were plenty of stronger tests ahead.

Spain finished top of Group H after a scrappy 2-1 victory over Chile, which was possibly their worst performance yet. Chile had looked comfortable and were enjoying a larger percentage of possession when a poor clearance from keeper Claudio Bravo allowed Villa to fire into an open goal from distance.

Spain improved from there on and before the break Iniesta doubled the advantage but it was still not all over as even with Chile a man down, a deflected goal brought them back into the game.

In the last 16, Spain faced a rival they knew very well, their Iberian cousins Portugal, who had finished second to Brazil in Group G.

The main concern was the threat from Portugal's star man Cristiano Ronaldo although despite his high-profile status he had done little in the tournament.

Ronaldo was desperate to steal some of the limelight back from Leo Messi after a low key season at Real Madrid but when his country needed him the Portuguese was unable to deliver.

In his first and last games during the group stage, against the Ivory Coast and Brazil, he was largely anonymous and in the other match, against a weak North Korea side, he scored the final goal in a seven-goal rout.

Still, Spain isolated Ronaldo as the key danger ahead of the game.

"Portugal have a very good side but to this is also added Cristiano Ronaldo. So it is almost a case of having him and then a team behind him. We don't know whether he is going to play on the wings or through the centre and so we will have to prepare the game with this in mind," said Del Bosque.

"We know them well and we have studied them closely in their last three matches. They arrived at the World Cup through the play-offs but Carlos Queiroz (the Portugal coach) has done an excellent job and they have got stronger as they have gone along.

"I realise that there have been a lot of debates about the national team and that I have used a lot of players because I am uncertain but I am not going to enter into that and I can say we have had very few slip-ups.

"Most importantly we have achieved our aims even though we have suffered doing so. The defeat against Switzerland was a big blow and it has taken a lot for us to come back from that but the key is that we did.

"After the Switzerland game everyone was quiet and there was too much tension which came from the responsibility and the desire to win."

In the match both sides cancelled each other out in the first half as Spain looked short of ideas on how to break down a dogged Portugal side. The change in the second half came as a result of Fernando Llorente, Athletic Bilbao's beanpole striker, coming on for Torres, who was still struggling for form, and Spain began to look more dangerous. Llorente had a close-range header blocked and Villa went close before the latter gave Spain the only goal of the game, sweeping the ball home after the keeper denied him the first time.

Portugal's tactic had been to pack the defence and launch long balls forward on the counter-attack but Ronaldo, despite the hype, barely touched the ball.

"It was a tense game. We had more depth in the second half and when we play like that it is difficult for the opposition to stop us," said Del Bosque.

"We want to make history and the players are motivated. This is a long tournament but we are ready to do it."

Next up for Spain were Paraguay, and Del Bosque denied it would be a walkover against the South Americans, who had knocked Japan out on penalties in the last round.

"We have the upmost respect for Paraguay and we are certain that it will not be an easy game. We must ignore those who claim that they are under-dogs because in football there are not such big differences between teams," he said, although adding: "the most important games are still to come and we cannot put limits on our expectations. Our aim is not just to win but to do so in a way which leaves a good taste in the mouth."

Once again Spain squeezed through to the next round by the narrowest of margins with Villa scoring his fifth goal of the tournament close to the end. They rode their luck, surviving a goal incorrectly called off-side and both teams had penalties saved.

The semi-final against Germany was billed as a match between two different styles of football. The disciplined and physically strong Germans faced the open flowing football of the Spaniards.

Few wanted to predict the outcome as the young Germans without their injured captain Michael Ballack had become the surprise package of the tournament as they swept past England and Argentina.

Spain, meanwhile, had stumbled into the semi-finals but had the quality in their team and the track record to beat any team in the world.

"Germany are the best team right now, but we will go out and give our best," said Del Bosque, "this is a great moment for Spanish football and although we did not play well against Paraguay we know our capabilities. We play Germany and so it will be a match between two top sides but while we respect them we do not fear them."

It was also a repeat of the 2008 European Championship final, and the Germans were gunning for revenge.

But there was one reason why Spain could afford to feel confident.

A German octopus called Paul had become famous for calling the results of his national football team. From his tank at Aquarium Sea Life in Oberhausen, Paul had so far got all Germany's World Cup results correct including the defeat by Serbia in the group stage.

Paul, nicknamed the 'psychic octopus', would be given two glass cubes with a mussel inside and on the front would be a nation's flag.

Given the choice of Spain or Germany, Paul initially appeared undecided, hovering over each container for a short while before finally going for Spain.

From the start at the Moses Mabhida Stadium in Durban, Spain looked in control as their strong technique and flexible movement made it difficult for the Germans to rob the ball off them.

Germany had destroyed Argentina 4-0 playing a solid system, which took advantage of their opponents' individualism and their disorganisation at the back.

Spain were a very different proposition and they played their strongest game against their toughest rivals.

The scorer of the winner against Germany in the European Championship final two years before, Torres, had been finally dropped after a poor tournament and Pedro Rodriguez took his place.

Spain still struggled to break down the Germans while they could easily have been reduced to ten-men when Sergio Ramos was lucky to escape a second yellow card.

Del Bosque's side raised the tempo in the second half and got the goal that their dominance deserved when Puyol thundered home a Xavi corner.

It was enough to see Spain through to their first ever World Cup final where they would play Holland, twice runners-up but never winners.

Holland had a well-balanced team with Wesley Sneijder inspirational in midfield not just for his creativity but also his tenacity. Along with him there was the attacking flair of Arjen Robben and the determined workhorse Marc van Bommel.

They had shown their credentials by eliminating Brazil, one of the pre-tournament favourites, and then in the semi-finals they knocked out a battling Uruguay side.

The final brought together two countries with long-standing cultural ties dating back to the 15th century and the time of Ferdinand and Isabella of Spain who both admired Flemish art.

The two countries were united under Charles of Ghent in 1516 but it was not to last as the Dutch fought the 80 Years' War for independence. In 1648 a deal was struck through partition and the seven northern provinces broke away to become the Netherlands and the other part that would later be known as Belgium remained with Spain but as an autonomous state.

To this day though the words to the Dutch national anthem reflect their battle against the Spanish.

The cultural links between the countries extended to football with the arrival of Rinus Michels and Johan Cruyff to Barcelona in the 1970s.

The irony now was that Holland were playing a more physical and defensive game, while Spain were the pervaders of 'total football', something not lost on the Dutch coach Bert van Marwijk.

"The Netherlands teams of '74 and '78 are our inspiration but you cannot compare this team with something that happened 28 or 32 years ago. We just play for everybody in Holland," he said.

"Over the last five weeks I've talked with Ruud Gullit and for a long time with Johan Cruyff. Also, from the first day we started to train here Rudi Krol has been involved.

"He's been to every training session, sitting on the bench and we have talked a lot about the past and the way we play now. I have had a lot of contact with those guys.

"I like the way Spain play. There are seven Barcelona players in the Spain side and I've often said that Barcelona and Spain are almost the same. They have the same style and way of playing.

"Maybe Spain is influenced by Barcelona and Barcelona influenced by Johan Cruyff and Rinus Michels. That's a big compliment to Dutch football."

Back in Spain, the country was gearing up for the final with giant screens put up in towns and cities. Even in Barcelona, with its pro-Catalan sentiment, many people had finally got behind the team and a mass turnout was guaranteed to watch the match in Plaza España.

The match didn't live up to expectations. Holland turned their back on 'total football' by playing an aggressive game, which worked to unsettle Spain. The common feeling in the

Dutch camp was that the opposition had better players and so the only way to beat them was to break-up their passing.

Van Bommel, intriguingly a former Barcelona player, was the main hitman making a constant stream of niggling fouls while Nigel de Jong could have seen more than a yellow card for a wild chest high tackle on Xabi Alonso.

It worked in that Holland had the clearest chance of the opening 90 minutes when Spain keeper Iker Casillas blocked a shot by Robben who was clean through on goal.

In extra-time Johnny Heitinga was sent off for a second yellow card and Spain were able to make the most of the man extra with Andres Iniesta becoming an instant hero with his goal after 115 minutes.

He controlled a pass from Cesc inside the area and slotted home. He celebrated by revealing a t-shirt in memory of Daniel Jarque, the Espanyol defender who had died a year earlier from heart failure, aged just 26.

There were recriminations afterwards from both sides over the handling of the game by English referee Howard Webb, but it had been a tough match to officiate and neither country could say they had been particularly prejudiced. While Spain complained about the fouls from Holland, the Dutch could also say that Carles Puyol should have been dismissed for a professional foul on Robben.

For Iniesta, it was another memorable goal like that he scored against Chelsea in the semi-final of the 2009 Champions League.

"It is difficult to explain how I feel but the important thing is that I have made millions of people very happy and that doesn't have a price," he said.

"It all happened very quickly. To begin with I thought I was offside, then I thought I must score as penalties would have been terrible. It has all been a very emotional experience particularly as we came back from losing the first game. We knew we had a great chance due to the exceptional players and I am just happy to be a part of a historical moment.

"It is something to be proud about that there were so many Barcelona players in the team. There are a lot of similarities between the way Spain play and Barcelona but this is logical considering that so many of us play for Spain."

The national team returned to a rapturous welcome as fans celebrated across the country. The psychic octopus Paul became a hero as he also predicted Spain would win the final and plans were made to try and bring him to Madrid and give him a luxurious aquarium. Not everyone was a fan though of Paul and one Argentine newspaper offered a reward for him to be killed as he had predicted their defeat.

Del Bosque was given a special reception on returning to his hometown of Salamanca.

"I am not very emotional or very theatrical but I am delighted to see the support for la roja. This will always be in my heart," he said.

Writing in the Catalan newspaper El Periodico, Johan Cruyff was very critical about the way Holland had played the final.

"Iniesta's goal represented the best aspect of Barça as it showed he is a talented player but also somebody who works hard. It was always going to be a big disappointment for who lost the game which stayed 0-0 for so long because Holland did not want to play football but just unsettle Spain," he said.

"Holland were very dirty and should have been reduced to nine men very early on. There were two very poor challenges that could have done a lot of damage. Spain played very well in the opening 20 minutes but then succumbed to the provocation.

"The reason why they played anti-football was because they thought that was the only way they could win.

"Iniesta has had a difficult year with the injuries which prevented him from playing for Barça. He lost a close friend in Daniel Jarque and showed a lot of courage to dedicate the goal to him.

"This was a Spanish game won by Iniesta and in Barça style. Iniesta was made into a footballer at the Masia, the

275

Barça youth academy, and one of the best schools in the world."

After the tournament Barça received considerable credit for Spain's achievement but Guardiola tried to play this down.

"The Barça players had an important part to play and while I am very happy for that they were also managed by a very good coach. Not even drunk would I have thought at the start of the season that Pedrito and Busquets would have won the World Cup," he said.

"But it is wrong to say this was a triumph for Barça. It is a triumph for all the teams that have played good football from the 'Quinta del Buitre' (the famous Real Madrid side of the 1980s), Victor Fernandez's Zaragoza side, to Lendoiro's Deportivo (la Coruña) and all the other side's. We took something from these teams as all take ideas from others. "

Chapter Sixteen

Streamlining and austerity

While there was little change on the pitch, the arrival of Sandro Rosell as president ushered in a new era at boardroom level. Gone was Laporta the showman who craved attention and courted controversy and he was replaced by a pragmatic leader who at least on the surface looked to bring people together and cut back on the club's spending.

During the elections the Rosell camp had spoken of the burgeoning debt which the club was saddled with due to the profligate spending of Laporta and they followed this up with an audit by Deloitte at the end of June, 2010, which revealed an alarming state of affairs.

The Laporta board bowed out claiming a final year profit of 11m euros but new financial director Javier Faus painted a very different picture announcing the club had an overall debt of 442m euros following a loss of 77.1m euros from the previous season.

It paved the way for austerity measures that would limit the club's spending power in the transfer market at a time when they sought to maximise their marketing potential.

On July 1st Rosell chose to be inaugurated outside the La Masia, the youth academy, a clear attempt to show that he would continue to back the club's policy of bringing through their own home grown players.

Carrying on from his election manifesto he spelt out his desire to mend bridges and that fans with different points of view would all be represented.

Referring to the acclaimed South African statesman Nelson Mandela he said: "I am not making a comparison with Mandela at all but I want to install his spirit in Barça; if we achieve just one percent of what he did then it will be a big success.

"Cruyff is Cruyff, Núñez is Núñez and Laporta is Laporta but what is important is that they are all for Barça."

There were smiles at the handover as Laporta was given his moment to speak and Rosell shook hands with Cruyff. The new president also praised Laporta for his commitment to youth, the agreement with Unicef and the way that he had worked to eradicate the violent Boixos Nois fans.

But despite the grand show of togetherness there was no sudden miraculous peace and Rosell was quick to demonstrate he was keen on revenge.

There was to be no backtracking as he carried out his threat to sue Laporta for the accusations in his book 'Un Sueño para mis Hijos' where he claimed that Rosell as vice-president had offered him 10m euros in his back pocket if they agreed a move to Chelsea for Ronaldinho. Rosell had already started legal action against his fellow election candidate Marc Ingla who claimed that the new president's company Bonus Sports Marketing was involved in corruption in Brazil.

The way that the board removed Cruyff's new position of honorary president left the impression of a childish spat and ultimately reflected badly on the board. Repeating what was pointed out during the election campaign, the board's spokesman Toni Freixa, said that as the post had not previously existed it would need to be first passed at the members' assembly.

However, just a day after shaking hands with Rosell at his presentation, Cruyff turned up unexpectedly at the club's offices and returned the honorary president's insignia.

"These things take a lot to earn them but little effort to return. If I am so important that this was discussed at the first meeting of the board then I would prefer not to be involved and I think this is for the best," said Cruyff.

The president was told about the unexpected development during a press conference and said: "Well, I would have done the same, if you are given a title that doesn't exist then you return it. I suppose he will have consulted his lawyers."

Later Cruyff washed his hands of the matter: "Rosell phoned me to talk about the position but I don't know what there is to discuss. I have never seen a circus like this before; when (Bobby) Charlton or (Franz) Beckenbauer were given a similar position at their clubs there didn't have to be votes from members.

"The subject is now closed, there is no need to have a vote in the assembly because I don't want to have anything more to do with this joke."

The most significant news to come out of the elections though was no doubt the revelation that the club was in serious economic trouble. On a broader scale it had ramifications which went to the heart of the club as the Barcelona model had been sold around the world as being near on perfect and yet it was in massive debt.

The policy of developing their own players was supposed to be the answer to big spending Real Madrid but in reality it was only the size of Barcelona and its capacity to receive massive loans that was keeping it afloat.

"It is a delicate situation which means that if we behave as though nothing is wrong then at some point there will be a problem," said Faus over the debt of 442m euros. "There is no reason for fans to worry and we will still have money to sign players."

The club's finance director stood back from saying that the previous board had made up their figures but rather that they had made them look more healthy.

"The problem that we have is not a case of something illegal last year but generally that the board members involved in financial planning were not doing their job well," he said.

Rosell also moved to calm supporters: "we have found the club in debt but we are not bankrupt. We will do what we can to introduce austere measures which will mean saving in some areas which are not vital so we can continue to make important payments like those for the players."

For the previous board this was a deliberate move to discredit them and besmirch their record. Former director Joan Oliver claimed it was a case of interpretation of the figures and that the Rosell board were not taking into consideration factors such as the financial benefits of the youth policy and the value of players like Messi.

The news led the board to arrange loans of 155m euros to pay for debts and costs which included the players' salaries from the previous month. Faus revealed an economic package where the board would seek to gradually cut back the debt.

"To get rid of it we need to pay off 50m euros each year and build up an income of 500m euros although 70 per cent of the costs at the moment are fixed," he said.

The implications on purchasing power were clear on what was a new look footballing department.

As expected sports director Txiki Begiristain had chosen to stand down at the end of the Laporta presidency and so the club had needed to find a replacement who would work between the board and the coaching staff.

At the end of June it was director Joan Oliver who announced in a press conference that Begiristain did not want to work for another president. The former Dream Team player had a crucial role in one of the most successful periods in the club's history but he knew the time was right to take a break.

"This is a good moment to do it with the end of Laporta as he is the person who had the most confidence in me and backed me at the right time. I need some time off now and then I will start again," he said. Interestingly he considered the renewal of keeper Victor Valdés when he appeared to be on his way out of the club to be his biggest achievement and his worst choices were the signings Gianluca Zambrotta and Alexander Hleb. In total he signed 38 players from the first Ricardo Quaresma through to David Villa.

Laporta said on several occasions that the appointment of Begiristain was the best decision he ever made and he worked well with Cruyff, his former coach, behind the scenes. Normally a hard working, serious man, Begiristain did show rare emotion after the Champions League victory in Rome, which he felt was a very personal achievement following his appointment of Pep Guardiola the summer before.

Rosell had anticipated the departure of Begiristain and his likely replacement by former Spain and Barcelona keeper Andoni Zubizarreta was a poorly kept secret. The changeover was smooth as the Basque player retained the link to the Dream Team and had the same footballing philosophy as Guardiola.

In a celebrated career, Zubizarreta won two leagues in Javier Clemente's physical Athletic Bilbao side but it was good performances at the 1986 World Cup which convinced Barça to sign him and he became a solid if not outstanding keeper. He was imposing and good in the air but he had his critics despite accumulating 126 international caps.

Many Barça fans were upset at the way he left after the club's 4-0 defeat in the 1994 European Cup final against AC Milan where he was blamed heavily. He was unceremoniously shown the door by coach Johan Cruyff and moved to Valencia where he stayed until he finished his career in 1998.

He had some experience as a sports director at Athletic Bilbao from 2001 to 2004 before working in the media as a television pundit and newspaper columnist.

On his new appointment he was quick to praise Begiristain: " I want to first mention those who were here before me, starting with Txiki. They achieved a lot and built a great team and my job now is to maintain this high level."

The transfer target on everyone's lips was Cesc Fabregas and with the player openly stating he would like to return to the Nou Camp, the question was whether they could negotiate a deal with Arsenal.

Rosell knew that the club was not in a particularly good bargaining position.

"This is more complicated due to the high transfer fee that the seller is looking for. Everyone knows that he wants to come here and so you can imagine what advantage Arsenal can take from that," said Rosell.

In May, Cesc had made it clear that Barça was where he saw his future.

"At the moment I am an Arsenal player but if one day I leave then I would like to go to Barça, it is a dream of mine which I would like to achieve," he said.

Later he admitted it was a mistake to be so frank as it only stirred up more transfer gossip and there seemed no end to the saga as Arsenal held their ground and denied Cesc was for sale. Arsenal coach Arsene Wenger resented the way that there was so much talk coming from the Catalan club over Cesc which was unsettling him. Barça players spoke unreservedly about how much they would like to see him at the Nou Camp and Carles Puyol and Gerard Pique joked with Cesc by forcing a Barça shirt on him during victory celebrations after the World Cup.

There was money available for transfers and the kitty had been boosted by the sales of Yaya Toure and Dmytro Chygrynsky.

The physically imposing Toure had proved himself to be a valuable member of the team and a fans favourite but was not happy about having fallen down the player order. Busquets was now ever present in the team alongside Xavi and Iniesta while Seydou Keita was also ahead of him as a stand-in. The club had become irritated by the constant rumour mongering from Toure's outspoken agent Dimitri Seluk but were reluctant to let him go even though Guardiola could not guarantee him first team football.

There were several clubs interested in the signing of the Ivory Coast midfielder but Manchester City's petrol dollars swung the balance. His 24m pound transfer would see him earn 221,000 pounds a week as well as 1.65m pounds annually through image rights and 823,000 pounds each season City qualified for the Champions League

The sale of Chygrynsky completed a poor piece of business with the Ukranian defender ushered out of the back door after a disappointing campaign. Fans had thought Guardiola had picked out an unlikely jewel from Shakhtar Donetsk but instead found a clumsy centre half lacking in confidence. They sold him back to Shakhtar for 10m euros less than the 25m euros they bought him for.

Also leaving the club were veterans Thierry Henry and Rafa Marquez who both signed for New York Red Bulls. Marquez was one of the first signings of the Laporta presidency and although not always the most disciplined in training he had been an important member of the rearguard. Henry, though, on reflection had been a disappointment as his performances and commitment never lived up to the expectation when he signed in 2008 from Arsenal.

There was an unfamiliar look to the team as they turned up to the first day of pre-season training at Sant Joan Despí as the World Cup was still in full swing and some of the players would not return until well into August as they were given a month off. It was a chance though for youngsters like Thiago, Marc Bartra and Jonathan Dos Santos to catch the eye of Guardiola.

The board listened to Guardiola who wanted to cut back on the amount of travel during the summer but the opportunity to boost the club's revenue saw them play a friendly in Oslo before embarking on a tour of Asia beginning in Seoul.

Guardiola insisted on fielding youth players which led to resentment in the tour countries and in China this threatened to boil over. There was talk of the trip being called off as having paid 1.5m to bring over the team, officials complained Barça failed to comply with their commitments, and newspapers branded the Catalan club's antics disrespectful.

Full stadiums were greeted by a Barça second string while the fans were never given the chance to meet their idols off the pitch. In one press conference Messi even appeared to be asleep.

There was particular outrage at an event organised by Unicef and club sponsors where children who survived the Sichuan earthquake in 2008, which killed more than 70,000 people, waited excitedly to meet the Barça players but were denied the chance to talk to them by a club press officer who said it was not in the contract.

Returning home there was more friction, this time from the club who slammed the Spanish football federation after seven Barcelona players were called up for an international friendly away to Mexico just three days before the first-leg of the domestic Super Cup.

Guardiola was furious and new sports director Andoni Zubizarreta said: "the players are not ready to play even ten minutes without training at that height and heat. It is the first time in history that a list of players who are on holiday have been called up."

The federation were making the most of the financial rewards from being world champions and less than a year after lifting the cup in South Africa they had made over 100m euros through matches, sponsorship and television deals.

Barça crashed 3-1 away in the first leg of the Super Cup against Sevilla as Guardiola rested key players and afterwards he complained at the way that commercialism was taking precedence over sport.

David Villa made his debut in the return leg and a full strength side turned around the tie with a Leo Messi hat-trick helping them to a 4-0 victory.

At the end of August, Villa scored his first goal for the club in the Joan Gamper trophy against AC Milan and Ronaldinho was given a warm welcome on his return to the Nou Camp.

Zlatan Ibrahimovic also played but his departure was around the corner and finally he signed for Milan for a figure of 24m euros.

The signing of the Swede had been an even bigger disaster than that of Dmytro Chygrynskiy financially as the club had made a loss of around 40m euros.

Ibrahimovic had a reasonable return of 21 goals from 41 games but he never seemed to fit in and had stuttered to the end of the previous season. His poor relationship with the coach was summed up by the way he complained to Italian journalists after the Joan Gamper match.

"I don't know why Guardiola doesn't want me. He never speaks to me, he has only spoken to me twice in six months," he said.

An irritated Guardiola replied: "If I have only spoken to him twice in six months then it is for a good reason. I am the trainer of the team not just one player and while I have no complaints about his commitment in training, as he has always been an example professionally, we are talking here about the person not the player."

Sevilla utility man Adriano Correia had been the Rosell board's first signing and while they had a replacement for Ibrahimovic in Villa, Guardiola was still looking to reinforce the midfield with Liverpool's tough tackling Argentine, Javier Mascherano, the first name on the list.

Although Mascherano had become an influential figure for the Merseyside club he had made clear his desire to play in Spain before and this time around he was prepared to force his departure. The final straw was his refusal to play a Premiership game against Manchester City and days later he signed for Barcelona in a 17.5m pounds deal.

Guardiola now had in place the squad he had asked for as he faced an ominous new threat from Real Madrid in the shape of Jose Mourinho who had been brought in by president Florentino Peréz as he continued his relentless bid to topple Barça's hegemony.

Mourinho was described in the Spanish tabloids as the Guardiola antidote after his Inter side had found a way to beat Barcelona and he had also seemingly rattled Guardiola with his comments before and after the Champions League semi-final ties the previous spring.

It was a new look Real as talismen Raul and Guti departed after 16 years with the club and fresh blood arrived including Ángel Di María, Sami Khedira and Mezut Ozil.

Mourinho's name was already courting controversy before his arrival as Real were attempting to paper over a previous spat between sports director Jorge Valdano and Mourinho, where the former had been critical of the Portuguese's style of football.

"I know that I have not always liked the way that Mourinho's teams play but my responsibility is now Real Madrid and the best for Real Madrid is Jose Mourinho," he said, but it was to be the start of a stormy relationship.

Mourinho in his presentation denied there was any particular tension between himself and FC Barcelona.

"I am not against them, I am coach of Madrid and I am only worried about Madrid. They are a great rival but that is it, if they hate me then that is a problem for Barcelona. I respect them but fear is not a word in my dictionary," he claimed.

Barça made a winning start to the season with Villa scoring in a 3-0 victory over Racing Santander but a home defeat against Hercules raised eyebrows. Critics claimed that Guardiola's tactics had been found out and the answer was to pack the midfield and so prevent their playmakers having time on the ball.

It sounded simple and an obvious over-reaction from a Spanish media desperate for stories to fill their delay sports papers. Barça bounced back although they were still not at their best as they continued to drop points against weaker sides.

Importantly as they came up to the first clasico they hit form with a 5-0 win over Sevilla and then an 8-0 victory against Almeria, the biggest away win in la liga since they defeated Las Palmas in 1959.

The match against Real at the Nou Camp was the first real test of the season and there was plenty of tension at the ground as fans warily jeered the arrival of Mourinho. No one was expecting the resounding 5-0 walkover which put them top of the table.

More than the result, it was the manner of the win which emphasised the quality of Barça's passing and linkup play and it has been described as one of the finest performances ever on a football pitch. Real were left bemused and utterly frustrated and their mood was summed up by Sergio Ramos who was dismissed for thrashing out at Messi.

As critics now began to ponder whether Barcelona could possibly be the best team of all time; Messi, Iniesta and Xavi occupied the three-man shortlist for the Fifa World Player of the Year. Some claimed it was a case of favouritism as a player like Wesley Sneijder who won the treble with Inter Milan and reached the World Cup final was not even shortlisted, but it really demonstrated the domination of Barça even if they did not win the 2010 Champions League.

After scoring the winning goal in the World Cup final, Iniesta had a strong claim to the award but even he was overshadowed by the dribbling skills of Messi who had notched up 42 goals in 36 league games during 2010.

The eulogies for Messi continued to flood in as he scored yet another hat-trick which gave Barça a 3-0 victory over Atletico Madrid, their 16th consecutive win, and so breaking Real Madrid's record run inspired by the great Alfredo Di Stefano, 50 years earlier.

The club was changed for ever in December, 2010, as the board agreed a deal with the Qatar Foundation for it to be the first shirt sponsor in its history.

While Laporta had admitted that he would do it if he felt it was necessary, Rosell felt the club needed the 150m euros from five years of sponsorship which would see the Qatar Foundation name on the front and the Unicef name relegated to the back.

The figure was the highest ever for a club shirt contract but what was puzzling was why Barcelona had chosen them with similar deals available and equally there was a question why the Qatar Foundation was interested in sponsorship.

The Catalan club had made a lot of effort to push the image of a humanitarian club and had paid 1.5m euros to have Unicef on their shirts so it was in stark contrast to now associate themselves with an organisation which has courted controversy.

Qatar has a poor standard of human rights where homosexuality is illegal and whose sponsorship laws for workers are little different to slavery. The state funded foundation was set up in Qatar in the mid-1990s to help boost education and development generally in the country but its alleged link to extreme Islamic groups and claims they have given money to the cleric Yusuf al Qaradawi, an advocate of terrorism, has tarnished its image.

Perhaps the interest in sponsorship was to boost Qatar's image, as it sought the 2022 World Cup, by associating it with Barcelona but Rosell's claims of debt, the need to cut spending and sell players has seen opponents question his integrity and similarly the deal with Qatar has led to rumours that he has business concerns, which he has entirely denied.

Rosell assures that he sold his company Bonus Sports Marketing to a Saudi Arabian company in July 2010 and so has no conflict of interests with the club's sponsorship deal. He admits having done business in Qatar since 2006 and that his contacts there helped Barça to arrange the sponsorship deal.

"We thought the best way to improve the finances was through marketing and I asked the people that I knew in Qatar if they could help us."

One of the fiercest critics of the deal was Joan Laporta, who since stepping down from the presidency had set up a new political party called Democràcia Catalana seeking independence from Spain.

"Initially I wasn't interested in politics but I had a passion for Barça and a passion for our liberties, and that is what led me into politics. Barcelona is the national team of Catalonia and as president I sought to look after its interests and promote our rights.

"With the problems that Catalonia faces the only solution is for independence so that we can make the right decisions and develop a better life. The structure which is here at the moment is not working and we want an independent state in the European Union.

"This is the most successful period in the club's history and we are the best team in the world, but the sponsorship is another example of how the new board are destroying everything that we achieved.

"The board talked about transparency but in my time there was more than there is now as the model was very open. (For example) Rosell said he would stop running his sports company if he became president but nobody knows what he is doing and I personally don't think he is telling the truth.

"I don't know whether Rosell is still involved in politics in Brazil but during the presidential elections it appeared as though he was involved in a bad case of corruption.

"We concentrated on bringing through young players and showing that we were a club that was open to the world by having Unicef on our shirts. We were more than a club but that is no longer the case.

"My legacy is that is that I returned Catalanism to Barça and it was the most Catalan that it has been in its history while also aiming for world solidarity. I am very proud but at the same time I am very sad that these people are doing what they can to destroy this legacy and they are acting like children."

While Real Madrid and Barcelona can raise passions across Spain, one of the downsides to their size and influence is that there is a lack of competitiveness across la liga and this has grown in the modern era with the injection of money into the game to the extent that it is now a two horse race.

Other clubs have lobbied for change and a fairer distribution of wealth which could breathe new life into the competition. The ever rising financial stakes have meant that many Spanish clubs have built up considerable debts as they try to compete and there has been talk of changing the television rights which favour the top two. Unlike the situation in other major football leagues, Barcelona and Real negotiate their own television contracts and take home 50 per cent of the 600m euros for coverage of Spanish football.

Real may have been overshadowed by Barcelona but they still possessed a magnificent array of talent and remained on the shoulders of the Catalan side.

Guardiola's men rode their luck in the Last 16 of the Champions League against Arsenal when the harsh dismissal of Robin van Persie, for a second yellow card after kicking the ball away, turned the tide in their favour and they passed through 4-3 on aggregate.

The added strain of the Arsenal double header took its toll in the league as they drew away to Sporting Gijon and then struggled to beat Athletic Bilbao, with Messi hitting a late winner. It proved to be an important victory as with Real only drawing away to Deportivo la Coruña they went into March with a seven point lead.

Barcelona were coping without their captain Carles Puyol who had picked up a knee injury at the end of January and but for a comeback against Real Madrid three months later missed the rest of the campaign. While his marauding spirit could never be fully replaced, full back Eric Abidal had moved across effortlessly to centre half alongside Gerard Pique.

Abidal was enjoying his best run in the team when news broke that he would have to undergo emergency surgery after a liver tumour was discovered in a routine medical. The French international underwent an examination after saying he felt unwell and the results left the club reeling.

"This is the toughest time I've had here but Abidal will get over this as he is one of the strongest people mentally that I know," said Xavi.

Abidal was inundated with get well messages as he recovered in hospital, while the team entered the crucial stage of the campaign with half their defence missing and cover thin on the ground.

Along with this the club found its reputation harmed by a drugs slur from a right-wing radio station. The Catalan side's success had clearly led some to believe it was unnatural.

A late-night programme on Cadena Cope revealed that Real were going to approach the Spanish football federation calling for stronger drug testing with the suggestion that players at Barcelona and Valencia were taking illegal substances.

The announcement was completely unsubstantiated and understandably angered the Catalan club and they were further irritated at the way that Real initially made no efforts to distance themselves from the claims.

Later Cope backtracked in a statement saying that they never doubted the achievements of Barcelona and that the source of the news was from Real Madrid.

While Guardiola demanded to know where the story originated in a press conference, it strained the good relationship between Rosell and the Real board but Laporta felt that his replacement should have taken a firmer line to protect Barcelona.

"He should defend the players better and I want more from the president than simply his saying that they have a statement from Real claiming they are not behind it," said Laporta.

It was the latest confrontation in the stand-off between Rosell and his predecessor which was also going to see them go to court over the financial management of the club.

Rosell had carried out his threat to raise the matter of the club's finances under the Laporta administration at the club's assembly of members the previous October and put to the vote whether legal action should be taken.

The due diligence report revealed extravagant sums had been spent on first class travel and 500,000 euros was paid out on tickets for board members for the Champions League final in Rome. A further 600,000 euros went on catering at matches in the Nou Camp during just one season.

Fans were divided as although they resented Laporta's lavish spending on luxuries, many felt that taking the unprecedented move of taking him and other former board members to court would be of little benefit to the club and harm its image.

In the end there was only a slender majority of 30 out of the 1093 at the assembly to take the Laporta board to court over the 48.7m euros which it was claimed had been lost during the seven years that he was president.

Laporta had refused to attend the assembly meeting saying that the new board manipulated the figures and did not allow him to present his own accounts which would have shown the club to be 11m euros in the black from his final year as president.

Countering the claims of excess he said: "this is false and it is very easy to throw stones and then run away, if they have the evidence of this then show it. There is nothing in the due diligence report to back up the statements that they have made. There was 420,000e spent on watches for players which were win bonuses and private planes were used to make the players' journeys more comfortable.

"This is defamation. I am used to certain sectors and above all the Spanish media doing it but what cannot be wiped out is the seven years of success at the club. Our record was impeccable and if you calculate the full length of our term then we are in credit and that includes losses from the previous board and the debts which the new board want to stick on us."

Laporta was planning to retaliate with legal action of his own claiming that the full details of the due diligence report should have been revealed and not just the results, and that the majority of only 30 at the assembly of members was not sufficient to take him to court.

There were further twists and turns to come in the title race but Barça always maintained a comfortable cushion and they appeared a notch above Real in the quality of their football as Mourinho's side showed admirable fighting spirit but in many games scrapped their way to victory.

The league meeting at the Bernabeu was expected to be a title showdown like the year before but in the end it turned into a formality for the Catalans who carried an eight point lead into the game.

It was the first of four clasicos in the space of 17 days which would go some way to deciding the fortunes of both clubs' seasons. Such is the hype when Barça and Real meet that four matches within a month really captured the imagination and led to saturation coverage in the media.

After the league game came the final of the King's Cup and a double header in the semi-finals of the Champions League.

Contrary to his usual stance of taking centre stage and stoking up matches, Mourinho preferred to take a back seat for the league match and instead his assistant Aitor Karanka faced the media in the pre-match press conference.

His decision was analysed by journalists and pundits who tried to work out his tactics and how he was aiming to get an advantage or whether it was a cowardly decision with the team having already lost any real hopes of winning the league.

The match itself suggested the latter was not true as the hard-fought game, high on gamesmanship and foul play while low on quality football, ended in a 1-1 draw.

It was a very different scoreline to the 5-0 thrashing at the Nou Camp but Barcelona still had 70 per cent of the possession and got the result that they needed.

Afterwards Real looked for excuses and Mourinho criticised the dismissal of defender Raul Albiol.

"It was an even game when we played 11 against 11 but then as happens on a lot of occasions we found ourselves with 10 players and it was almost impossible for us," he said.

"Barcelona maybe the best team in the world when they have the ball but they had problems when it was 11 versus 11. When it was 11 versus 10 they could do what they liked but even then the referee showed a different approach as I don't know why Alves didn't receive a second yellow card. If he had committed the foul for the penalty 50 yards away from goal he would have been booked and it is even clearer because he did it in the penalty area."

Mourinho was rebuked for his defensive tactics but he gave the perfect response days later in the final of the King's Cup when an extra-time goal from Cristiano Ronaldo gave them a 1-0 win. It led to euphoric celebrations in Madrid and a victory parade through the streets of the capital which left Sergio Ramos red faced as he dropped the cup and the bus ran over it.

"Our mentality has been changed. Mourinho is a phenomenon," proclaimed keeper Iker Casillas as their hopes soared for the Champions League semi-final.

In Barcelona the tension was rising high and once again Mourinho's provocation hit a nerve and Guardiola lost his cool.

Mourinho had taunted him for complaining about the referee in the King's Cup final over a decision to correctly rule Pedro Rodriguez off-side.

"Tomorrow at 8.45pm we play a match on the field. Off the pitch he has won all year, this season and he will do in the future. Let him have his personal Champions League," ranted Guardiola.

"In this room (the press room) he is the king, he is the man and I can't compete with him. If Barcelona want someone to compete then they should look for someone else but that is what we as people and an institution don't do."

The scene was set for a tense couple of games with all manner of histrionics that did neither side any credit. To the many millions around the world they saw crude challenges, diving and other theatricals while every refereeing decision was contested.

Cynical fouls in the first leg by Pepe and Sergio Ramos were matched by playacting from Dani Alves and Sergio Busquets in particular. Pepe was eventually dismissed for a lunge at Alves which swung the contest towards the Catalans. Barça had been in charge but Pepe had been effectively employed by Mourinho as a destroyer in front of the Madrid defence who broke up Barcelona's attacks by fair means or foul.

With Pepe gone there was no one to stop Messi who followed up a close range finish with a delightful goal where he beat Casillas after slaloming through the defence.

The build-up to the return leg had further snipings from both camps with claims from Real of Uefa bias towards Barcelona. In particular they felt that the European governing body should have taken action over Busquets apparently shouting 'monkey' at full-back Marcelo.

The game ended 1-1 and Real had more complaints over a Gonzalo Higuain goal that was not allowed for a foul by Cristiano Ronaldo, although replays suggested he himself was pushed by Gerard Pique.

While Real were left feeling aggrieved there was no doubt that Barcelona had edged them in the quality of their passing and movement, and in Messi they have a player who is on another level to those around him.

Barcelona now had the chance to win their second Champions League in three years and they would play the final at Wembley, a ground with a particular sentimental attachment as it was where they won their first European Cup back in 1992.

Before that they tied up their third straight league title in low key fashion with a mid-week 1-1 draw away to Levante. It was an emotional match for Abidal who was a surprise inclusion in the starting lineup but demonstrated his mental resolve at returning so quickly to action and also the support he had been given by Guardiola.

As all eyes centred on Wembley at the end of May, there was plenty of confidence in Catalonia that they would beat an ageing Manchester United side which had won the Premiership but were a steady rather than remarkable side. It was also the club which Barça had beaten relatively easily two years earlier in the Rome final when they were arguably a stronger side which included the then World Player of the Year Cristiano Ronaldo.

Barça had defensive problems as Carles Puyol was not ready to start and so Javier Mascherano, despite his lack of height was chosen to partner Gerard Pique at the back. Guardiola also put his confidence in Abidal at left back even though he had only just returned to regular first team action.

The strength of the team lay in midfield and especially attack where Messi was bringing to an end another record-breaking season. He had become the first player to score 50 goals in a Spanish season, breaking the record set by Real Madrid's Ferenc Puskas in the 1959-60 campaign.

Messi had fought a goal scoring battle with Cristiano Ronaldo all season and the Portuguese had finally gone ahead on 53 goals while Messi had one less going into the Champions League final.

After a lively start by United, similar to the final in 2009, Barcelona took control of the game by out-passing them in midfield. Rather than seeking a method to break up Barça's rhythm in the middle of the pitch, United coach Alex Ferguson played his regular formation and they appeared doomed from the outset.

Although Real were beaten, Mourinho had looked for a way to stop Barça by employing Pepe as a destroyer in midfield, but Ferguson's team lost the game almost limply as Michael Carrick and Park were never going to hold their own in midfield. Then on the left wing was the 37-year-old Ryan Giggs up against the energetic Dani Alves.

Barça went ahead through Pedro as United showed they could not compete technically at playing one touch football. A well-worked move did see Wayne Rooney equalise but United were on the back foot throughout the second half with Messi and Villa giving Barcelona a comfortable 3-1 victory.

In a symbolic gesture to recognise Abidal's cancer battle, captain Carles Puyol gave the Champions League trophy to the Frenchman to lift.

"He has recovered well and we have all tried to show how important he is to the club. As a coach it is important to see this kind of thing happen and it was very thoughtful of Puyol to do it," said Guardiola.

Abidal himself explained: "When doctors give you the news then you automatically think the worst but then I thought about what we say to sick children in hospital when we visit and that they have to fight and I knew that this was the situation now for me.

"I would say that I do now appreciate more being a professional footballer and the quality of life that I have."

It had been another successful season on the pitch in Rosell's first year as president and he had fulfilled many of his pledges which included having a lower media profile but many fans were disappointed at the way he continued the almost petty point scoring with Laporta and the methods he was using to increase revenue at the club even though he claimed it was necessary.

The Qatar Foundation sponsorship continued to be a point of fierce contention.

"There will always be people in favour and against with a club the size of Barça. Everyone knows who Qatar are, they come from the Middle East and they are looking towards the West to help them open up. We can help them to become more democratic," said Rosell.

Further austerity measures which meant cutting back on other sporting sections of the club and closing down their baseball team was greeted by anger from many, principally because in his election message he stated he would support them.

Although now committed to politics and with his party having won four seats in the Catalan Parliament, as well as fighting legal cases with the new Barça board, Laporta was also in dispute with the football agent Bayram Tutumlu who alleged he was owed three million euros for arranging the controversial deal in 2008 where Barça were to play FC Budyonkor of Uzbekistan. In the end the two games never took place and instead there was just a training match at Barcelona's Ministadi.

The court case, which is likely to see several first team players giving evidence, has been described by Laporta as a sham.

"These are lies and untruths. I've seen this man three times in my life and there were no verbal agreements or anything signed," he said.

Although offering a new brand of presidency it is clear that the divisions and personal conflicts over the leadership of the club which have dogged Barça in particular since the latter days of the Nuñez presidency remain very much in place.

Rosell has had no intention to draw a line over what has happened in the past and Laporta, with the support of Cruyff, is vociferous in his criticism of the new board.

"At the moment the club is continuing to win but on an institutional basis it is deteriorating as decisions are being taken out of spite and immaturity. The board now have tried to ruin our image and we are being forced to go to court to clear our names," said Laporta.

"The present board has connections to powerful economic and political groups whose interests are in preventing any political change and so that is why they are trying to damage my name.

Whether the allegations from Laporta are true or not it is clear that for good or bad Barcelona is now run on a more business footing and as such the club has lost some of its romanticism. Rosell chooses his words carefully even to the point where fans have complained that he should be more vocal in defending the club for example against the drugs accusations or the claims emanating from Real Madrid of histrionics during the el clasico clashes at the end of the season.

The club's image has been changed forever with the shirt sponsorship and its values perhaps tarnished by a deal with the Qatar Foundation but it reflects the way football has become a major business and not even Barça can escape this.

On a positive note the club has continued to triumph with its brand of open attacking football and with a young squad the future is looking bright. The main doubt is over the position of Guardiola who has never planned to stay long at the helm and is only prepared to sign one-year contracts. Although he claims that his own achievements will never match those of Johan Cruyff's, who introduced a new approach to football, he has adapted that style to the modern game and as well as having world class players at his disposal, his motivation and discipline have been immense in bringing about the success.

Other Peak Platform Titles

Red, White and Khaki: The Story of the Only Wartime FA Cup Final

Author: Matthew Bell
ISBN: 9781907219
Format: Paperback

When, on April 24th 1915, Sheffield United captain George Utley lifted the FA Cup, it brought to a close one of the most controversial football seasons in history. The same day, thousands of allied troops were killed or injured in a German poison gas attack near Ypres. The two contrasting scenes underlined the fierce debate that had endured for many months about the continuation of professional football whilst innumerable young men were being sacrificed in the name of freedom and democracy.

Fit and Proper? Conflicts and Conscience in an English Football Club

Author: Matthew Bell and Gary Armstrong
ISBN: 1907219110
Format: Paperback

Based on years of research by its two authors, Fit and Proper? details the history of the boardroom of Sheffield United Football Club, focusing particularly on the foibles of the men who over three decades from 1980 tried, and largely failed, to turn the 'Blades' into a profitable business and a successful club.

Matthew Bell is a mechanical engineer by trade and spends every spare moment writing about Sheffield United. He has edited the United fanzine, 'Flashing Blade' for over twenty years and has written a weekly column in the Green 'Un since 1993. He was co-editor of 'Blades Tales' and 'Blades Tales 2' and has written articles for 4-4-2 magazine and the 2003 Sheffield United v Arsenal FA Cup semi-final programme.

Dr. Gary Armstrong is a Reader in the School of Sport and Education, Brunel University, London. He previously lectured in Criminology at the University of Westminster and the University of Reading. His research into sports-related matters has produced various publications including: Football Hooligans: Knowing the Score, Blade Runners: Lives in Football, and Sheffield United FC: The Biography.

I Hate Football: A Fan's Memoir

Author: John Firth
ISBN: 9781907219021
Format: Paperback

It is easy to support a successful football team, but it takes guts, loyalty and a whole heap of stupidity to follow one of the also-rans. "I Hate Football" is the story of such a group of fans who are unfortunate enough to follow Sheffield Wednesday. It is a record of the fortunes of the club from 1970 through to 2009, as seen through the eyes of the fans; fans that live and breathe every kick. This is the autobiography of almost every fan in the country - a must read for all football fans.

About John Firth

John Firth grew up in Sheffield and now lives in Wakefield. He is married with a seven year old boy who has Autism. When his son was diagnosed with Autism, he resigned his position to give the care and support that their son desperately needed. He then started up a plumbing business that is now flourishing. What precious spare time that he has is taken up by writing and obviously following Sheffield Wednesday, which is a huge passion in his life.

Paying on the Gate: A Bantam's journey into the heart of lower league football

Author: Jason McKeown
ISBN: 9781907219252
Format: Papaerback

They say you should never change your football team; but when Jason McKeown happens to stumble upon his local club, Bradford City, he instantly finds greater enjoyment from swapping the so-called glamour of Manchester United for the deeper substance of lower league football. As he grows up from excitable teenager to young adult, the strong bond with the Bantams proves both a hindrance and help in shaping his future.

Paying on the gate celebrates the virtues of supporting your local, less glamorous football club as opposed to the superficial nature of following one that wins more often, but with whom you have no relationship. The glory may be in short supply, but Jason's decision to break the golden rule helps him learn what being a football supporter is really about.

Playing For England: England Supporters Band Early Years

Authors: John Hemmingham & Stephen Holmes
ISBN: 9781907219108
Format: Hardback

In the spirit of 'Fever Pitch', 'The Full Monty' and 'Brassed Off' this is the story of the Sheffield based England Band supporting the England team since 1996. This inspirational band, aged between 10 and 80 plus, play with passion in support of their country and have now 'Played for England more times than Beckham'. Richard Branson personally persuaded them to sign up for their first chart making record deal and the Band have since released many others plus three singles and an album for the World Cup 2010. They have made numerous TV and Radio appearances. Our dream is to play for England at the World Cup Final one day.A"

About John Hemmingham
Give me the child until he is seven and I'll give you the man'. So it was that as a seven year old boy growing up in Sheffield within sight of his team's ground, John was already obsessed with football and playing the bugle, in that order. In typical style John took a bugle to a match in 1993 'just for a laugh'. The mystery bugler was identified and asked to form a football terrace band. John and the band were then given the honour of being asked to play for England. Musically challenged, perhaps, but the most passionate, determined and best at generating an atmosphere anywhere on the planet. John is in the process of writing his second book.